THE NUCLEAR AGE

TimeFrame AD 1950-1990

EUROPE

THE UNITED STATES AND THE SOVIET UNION

TimeFrame AD 1950-1990

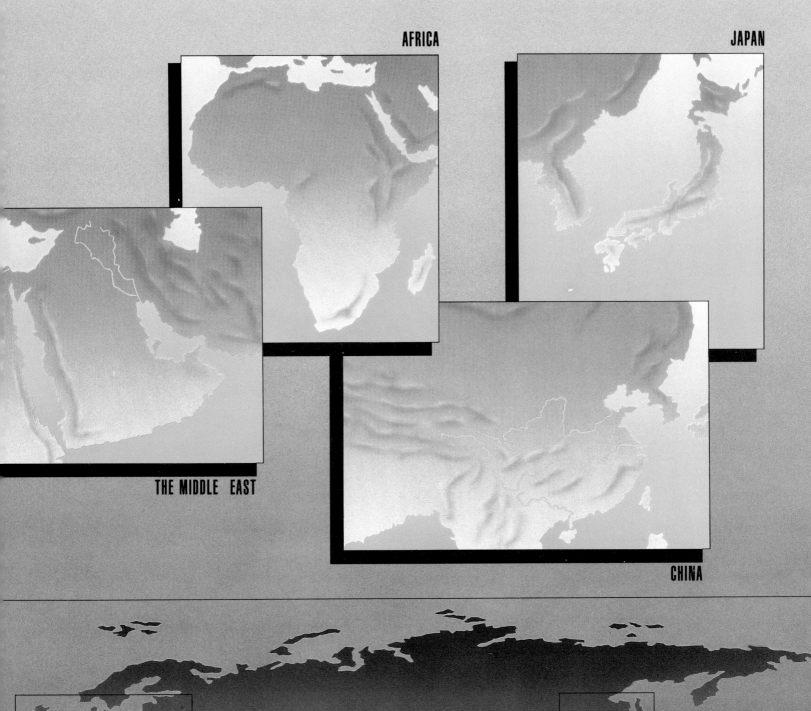

AFRICA

JAPAN

THE MIDDLE EAST

CHINA

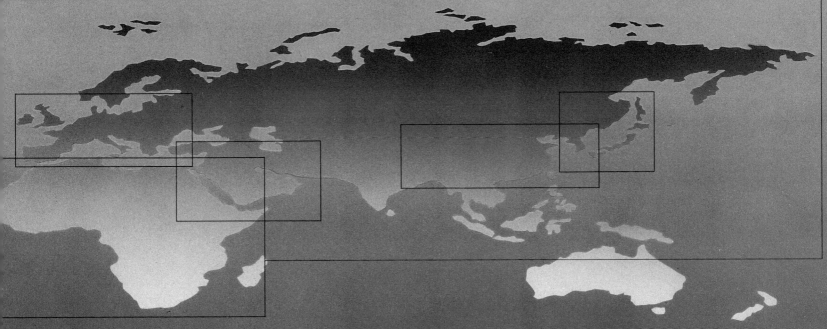

TIME® LIFE BOOKS

This volume is one in a series that tells the story
of humankind. Other books in the series include:
The Age of God-Kings
Barbarian Tides
A Soaring Spirit
Empires Ascendant
Empires Besieged
The March of Islam
Fury of the Northmen
Light in the East
The Divine Campaigns
The Mongol Conquests
The Age of Calamity
Voyages of Discovery
The European Emergence
Powers of the Crown
Winds of Revolution
The Pulse of Enterprise
The Colonial Overlords
The World in Arms
Shadow of the Dictators

THE NUCLEAR AGE

TimeFrame AD 1950-1990

BY THE EDITORS OF TIME-LIFE BOOKS

TIME-LIFE BOOKS, ALEXANDRIA, VIRGINIA

Time-Life Books Inc.
is a wholly owned subsidiary of
THE TIME INC. BOOK COMPANY

President and Chief Executive Officer:
Kelso F. Sutton
President, Time Inc. Books Direct:
Christopher T. Linen

TIME-LIFE BOOKS INC.

EDITOR: George Constable
Director of Design: Louis Klein
Director of Editorial Resources:
Phyllis K. Wise
Director of Photography and Research:
John Conrad Weiser

EUROPEAN EDITOR: Ellen Phillips
Design Director: Ed Skyner
Director of Editorial Resources:
Gillian Moore
Chief Sub-Editor: Ilse Gray
Assistant Design Director: Mary Staples

PRESIDENT: John M. Fahey, Jr.
Senior Vice Presidents: Robert M.
DeSena, Paul R. Stewart, Curtis G.
Viebranz, Joseph J. Ward
Vice Presidents: Stephen L. Bair,
Bonita L. Boezeman, Mary P. Donohoe,
Stephen L. Goldstein, Andrew P. Kaplan,
Trevor Lunn, Susan J. Maruyama, Robert
H. Smith
New Product Development: Trevor Lunn,
Donia Ann Steele
Supervisor of Quality Control: James King

PUBLISHER: Joseph J. Ward

Correspondents: Elisabeth Kraemer-Singh
(Bonn); Christine Hinze (London);
Christina Lieberman (New York); Maria
Vincenza Aloisi (Paris); Ann Natanson
(Rome). Valuable assistance was also
provided by: Betty H. Weatherley
(Alexandria, Virginia); Jaime Florcruz
(Beijing); Sasha Isachenko (Moscow);
Elizabeth Brown (New York); Michael
Donath (Prague); K.C. Hwang (Seoul);
Dick Berry (Tokyo).

TIME FRAME
(published in Britain as
TIME-LIFE HISTORY OF THE WORLD)

SERIES EDITOR: Tony Allan

Editorial Staff for *The Nuclear Age:*
Editor: Tony Allan
Designer: Mary Staples
Writers: Chris Farman, Christine Noble
Researchers: Paul Dowswell, Caroline
Smith
Sub-Editor: Frances Willard
Design Assistant: Rachel Gibson
Editorial Assistant: Molly Sutherland
Picture Department: Amanda Hindley
(administrator), Zoë Spencer (picture
coordinator)

Editorial Production
Chief: Samantha Hill
Traffic Coordinator: Emma Veys
Editorial Department: Theresa John,
Debra Lelliott

U.S. EDITION

Assistant Editor: Barbara Fairchild
Quarmby
Copy Coordinator: Ann Lee Bruen
Picture Coordinator: Barry Anthony

Editorial Operations
Production: Celia Beattie
Library: Louise D. Forstall

Computer Composition: Deborah G. Tait
(Manager), Monika D. Thayer, Janet
Barnes Syring, Lillian Daniels

Special Contributors: Windsor Chorlton,
John Cottrell, Neil Fairbairn, Ellen
Galford, Alan Lothian, John Man (text);
Timothy Fraser (research); David E.
Manley (index).

CONSULTANTS

General:
GEOFFREY PARKER, Professor of History,
University of Illinois, Urbana-Champaign,
Illinois

CHRISTOPHER BAYLY, Reader in Modern Indian History, Saint Catharine's College, Cambridge University, Cambridge,
England

The Cold War:
DAVID REYNOLDS, Fellow and Director
of Studies in History, Christ's College,
Cambridge University, Cambridge, England

Europe:
RICHARD OVERY, Reader in History,
King's College, London, England

China:
DENIS TWITCHETT, Gordon Wu Professor of Chinese Studies, Princeton University, Princeton, New Jersey

PENNY BROOKE, Current Affairs Orga-
nizer, Chinese Service, BBC World Service
(1988-1989)

Africa:
RICHARD RATHBONE, Lecturer in African History, School of Oriental and African Studies, University of London, England

The Middle East:
ROGER OWEN, Lecturer in the Recent
Economic History of the Middle East, Saint
Antony's College, Oxford University, Ox-
ford, England

Japan:
ANN WASWO, Lecturer in Modern Japanese History, Saint Antony's College, Oxford University, Oxford, England

**Library of Congress Cataloguing in
Publication Data**

The Nuclear age: TimeFrame AD 1950-1990 /
by the editors of Time-Life Books.
    p.   cm.
    Includes bibliographical references (p.
    Includes index.
    ISBN 0-8094-6475-6 — ISBN 0-8094-6476-4
    1. History, Modern—1945- I. Time-Life Books.
D840.N83 1990
909.82—dc20   90-11201
                                           CIP

CONTENTS

THE COLD WAR

On Saturday September 3, 1949, while most of the United States prepared to enjoy the Labor Day weekend, a converted B-29 bomber was carrying out a routine weather reconnaissance between Japan and Alaska. Its crew was keeping an eye on more than just meteorology: For more than a year, the U.S. Air Force had been sampling the atmosphere for traces of radioactivity that might help U.S. scientists monitor the progress of the Soviet Union's atomic weapons research. This was a needless precaution according to many, who were convinced that the Soviets lacked the technology to make a bomb and that America's nuclear monopoly would endure for years. But more than 18,000 feet above the Kamchatka Peninsula, traces of exotic dust set Geiger counters clicking. The filter papers that the bomber brought back would ruin the holiday weekend for America's government, its Atomic Energy Commission (AEC), and its military staffs. For the isotopes they had scooped up were definite proof that the Soviet Union had exploded an atomic bomb of its own—and a bomb of an advanced type, better than America's own first effort. America's lead had lasted precisely forty-nine months. Now its greatest enemy, too, was armed with the terrible weapon that had destroyed Hiroshima and Nagasaki in August 1945.

The last time the bomb had been used, the Soviet Union and the United States had been allies. But within a remarkably short time of their joint victory in World War II, cooperation had turned into mistrust, and mistrust had deepened into an unprecedented state of peacetime hostility, which the U.S. columnist Walter Lippmann had aptly and indelibly entitled the Cold War. The reasons for the abrupt change, as the United States and its allies saw them, were as simple as they were numerous. Essentially, the Soviet dictator Joseph Stalin—the bluff, mustached "Uncle Joe" of inter-Allied propaganda—had revealed himself obdurate and implacable in the face of postwar pleas for cooperation, while his state seemed even more totalitarian and at least as territory-hungry as Hitler's late and unlamented Germany had ever been. While British and American forces were demobilized as fast as transport could be organized to bring the soldiers home, a vast Red Army still lay sprawled across its Eastern European conquests: Poland, Czechoslovakia, Bulgaria, Romania, Hungary, and the Russian zones of a divided Austria and Germany. Yugoslavia and Albania, although free of Soviet troops, were further Communist bastions.

Against the tanks and artillery of the all-conquering Red Army, the United States had been able to position its nuclear weapons and the air force needed to deliver them. It was an unhappy balance, not at all what Americans had fought for in World War II, but it was a balance; on its stability rested the painfully created policy of containment, by which the United States hoped to prevent any further Soviet expansion. It was formally enunciated in the so-called Truman Doctrine of 1947, by which America was pledged to support "free peoples who are resisting attempted

Separated only by a worried interpreter, U.S. Vice President Richard Nixon and Soviet leader Nikita Khrushchev engage in head-to-head argument over the merits of their countries' respective political systems. The impromptu Kitchen Conference—so called from its venue, beside a model kitchen display in a 1959 American exhibition in Moscow—displayed the Cold War relationship in miniature. "We have means at our disposal that can have very bad consequences," warned the anticapitalist Khrushchev. "We have too," retorted anticommunist Nixon. Although the encounter ended amicably, three years later Khrushchev led the Soviet Union into the terrifying Cuban missile crisis.

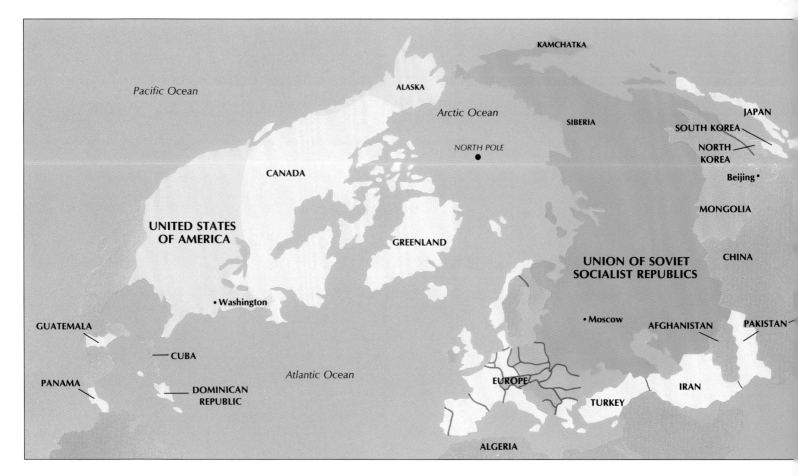

subjugation by armed minorities or by outside pressures." It was a tall order, a commitment open-ended in time as well as space, to be continued until there came about, as the veteran U.S. diplomat George F. Kennan put it, "the gradual mellowing of Soviet power." But it was better than outright war.

Harry S. Truman himself accepted the Soviet Union's new nuclear status with greater equanimity than many of his advisers. The president had always had doubts as to the practical utility of the new weapons, even though—or perhaps precisely because—he was the only man who had ever authorized a nuclear attack. The destruction wrought in Japan had convinced him that the atomic bomb was no normal military weapon; and he had irked U.S. military planners by keeping it under strict presidential control; he would not, he told his defense secretary, let "some dashing lieutenant colonel decide when would be the proper time to drop one." Still, the president was equally convinced—or so he declared to the director of the Atomic Energy Commission—that without the bomb, "the Russians would have probably taken over Europe a long time ago."

One immediate result of the Soviet test came a few days later at an AEC meeting to discuss America's future weapons program. For months, scientists, soldiers, and politicians had debated the wisdom of producing a new type of nuclear explosive based not on splitting but on combining atomic nuclei—fusion rather than fission.

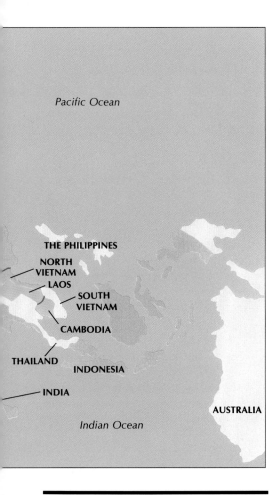

Pacific Ocean

THE PHILIPPINES
NORTH
VIETNAM
LAOS
SOUTH
VIETNAM
CAMBODIA
THAILAND
INDONESIA
INDIA
AUSTRALIA
Indian Ocean

The United States and the Soviet Union confront each other across the roof of the world, where the state of Alaska is only fifty miles from Soviet territory. As relations between the two countries deteriorated, each strove to build up a global network of alliances. The United States very nearly achieved its aim of encircling its Communist counterpart with allied countries (shaded pale yellow). The Soviet Union found fewer friendly nations (shaded pale green), but it established a foothold in America's backyard through its comradeship with Cuba. This map shows the web of alliances at the time of the Cuban missile crisis of 1962.

Such a thermonuclear device—the hydrogen bomb—would have a destructive capacity perhaps a thousand times greater than existing atomic weapons; U.S. Air Force generals even doubted whether its use could ever be justified. The decision, however, was made after a few minutes of discussion: The H-bomb would be built.

Nuclear weapons were no help a few months later, when the prolonged Chinese civil war was won by Mao Zedong's Communists. Although no conceivable U.S. action could have prevented Mao's victory, it was still seen as an American defeat. The State Department did what it could to avoid a rupture with China's new rulers, but few doubted that the Soviet Union had received a massive reinforcement.

Truman's European allies had no qualms about U.S. nuclear strength, and few doubts as to its value. Like most American soldiers and diplomats, they believed that in 1948, when the Russians had blockaded the Western powers' enclave in Berlin, it was only the dispatch of American bombers to forward bases in Britain, together with the accompanying airlift of supplies to the besieged city, that had restrained Soviet military action. Then, the deployment had been a bluff: Only a handful of nuclear bombs existed in the U.S. armory, and none of the bombers sent to Britain were capable of carrying them. But Europe's desire for the protection of the American nuclear umbrella had led in April 1949 to the formation of the North Atlantic Treaty Organization (NATO), a mutual defense pact that formally linked the security of Western Europe to U.S. power.

The view from Washington, though, was gloomy. The division of the world between two competing superpowers seemed dangerously unstable. Yet such fears were to prove groundless. Although there would be no lack of fighting around the world in the years ahead, the peace between the superpowers would hold, as firmly as any peace on earth ever had. And at the same time, a greater prosperity than the world had ever previously known would spread through the developed lands, with the losers of World War II, Germany and Japan, among its greatest beneficiaries. Outside the charmed circle of the wealthy nations, former colonies would win political independence, although economic success would continue to elude them. By the closing decade of the millennium, new problems, born of success, would be confronting the world: how to feed a global population that had doubled in less than four decades, and how to direct and restrain growth so as to avoid irreparably depleting the planet's resources.

None of this could even have been guessed at in 1950. The prospect from Moscow in that year appeared even less promising than that from the United States. In Soviet eyes, the United States had come out of World War II relatively unscathed, with its homeland undamaged and an exuberant industrial economy that outproduced the rest of the world put together. In contrast, the Soviet Union had been grievously weakened by the conflict. It had lost one-tenth of its population, and its industry and agriculture had suffered appalling damage; about one-fourth of the nation's capital assets had been lost. Heavily engaged in a colossal program of reconstruction merely to regain its 1941 position, the Soviet Union was in poor shape for any major confrontation with the superpower across the Atlantic. And with labor desperately needed in resurgent industry, there was no possibility of retaining the tank armies that had destroyed Hitler's Wehrmacht in the East: By 1948, the much-feared Red Army, 11 million strong in 1945, numbered fewer than 3 million men.

In Soviet eyes, it was the United States that threatened world peace; the Russian bomb simply restored equilibrium to Great Power relations. To Moscow the U.S. policies of containment and deterrence meant something quite different. In translation, the words came out as "keeping out" and "intimidation" and added up to one thing: encirclement. Particularly alarming was the creation in May 1949 of a strong West German state out of the British, French, and U.S. zones of occupation. The Russians feared that America was promoting the likelihood of a third German war.

The fragility of world peace was clearly demonstrated as the new decade began. In a January 1950 speech on his government's containment policy, Secretary of State Dean Acheson outlined a boundary to U.S. vital interests that apparently excluded the non-Communist southern half of the Korean peninsula, divided in 1948 along the 38th parallel between U.S. and Soviet occupying troops. In June of 1950, a huge North Korean army launched an invasion aimed at reuniting the country and within weeks had almost driven the defenders into the sea.

But the South Koreans were not fighting alone. For the United States there was an inescapable connection between Acheson's speech and North Korea's response; the Americans were certain that the attack was carried out with Chinese and Soviet encouragement and quite probably at Moscow's direct order. Truman at once reinforced the small American garrison in Korea, and took advantage of a Soviet boycott of the United Nations (UN) to gain a Security Council resolution calling for armed assistance to the victim of aggression. The United Nations army that went on the offensive was composed predominantly of U.S. troops, but it also included contingents from Canada, Britain, and France, among other U.S. allies, and was commanded by Douglas MacArthur, victor of the Pacific war. Overwhelming American naval power allowed a seaborne landing that attacked the North Koreans from the rear, and soon the Communist forces were in full retreat.

U.S. success brought a policy dilemma: Should the army be allowed to advance across the 38th parallel, enforcing its own reunification of the peninsula? As the skeptical George Kennan warned, once engaged in mainland Asia, "we have about a 10,000-mile walk if we keep on going, and we are going to have to stop somewhere." Others, notably MacArthur, recommended pushing into China itself. Truman and many of his advisers feared that the whole Korean conflict was no more than a Soviet ploy to draw U.S. attention from Europe; with misgivings, he authorized an advance across the former border.

In November 1950, the UN forces, spread out by their rapid progress and disorganized by the snow and bitter cold of the Korean winter, neared the Yalu River border with China. It was too much for Mao: Chinese "volunteers" flooded across the border by the hundreds of thousands. Overwhelmed, MacArthur's army retreated southward even faster than it had advanced—a near-debacle that did not improve the general's worsening relationship with his president. A UN counteroffensive in March 1951 painfully clawed its way back to the 38th parallel but could make no further headway, and the fighting lapsed into an ugly war of attrition for more than two years while an armistice was negotiated.

In the meantime, U.S. military expenditure almost quadrupled. The first hydrogen bomb was tested in 1952, while conventional armaments and the nuclear stockpile alike were vastly expanded. Overseas bases multiplied, and military aid was lavished on America's allies—a lengthening list that would soon include most non-Communist powers on the globe. Fearful of communism spreading across Southeast Asia, the United States began to support the French in their drawn-out colonial war in Indochina. It was the price of French support in Europe and Korea, but it was the beginning of the most regretted foreign involvement in U.S. history.

The Soviet economy could not match the American increase; even so, Soviet defense spending rose by two-thirds, and it would continue its uninterrupted growth for a decade. Soviet-American relations, already icy, became glacial, and diplomatic communications seldom rose much above the level of insult and invective.

Tensions were aggravated by American domestic policy. Vitriolic anticommunism, silent during World War II, had thrived since the late 1940s; the Truman administration had launched a "loyalty program," designed to winnow left-wing Americans from positions of influence, and a series of treason trials in the late 1940s had increased public disquiet. But in 1950, the United States began to indulge itself in the kind of ideological purge that had hitherto been a Soviet monopoly. In a Republican senator named Joseph McCarthy, America found its own grand inquisitor. Aptly described by Truman as a "pathological character assassin," he made a political living from hysterical denunciations of specified (but never substantiated) numbers of card-carrying Communists in America's governmental institutions. As chairman of the ominously named Permanent Subcommittee on Investigations, he used the new medium of television to hound his suspects. Some had indeed had links with the American Communist party and associated organizations, generally back in the 1930s, but almost all of them were innocent of the treason charges that were the stock in trade of McCarthy's rhetoric. Fear bred fear, however; lives and careers were ruined by the hundred, while McCarthy and the politicians who supported him created a lobby that no president dared ignore.

But the situation was changing. While the Korean negotiators were patching together a brittle cease-fire along the 38th parallel, the main Cold War protagonists left the scene. In the United States, MacArthur was fired in April 1951: His increasingly public demand for the use of the atomic bomb against mainland China delighted McCarthy but infuriated Truman, who feared the effect on his nervous allies—and the Russians—of even discussing such a strategy. Truman himself, exhausted by constant crisis at home and abroad, did not run for reelection in 1952. In his place, the United States chose Dwight D. Eisenhower, World War II supreme allied commander and America's first Republican president in twenty years.

The most dramatic departure was in Moscow. On March 5, 1953, after almost thirty years as dictator, Joseph Stalin died. Thousands of bereft Russians sobbed in the streets of Moscow. Many were crushed to death as they mobbed Stalin's bier; later he would be embalmed and placed beside his supposed mentor, Vladimir Ilyich Lenin, in the mausoleum in Red Square. Others, however, remembered the millions imprisoned and killed under his rule and felt more hope than grief.

Even before the funeral obsequies ended, the struggle for succession began in Moscow. Meanwhile, in Washington, John Foster Dulles, Acheson's successor as secretary of state, telegraphed U.S. embassies worldwide: It was time "to sow doubt, confusion, uncertainty about the new regime not only among both Soviet and satellite elites and masses, but among local Communist parties outside the Soviet Union."

The doubt and confusion already existed, without any intervention. In June 1953, there were workers' riots in East Berlin, spreading rapidly throughout East Germany and into Poland. As Red Army units moved to quell the riots, the U.S. administration backed away from confrontation: There was no question, Eisenhower declared, of "taking any physical action of any kind that could be classed as intervention."

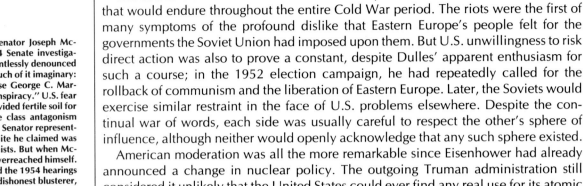

The events themselves and the American response to them marked two features that would endure throughout the entire Cold War period. The riots were the first of many symptoms of the profound dislike that Eastern Europe's people felt for the governments the Soviet Union had imposed upon them. But U.S. unwillingness to risk direct action was also to prove a constant, despite Dulles' apparent enthusiasm for such a course; in the 1952 election campaign, he had repeatedly called for the rollback of communism and the liberation of Eastern Europe. Later, the Soviets would exercise similar restraint in the face of U.S. problems elsewhere. Despite the continual war of words, each side was usually careful to respect the other's sphere of influence, although neither would openly acknowledge that any such sphere existed.

American moderation was all the more remarkable since Eisenhower had already announced a change in nuclear policy. The outgoing Truman administration still considered it unlikely that the United States could ever find any real use for its atomic arsenal and, during the Korean War, had sought to increase America's conventional forces. Eisenhower, conscious of election promises that he would reduce military spending, thought otherwise: Compared with the cost of maintaining a large and well-equipped army, atomic bombs were cheap. But if the administration was not prepared to use the weapons—or publicly threaten their use—they would be politically worthless. "Atomic weapons," the president therefore warned the United Nations, "have virtually achieved conventional status within our armed forces." European land defenses would rely on newly designed miniature bombs, some small enough to be fired from an artillery piece. With these so-called tactical weapons, weak U.S. forces could hold off any Russian onslaught. The word "tactical" reassured Western European soldiers and political leaders alike; no one had yet given much thought to what their homelands might look like after the weapons had been used.

Fortunately, Eisenhower was far less enthusiastic in private, especially after the Soviet Union tested its own first H-bomb in August 1953. Although the United States still had a vast nuclear superiority—for whatever the size of their stockpile, the Soviets had nothing to match the U.S. Strategic Air Command, with its hundreds of long-range bombers deployed worldwide—it was grimly obvious that any use of nuclear weapons could escalate unpredictably into a cycle of retaliation and counterretaliation, and that America, too, might suffer griev-

FORTY YEARS OF CONFLICT

АМЕРИКАНСКИЙ ОБРАЗ ЖИЗНИ

КАЖДЫЕ 9 МИНУТ-ОГРАБЛЕНИЕ

КАЖДЫЕ 3 МИНУТЫ-УГОН АВТОМОБИЛЯ

КАЖДЫЕ 100 СЕКУНД-КРАЖА СО ВЗЛОМОМ

КАЖДЫЕ 21 СЕКУНДУ В США ПРОИСХОДИТ СЕРЬЕЗНОЕ ПРЕСТУПЛЕНИЕ /ИЗ СООБЩЕНИЙ АМЕРИКАНСКОЙ ПЕЧАТИ/

КАЖДЫЕ 44 МИНУТЫ ПРЕДУМЫШЛЕННОЕ УБИЙСТВО

ЕЖЕГОДНО БЕССЛЕДНО ИСЧЕЗАЮТ

A 1950 Soviet propaganda poster purporting to show the American way of life draws on U.S. crime statistics to reveal that "every twenty-one seconds in the U.S., a serious crime takes place." During the worst of the Cold War, each superpower systematically vilified the other. Yet even harmful information could sometimes perplex its recipients; if, as the poster also claimed, "every three minutes, a car is stolen," Soviet citizens noted that the American capitalists had an auto industry more productive than theirs. But when they read that "in New York City, 13,000 people disappear every day," they were on familiar ground: Under Stalin, Soviet citizens had disappeared in uncounted numbers for twenty years.

ous losses. While Eisenhower continued to deny that a nuclear threshold existed, he would prove as reluctant to cross it as Truman had been.

Tensions in fact eased after Stalin's death. His successor, Georgi Malenkov, was anxious to improve the Soviet standard of living, which meant switching at least some resources from heavy industry and arms production and seeking technical aid from the West. In Korea the armistice held. But there were other conflicts in the world. Despite American aid, the French were steadily losing their war against Communist guerrillas in Vietnam. Matters came to a head in March 1954, when a French army was isolated and besieged at Dien Bien Phu. The French government had pleaded for months for U.S. air support; now their army faced certain defeat without it.

Eisenhower, backed by most of his military and faced with a noninterventionist Congress, wanted nothing to do with the conflict. American involvement in Southeast Asia, the president declared, "would absorb our troops by the divisions." A Pentagon plan to use atomic weapons to rescue the beleaguered French was quietly abandoned. The garrison surrendered in May, and the resulting Geneva conference divided the country on the Korean model, with a Communist north and a U.S.-oriented south. The artificial division was a sop to French pride: The Vietminh accepted the deal on the advice of their Chinese allies, who pointed out that reunification of the country under Communist rule was only a matter of time.

The United States, still following a policy of containment, made the best of the new situation by setting up the Southeast Asia Treaty Organization (SEATO), including most of the region's remaining non-Communist states; SEATO was complemented in the Middle East by the British-led Central Treaty Organization, brought together by the Baghdad Pact. Both were modeled on NATO, but neither had a fraction of the military power or political solidarity of that 1949 alliance.

Meanwhile, relations with the Soviet Union continued to improve. Malenkov was ousted early in 1955 by Nikita Khrushchev; although Khrushchev denounced Malenkov for his softness toward the West and his military reductions, once in power he soon adopted similar policies. By agreement, Soviet and Western occupying troops left Austria in May 1955, in exchange for the country's neutralization. The new leader went further: Starting with oblique references to the cult of personality and culminating in a secret speech to the Twentieth Party Congress in February 1956, he began

1950

FEBRUARY. Senator Joseph McCarthy launches a crusade against alleged Communist infiltration of the U.S. State Department. Joseph Stalin and Mao Zedong conclude a formal alliance between the USSR and China.

JUNE. Communist North Korea invades South Korea. The United Nations—boycotted at the time by the USSR—condemns the invasion and sanctions armed intervention to repel it.

OCTOBER. Chinese Communist troops invade and occupy Tibet. The Dalai Lama is forced into exile.

NOVEMBER. In Korea, UN troops reach the Chinese border, prompting massive intervention by China in support of North Korea.

1951

JANUARY. North Korean and Chinese Communist forces capture Seoul, the principal city of South Korea.

1952

NOVEMBER. Dwight D. Eisenhower (below) wins the U.S. presidential election. The U.S. explodes the world's first hydrogen bomb on Eniwetok atoll in the Marshall Islands.

Soviet shoppers covetously examine a mannequin displaying 1950s high fashion, Moscow-style. Such sights were rare that decade: The massive efforts made by the Soviet Union to repair war damage left few resources for consumer goods of any kind. Even after the reconstruction period, though, shortages of all but basic necessities continued to irk Soviet citizens, and when goods were available, their quality remained low.

1953

JANUARY. Nine distinguished Soviet Jewish doctors are arrested, prompting fears of new purges in the USSR.

MARCH. Soviet leader Joseph Stalin dies of a cerebral hemorrhage. He is succeeded by Georgi Malenkov.

JUNE. Julius and Ethel Rosenberg *(left)* are executed for selling atomic secrets to the USSR. Soviet tanks and troops crush workers' riots in East Berlin.

JULY. The Korean War ends in a stalemate, with more than two million dead in the three years of fighting.

AUGUST. The Soviet Union explodes its own hydrogen bomb.

1954

JULY. Following the surrender of a French garrison at Dien Bien Phu two months earlier, a peace conference in Geneva divides Vietnam between a Communist North and an American-backed South.

DECEMBER. The U.S. Senate condemns some of Joseph McCarthy's actions, signaling the end of McCarthyism as a major political force.

the de-Stalinization of the Soviet Union. Details of the speech circulated widely, as Khrushchev had intended. Millions of amnestied political prisoners returned to the mainstream of Soviet society, and Stalinist officials, in Eastern Europe as well as the Soviet Union, were steadily replaced by pro-Khrushchev moderates. Khrushchev had no doubts that world communism would triumph over capitalism; but it would do so without wars. "Peaceful coexistence" became the new Soviet watchwords.

The thaw in the Cold War even led to an amicable—though unsuccessful—disarmament conference at Geneva, where Khrushchev met with Eisenhower as well as British and French leaders. But a rearmed West Germany was now a member of NATO. Khrushchev, responding, had established the Warsaw Pact in 1955, a formal military alliance between the Soviet Union and its European satellites. Now he also pressed forward with the development of intercontinental ballistic missiles—long-range rockets against which there was no real defense. The world was still a frightening place.

How much so became apparent in 1956. Thanks to Khrushchev's de-Stalinization reforms, there was once more a dangerous climate of hope in Eastern Europe, and much unrest. The demonstrations and disorder that occurred in Poland and in Hungary throughout October 1956 quickly reached the dimensions of a popular revolt. On November 1, the Hungarian government announced its withdrawal from the Warsaw Pact. For a few days Khrushchev and his Kremlin advisers vacillated. Then, on November 4, the Red Army's tanks rolled into Budapest. At least 2,000 Hungarians were killed; another 200,000 fled into exile. Hungarian Premier Imre Nagy was arrested (to be executed months later, after a secret trial) and the reform movement was rigorously crushed.

As in 1953, the United States confined itself to verbal protests. But although news of the Hungarian repression was masked by the Suez crisis, which was unfolding at the same time, it had a searing effect on Communist parties and voters in Western Europe. Thousands threw away their party cards; others, shaken, began the long period of reflection that would lead to a Eurocommunism with no ties to Moscow.

Khrushchev's de-Stalinization program was also straining relations with China. Mao Zedong, who was busily establishing a personality cult of his own, rejected Khrushchev's denunciations; the Chinese were also highly critical of the Soviet Union's new openness toward the West. Underlying the developing rupture, though, was dissatisfaction with the level of Soviet aid to China, particularly Soviet assistance in China's own nuclear weapons program: Generous in the early 1950s, the flow had been rapidly cut back as Kremlin fears of Chinese independence grew.

As always, the decision-making processes at the center of Soviet power politics remained veiled. But there was nothing secret about the Soviet Union's growing

1955

FEBRUARY. In the USSR, Malenkov is ousted from power by Nikita Khrushchev *(left).*

MAY. The Warsaw Pact links all the Communist nations of Eastern Europe except Yugoslavia in a Soviet-led military alliance aimed at countering the forces of the North Atlantic Treaty Organization (NATO). In the United States, the Supreme Court rules that states must end racial segregation in the public-school system.

1956

FEBRUARY. Khrushchev denounces Stalin during a six-hour speech to the Communist Party Congress.

OCTOBER. Hungarians revolt against the Soviet presence in their country and their own security police *(left).* **The revolt is subsequently crushed by Soviet troops following bloody street fighting.**

military strength. Both the United States and the USSR had already equipped themselves with medium-range ballistic missiles, the best that contemporary technology could produce. But such weapons put the Soviets at a geographic disadvantage: While American missiles based in Britain, Italy, or Turkey could reach the Soviet Union, Soviet missiles could not harm the continental United States. In August 1957, Khrushchev announced the successful test of his first intercontinental missile; America's long-range rocket program was still beset by technical difficulties. And in October, the Soviet Union put the first artificial satellite in orbit around the Earth.

Sputnik 1 was more than a great scientific achievement: It was a propaganda triumph. While Khrushchev exulted publicly in the merits of dynamic communism versus decadent capitalism, the United States endured a staggering blow to its national pride. Eisenhower's opponents excoriated him for the low-spending policies that had led to such humiliation; by permitting a so-called missile gap between the superpowers, he had, they claimed, seriously endangered American security. Khrushchev, flexing his muscles, reinforced Eisenhower's critics. The Soviet leader energetically threatened U.S. allies with a rain of rocket-borne destruction, and he felt strong enough to risk a Berlin crisis in 1958, unsuccessfully demanding concessions that would have ended the anomalous status of the western half of the city.

Eisenhower was in a quandary. Since 1956, secret high-altitude reconnaissance flights over the Soviet Union had given him an accurate estimate of Russia's strength. Despite Khrushchev's boasts and the outrage of his own domestic critics, he knew that Soviet long-range missile production was still modest in quantity and quality: There was no missile gap. But the president dared not say so, for any public acknowledgment of the covert overflights would provoke a critical international crisis.

That was precisely what happened in 1960, when a missile brought a U-2 reconnaissance plane down over Russian territory. Khrushchev expressed outrage at the infringement of Soviet air space and used the incident to call off a summit conference planned to discuss the Berlin situation; an invitation to Eisenhower to visit the USSR was also withdrawn.

The imaginary missile gap was an important issue in the close election contest of that year between Vice President Richard M. Nixon and the Democrat victor, the forty-three-year-old John F. Kennedy. Surrounding himself with an equally youthful cabinet, Kennedy was determined to inject a new dynamism into American policy after what he saw as the lethargy of the Eisenhower years. Even after he had learned the true strength of the Soviet missile force, he increased spending on his strategic bomber force, his new land-based missiles, and his even newer submarine-launched missiles, the latter invulnerable to any Soviet strike. Within two years of taking office, he would need all the assurance that his nuclear strength gave him.

1957

JULY. With the support of the Soviet military, Khrushchev survives an attempt to depose him organized by opponents of his de-Stalinization policy.

SEPTEMBER. The U.S. government sends 1,000 troops to Little Rock, Arkansas, to enforce its desegregation policy at the local high school.

OCTOBER. The Soviet Union places the first man-made satellite in space. The launch of *Sputnik 1* heralds the beginning of the space race.

1958

JANUARY. The first United States satellite, *Explorer 1*, is put into orbit.

1959

JANUARY. After a two-year guerrilla campaign, rebel forces led by Fidel Castro *(right)* seize power in Cuba, deposing the American-backed dictator Fulgencio Batista.

In April 1961, Kennedy gave reluctant approval to an operation planned by the Central Intelligence Agency (CIA) under Eisenhower: an invasion of nearby Cuba by exiles, aimed at inspiring a popular revolt against the annoyingly pro-Soviet Cuban leader Fidel Castro. It was a risky undertaking, the more so since Kennedy forbade any involvement of U.S. forces in the landing, and in the event, the attempted invasion was a disaster. Castro was forewarned by poor security among the exiles: When they landed at the Bay of Pigs, they were quickly killed or captured. The new president was badly shaken.

Khrushchev met Kennedy two months later in Vienna, determined to keep up the pressure. Resurrecting his Berlin demands, he also announced that the Soviet Union would continue to give arms and support to various revolutionary movements throughout the Third World, allying itself with "just wars" of national liberation everywhere. It was an acrimonious encounter, but Kennedy proved harder to bully than Khrushchev had hoped. Announcing the mobilization of 25 percent of U.S. reserve forces, the president served notice of his determination to resist Russian threats; he also pointed out his considerable superiority in long-range weaponry. Khrushchev decided not to press the Berlin issue.

But the continued drain of East Germans escaping through the city to the West was a problem whose solution Khrushchev dared not long postpone. In August, the East German government built a wall across the center of the city. It was an improvised structure, thrown up overnight; in the months and years to follow, it would harden into a massive barrier of concrete blocks, barbed wire, machine-gun towers, and minefields. East Germany would end the troublesome outflow of its best talents by the simple method of killing them if they tried to leave.

The Berlin Wall did nothing for the Soviet bloc's international standing, and su-

1960

MAY. An American U-2 spy plane piloted by Francis Gary Powers is shot down over the Soviet Union. Ensuing recriminations lead to the abandonment of the Paris summit between the United States, USSR, France, and Great Britain.

JUNE. Sino-Soviet relations take a turn for the worse as Khrushchev publicly criticizes China's leadership and stops economic and military aid.

NOVEMBER. John F. Kennedy *(right)*, with running mate Lyndon B. Johnson, wins the U.S. presidential race, beating the Republican candidate Richard M. Nixon by less than 120,000 votes.

AGENTS OF OBLIVION

The first nuclear weapons were designed for delivery by the simplest means: Carried to their target in a piloted aircraft, they fell from a bomb bay toward the ground. The method had definite advantages: A manned bomber could always be diverted or even recalled at the last moment. And even if antiaircraft systems became more effective, only a single plane had to reach each target intact in order to destroy it.

Both superpowers, however, recognized that an unmanned missile, arriving with little warning and almost impossible to intercept, would make a far more effective—though less flexible—delivery vehicle. By the late 1950s, both had started to deploy substantial numbers of ICBMs—intercontinental ballistic missiles, which threatened to destroy conventional bombers before they left the ground.

It was obvious, however, that ground-based ICBMs might themselves be vulnerable to an aggressor's preemptive strike. One solution adopted by both sides was the mounting of ballistic missiles in nuclear submarines, which could remain concealed in the depths of the world's oceans for months at a time. But submarines added communications difficulties to the ICBM's inflexibility, so for maximum security, each power kept all three delivery systems—the so-called strategic triad.

In the 1960s, antimissile defense became possible. But offensive technology was also advancing. The next stage was to equip attacking missiles with MIRV technology—multiple warheads, including dummies, that reentered the atmosphere independently in sufficient numbers to swamp any defense. The development of cruise missiles—ground-hugging, pilotless planes whose on-board computers fly them with inexorable accuracy—left the advantage firmly with the offense. However, the proliferation of weapons systems meant that no conceivable attack would leave its victims without the power to launch a devastating retaliation.

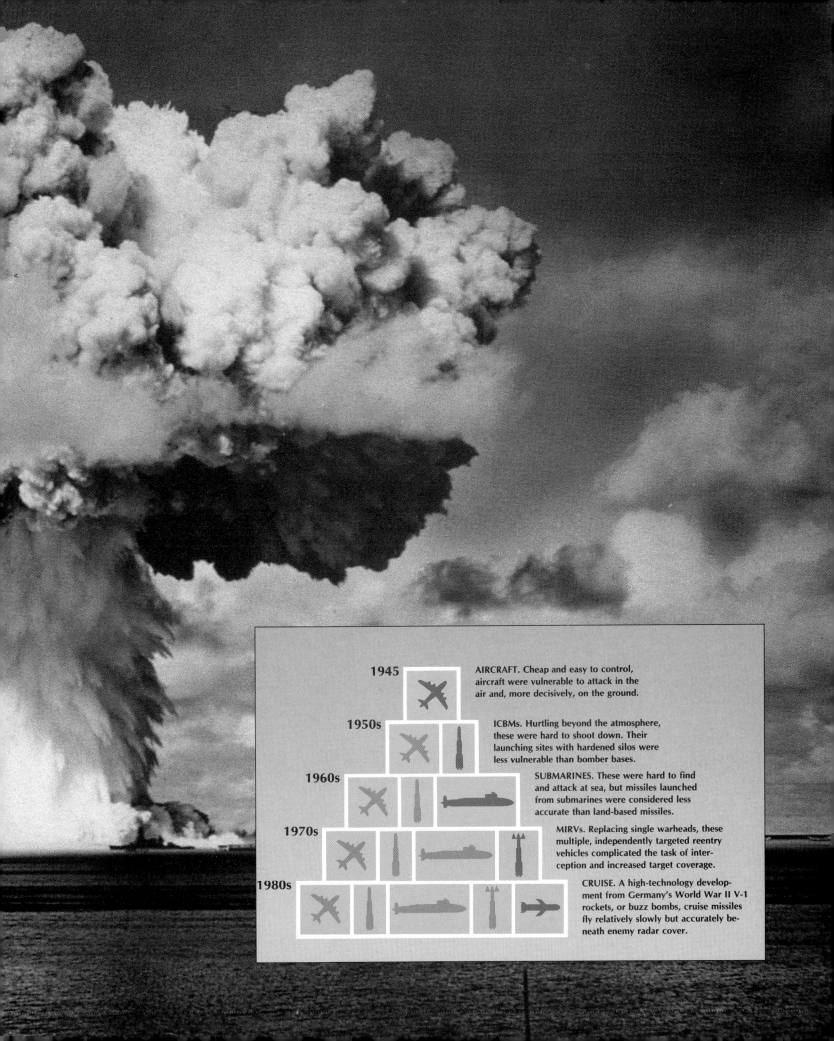

1945 AIRCRAFT. Cheap and easy to control, aircraft were vulnerable to attack in the air and, more decisively, on the ground.

1950s ICBMs. Hurtling beyond the atmosphere, these were hard to shoot down. Their launching sites with hardened silos were less vulnerable than bomber bases.

1960s SUBMARINES. These were hard to find and attack at sea, but missiles launched from submarines were considered less accurate than land-based missiles.

1970s MIRVs. Replacing single warheads, these multiple, independently targeted reentry vehicles complicated the task of interception and increased target coverage.

1980s CRUISE. A high-technology development from Germany's World War II V-1 rockets, or buzz bombs, cruise missiles fly relatively slowly but accurately beneath enemy radar cover.

A fearsome array of Soviet missiles passes in review during Moscow's 1964 May Day parade. In the 1960s, Soviet defense budgets regularly swallowed almost 10 percent of the national income, rising to more than 15 percent by the mid-1980s, at least twice the proportion the United States spent on its own military. According to some economists, the real costs were even higher: The largely unaccountable Soviet defense industry functioned almost as a state within a state, dominating investment priorities and absorbing up to one-third of metallurgical and machine-tool outputs.

1961

APRIL. U.S.-backed Cuban exiles fail to overthrow Fidel Castro's regime following an abortive landing at Cuba's Bay of Pigs.

AUGUST. East Germany builds the Berlin Wall.

OCTOBER. In the Soviet Union, Stalin's body is moved from its place of honor in the Red Square mausoleum to a small plot in the Kremlin.

NOVEMBER. The United States government announces that it is sending 15,000 military advisers to help South Vietnam in its struggle against Communist North Vietnam.

1962

FEBRUARY. U-2 pilot Francis Gary Powers is swapped for Soviet spy Rudolf Abel in Berlin.

OCTOBER. On learning that Soviet missile bases are being constructed in Cuba, President Kennedy announces an air and naval quarantine of the island. The crisis is resolved only when Khrushchev agrees to remove the bases under UN supervision.

perpower hostility remained perilously high. Despite the tension, Khrushchev decided to regain lost prestige through a Cuban adventure of his own, which was to prove far more dangerous than the Bay of Pigs fiasco. Ever since the aborted invasion, the Soviet Union had poured arms and advisers into Cuba. In 1962, Khrushchev began the secret deployment of medium-range nuclear missiles on Castro's island. Once installed, the weapons might have negated America's nuclear superiority.

Unfortunately for Khrushchev, an appalled Kennedy was presented on October 16 with clear pictures, taken from a U-2, of missiles, launchers, and their Soviet personnel. For six days, while U.S. nuclear and conventional forces remained on alert, he and his advisers debated their response: A full-scale invasion and a series of "surgical" air strikes were among the options considered. By October 22, when he told the American people of the crisis, Kennedy had made his decision. Cuba would be quarantined: The U.S. Navy would blockade the island, stopping approaching vessels and searching them for missiles. It was a canny choice: An attack on Cuba could easily result in a nuclear exchange, whereas a blockade not only provided time for diplomacy but put the responsibility for further escalation squarely on Khrushchev, who now had to decide whether to order his ships to press on.

For four days, the world waited in fear while the superpowers decided its fate. Declaring the blockade illegal, Moscow at first insisted that Soviet ships would refuse to be stopped; the U.S. Navy drew its ring closer, although for the time being, Kennedy made sure the only vessel searched was a Cuban ship he was reasonably sure carried no missiles. At last, on October 28, Khrushchev backed down: The missiles would be removed if the United States ended the blockade and promised not to invade Cuba. These were terms Kennedy was happy publicly to accept. (Secretly, U.S. missiles were also removed from Turkey, although Kennedy never admitted to a deal.) Soviet technicians began dismantling the Cuban launch sites.

The outcome was a definite victory for the United States. Khrushchev's rashness earned him much internal criticism, as well as abuse from Beijing. More important than any gain or loss of prestige, however, was the fact that both leaders had come close enough to nuclear war to frighten themselves—not to mention everyone else on the planet with access to a radio, a television, or a newspaper. Both recognized that their bad relations were simply too dangerous to continue, and the following year saw a striking improvement. The chronic Berlin crisis was considered resolved, however unsatisfactorily, by the infamous Berlin Wall; the following July, the United States, the Soviet Union, and Britain signed a treaty banning any further testing of nuclear weapons in the atmosphere; and a direct teleprinter link—the hot line—was installed between Moscow and Washington. The two powers' arsenals, it seemed, would ensure a certain stability—a doctrine of deterrence aptly summarized by Secretary of

1963

JUNE. In a speech at the Berlin Wall aimed at reaffirming U.S. support for West Germany, President Kennedy declares, "Ich bin ein Berliner."

AUGUST. A twenty-four-hour teleprinter hot line is set up between the Kremlin and the White House following delays in communications between the two powers during the Cuban missile crisis. Martin Luther King, Jr., makes his "I Have a Dream" speech at the Lincoln Memorial in Washington, D.C.— the most famous declaration of the civil rights movement.

NOVEMBER. President Kennedy is shot dead in Dallas *(left)*. Vice President Lyndon Johnson succeeds him.

1964

OCTOBER. Khrushchev is deposed by the Soviet Politburo, to be succeeded by the duumvirate of Leonid Brezhnev and Aleksei Kosygin *(right)*. Martin Luther King, Jr., is awarded the Nobel Peace Prize. China explodes its first atomic bomb.

NOVEMBER. Lyndon Johnson, with running mate Hubert Humphrey, wins the U.S. presidential election.

Fire hoses batter black protesters during a 1963 civil rights demonstration in Birmingham, Alabama *(opposite)*. The U.S. civil rights movement was inspired by racial segregation and the denial of voting rights, usually by means of rigged literacy tests, to 11 million blacks in the American South. The demonstrations, and the brutality with which they were often suppressed, shocked U.S. and world opinion, and they provided a rich vein of material for Soviet Cold War propaganda. President Kennedy and his successor, Lyndon B. Johnson, began a steady stream of civil rights legislation that would transform, at least on paper, the lot of black Americans. But the new legislation did not prevent ferocious urban rioting throughout the 1960s, and even a generation later, race relations in the United States remained a sensitive and highly charged issue.

Defense Robert A. McNamara's acronym MAD, for "mutual assured destruction."

There would be no further attempt at the kind of deception Khrushchev had practiced in Cuba. Nor could there be: Space technology, already far advanced from the days of *Sputnik 1*, now provided both sides with effective reconnaissance satellites. The newly opened skies did much to decrease the chronic mistrust between the superpowers; without it, the Nuclear Test-Ban Treaty would have foundered, as previous negotiations had done, on the difficulties of verification.

Kennedy did not live to enjoy the relaxation in superpower tensions after the Nuclear Test-Ban Treaty. In November 1963, he was assassinated in Dallas. His death shocked millions of ordinary people throughout the Western alliance: For better or worse, the United States would never again have a president who could inspire such affection abroad.

Kennedy himself had seen to that. For, despite his general success, he had left his country with one dreadful burden: a growing engagement in Vietnam. Although none of the signatories of the 1954 Geneva agreement had seriously expected the division of the country to last, quantities of American aid had flowed into the supposedly democratic Republic of Vietnam. According to reports from U.S. diplomats and military observers, the South Vietnamese regime appeared to be incapable of inspiring the loyalty of its people, most of whom would probably vote Communist if the all-Vietnam elections promised at Geneva ever took place. The elections, in fact, were postponed indefinitely: Washington and Saigon claimed, with some justice, that Communist coercion would make a free vote impossible. Hanoi used the repression of southern Communists, nonetheless, to justify a guerrilla campaign in the South, which made rapid headway against Saigon's badly led and unhappy troops.

Despite the messy historical background, American politicians increasingly saw South Vietnam as a critical test of America's global political power: In 1956, young Senator Kennedy himself described it as the "cornerstone of the free world in Southeast Asia." By 1960, U.S. subsidies accounted for 75 percent of South Vietnam's budget, yet Hanoi's ill-equipped Vietcong, modestly funded by China and the Soviet Union, were clearly winning the struggle.

Faced with Khrushchev's just wars policy, Kennedy decided to make Vietnam his sticking place against Communist aggression, and he poured arms, money, advisers, and, by 1962, combat troops into the country. It made little difference: Despite almost 500 U.S. casualties in 1963, the South Vietnamese could not be induced to fight effectively against the Vietcong. In November 1963, the frustrated Americans backed a coup in which South Vietnamese president Ngo Dinh Diem was assassinated. By then, Kennedy had severe doubts about the wisdom of his policy, hinting to friends that he would pull out once he had won the 1964 election. He never had

1965

JUNE. American troops in Vietnam *(left)* go on the offensive, attacking Vietcong jungle strongholds east of Saigon.

AUGUST. Twenty thousand National Guardsmen are called out to end racial rioting in the Watts section of Los Angeles.

1966

APRIL. Leonid Brezhnev assumes the Soviet Union's most powerful post—general secretary of the Communist party.

1967

MARCH. Stalin's daughter, Svetlana Alliluyeva, defects to the West.

JULY. U.S. paratroopers restore order in Detroit following three days of race riots. Puerto Ricans in New York also riot.

1968

APRIL. Martin Luther King, Jr., is assassinated in Memphis. His death sparks riots in New York, Detroit, Washington, D.C., and many other cities.

JUNE. Presidential candidate Robert F. Kennedy is assassinated in Los Angeles by a Palestinian angered by Kennedy's support for Israel.

AUGUST. Soviet and Warsaw Pact tanks and troops invade Czechoslovakia to eject the reforming government of Alexander Dubček *(left).*

NOVEMBER. Richard M. Nixon, with running mate Spiro T. Agnew, wins the U.S. presidential election.

1969

JULY. Americans Neil A. Armstrong and Edwin "Buzz" Aldrin, Jr., become the first men to set foot on the Moon *(right).*

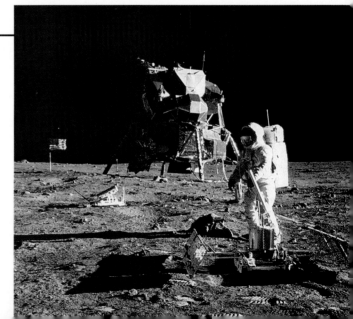

the chance: The Dallas shooting saw to that. The new president, former Vice President Lyndon B. Johnson, decided to continue and strengthen U.S. involvement.

It was a serious error of judgment. The foundations of failure were already laid, first and foremost in a double misunderstanding of the nature both of the enemy and of America's own strength. Secretary of Defense McNamara, a business genius who had come to the White House from the presidency of the Ford Motor Company, exemplified both misconceptions when he declared with characteristic confidence, "We have the power to knock any society out of the twentieth century." In fact, Vietnam scarcely belonged to the twentieth century in the first place, and certainly not to the twentieth century as perceived by people in the West. North and South Vietnam alike were poor, peasant societies, scarcely industrialized, and almost totally lacking targets against which America's devastating air power might have an obvious effect. The difference between them was that the Communist North was tightly organized, with an efficient army and a leadership endowed with a clear purpose; the South had neither of these things. In theory, the United States had the power to visit nuclear annihilation upon the Vietnamese; in practice, however, there was almost no way for Washington to impose its will upon Hanoi.

Meanwhile, the drafting of the nation's youth ensured the war's unpopularity at home. Casualties mounted—more than 50,000 Americans were to be killed, half again as many as in Korea—and a tide of antiwar protest rose with them. By 1968, Johnson was convinced that the war could be won only at a cost that was politically unsustainable. Refusing to run for reelection, he tried to make peace. But Hanoi saw no reason for compromise, and the United States was not yet ready to admit defeat.

Under Johnson's Republican successor, Richard Nixon, the war continued and even intensified. U.S. troops invaded neighboring Cambodia, while North Vietnam was scourged with more explosives than were used in the entire Second World War. Eventually, after Nixon's 1972 reelection, a peace of sorts was signed; the Americans withdrew, and Hanoi left the South alone for a brief period. In 1975, however, the North Vietnamese crossed the border; without American help, Saigon's armies melted away, and the war was finally over.

The United States had delayed a Communist victory by perhaps fifteen years, at a tremendous price. Its prestige had suffered a grievous blow. The extent and atrocity of the conflict had done enormous damage to the moral standing of the United States: For the first time, Europeans—and some Americans themselves—began to talk of the "moral equivalence" of the superpowers. War spending had created enough inflation to hurt even the U.S. economy. And politically, the nation was more divided than it had been since the Civil War more than a century before.

1970

APRIL. The United States sends troops to attack North Vietnamese positions in Cambodia.

OCTOBER. Soviet authorities prevent dissident author Alexander Solzhenitsyn (left) from traveling to Stockholm to receive the Nobel Prize for literature.

1971

SEPTEMBER. Nikita Khrushchev dies in Moscow at the age of seventy-seven.

1972

FEBRUARY. President Nixon meets Mao Zedong in Beijing, signaling a rapprochement between the United States and China.

MAY. President Nixon and Soviet leader Leonid Brezhnev meet in Moscow for strategic arms limitation talks. A treaty is signed in October.

SEPTEMBER. Seven men, including two former White House aides, are charged with breaking into Democratic party headquarters at the Watergate complex in Washington, D.C.

NOVEMBER. Richard Nixon roundly defeats Democrat George McGovern to win a second term as U.S. president.

U.S. marines carry their dead to a waiting Chinook helicopter during the siege of the Khe Sanh base in Vietnam in 1968. The Khe Sanh battle symbolized the tragic waste of the Vietnam War, which killed more than 50,000 Americans and uncounted Vietnamese. The base was exposed and strategically irrelevant; yet military planners were convinced that its retention was vital to American prestige. Almost 500 marines went home in body bags before the siege ended, after which the base was quietly dismantled.

The Vietnam War had one major beneficiary: the Soviet Union. America's long absorption in the conflict was a windfall for the Kremlin at a tense and difficult time. The USSR's least problem was its own leadership crisis, quickly and quietly resolved in 1964. Khrushchev, discredited not only by his risky foreign policies but also by disastrous failures of Soviet agriculture, was deposed and replaced as party secretary by the much more cautious Leonid Brezhnev; Aleksei Kosygin became premier.

The nation Brezhnev inherited faced a double danger. First, the split with China had turned into a gulf. Sino-Soviet relations were now so bad that large numbers of Soviet troops—and missiles—had to be deployed along the Chinese border, and shots

1973

APRIL. The Watergate scandal deepens as four of President Nixon's top aides resign. The following month, televised Senate hearings on the Watergate break-in begin.

SEPTEMBER. The Marxist government of Chile is overthrown by a CIA-backed military coup, in which President Salvador Allende is killed.

OCTOBER. Vice President Spiro Agnew resigns following charges of tax evasion. He is succeeded by Gerald R. Ford, Jr., Republican leader of the House of Representatives.

1974

FEBRUARY. Alexander Solzhenitsyn is exiled from the Soviet Union following publication in the West of his exposé of Soviet labor camps, *The Gulag Archipelago.*

AUGUST. President Nixon *(right)* resigns under threat of impeachment as a result of his involvement in the Watergate scandal. He is succeeded by Vice President Gerald Ford.

were regularly exchanged by border guards, a situation that in 1969 erupted into something like full-scale war on the Ussuri River boundary. Thenceforth, the Kremlin would have to live with the nightmare of a possible Chinese-American alliance—an eventuality that, to the Russians' relief, the Vietnam War made less likely.

The Kremlin's second major worry was less of an immediate peril. The European Economic Community (EEC) was proving an economic powerhouse, setting a distressing example to the vastly poorer Soviet satellites and clearly developing into a major source of political influence in its own right. Financially it was already drawing Eastern European leaders to seek loans to improve their own muddled economies—a dilution of Soviet influence that Moscow regarded with intense suspicion. Even here, though, America's Vietnam commitments helped the Soviet Union, as U.S. allies, dismayed at Washington's embroilment in Southeast Asia, developed increasingly independent relations with the East. France, always a maverick, had pulled out of NATO's command structure in 1966; now West Germany, deeply conscious of its status as a divided nation, introduced a new *Ostpolitik*—an attempt to improve relations with its Eastern European neighbors—which made it easier for the Soviet bloc to acquire Western goods and technologies.

Western Europe's affluence was one of the factors that encouraged the new Czechoslovakian party secretary, Alexander Dubček, to initiate in 1968 a series of political and economic reforms that were known as the Prague Spring. Brezhnev made certain there was no "Prague Summer": In August that year, a Russian-dominated Warsaw Pact army rolled into the country and crushed Dubček's ideas beneath its tank tracks. The repression was far less bloody than the invasion of Hungary had been in 1956, but it was just as effective. Dubček disappeared from public life to be replaced by Brezhnev's own appointees, and ordinary Czechs settled back down to surly and dejected obedience. The Brezhnev Doctrine—Moscow's unstated determination to keep its satellites in secure orbit around it—had been brutally enforced, at the cost of further alienating world opinion.

Nixon, and his German-born secretary of state, Henry A. Kissinger, were not entirely absorbed by the Vietnam War. Kissinger, a student of nineteenth-century diplomacy, was convinced that a straightforward Great Power relationship, unconcerned with ideology, could be negotiated with the Soviet Union. Since the Cuban crisis, the Soviets had steadily increased their nuclear armaments: By 1970, a missile gap of sorts did exist, although by then, both superpowers had more than enough weaponry to destroy each other several times over. A treaty limiting strategic arms seemed even more urgent than in Johnson's time; and Nixon, as a right-winger, was in a better position to negotiate it than a president with a liberal reputation.

1975

APRIL. Communist Khmer Rouge forces capture the Cambodian capital, Phnom Penh. Vietcong troops capture the South Vietnamese capital, Saigon.

JULY. Russian and American astronauts meet in space as part of the Soviet-U.S. détente agreement instituted by Nixon and Brezhnev in 1972.

OCTOBER. The Russian physicist and human-rights campaigner Andrei Sakharov is refused permission to travel to Oslo to receive the Nobel Peace Prize.

1976

NOVEMBER. Democrat Jimmy Carter *(right)*, with running mate Walter Mondale, wins the U.S. presidential election.

1977

JUNE. Leonid Brezhnev becomes president of the Soviet Union following the dismissal of his predecessor, Nikolai Podgorny.

A strategic arms limitation treaty (SALT) suited Moscow, too. Closer relations with the United States would benefit the Soviet economy and would also allow access to American grain surpluses, which were much needed, given chronic Soviet agricultural failure. So a new policy of détente was born, and Nixon gave his assent to the SALT agreement on a triumphant visit to Moscow in 1972.

The new rapport was put to a dangerous test the following year, when the Arab states launched an attack on Israel during the nation's holiest day, Yom Kippur. After initial near-disaster, Israeli forces, massively replenished by a U.S. arms airlift, counterattacked, and the Egyptians faced battlefield disaster. Brezhnev threatened to use airborne troops to restore the balance; the United States responded by putting its nuclear forces on a worldwide alert, the first since the days of Cuba. In fact, neither side was anxious for a showdown over what each regarded as troublesome allies. Both backed down. Kissinger, in a flurry of shuttle diplomacy, organized a cease-fire that deprived the indignant Israelis of what they regarded as their rightful spoils; the Soviet Union rearmed the Arabs. The Middle East remained a dangerous flash point.

Nixon's resignation in 1974, to avoid impeachment as a result of the Watergate scandal, undermined presidential authority, once more to the advantage of the Soviet Union. By the time Jimmy Carter was elected in 1976, Moscow—convinced that détente reduced the risk of Third World adventures—had made the most of its opportunities. A newly expanded navy was used to project Soviet power worldwide, establishing bases in Vietnam and Yemen. In Africa, Cuban troops under Moscow's control—Castro had to pay a price for the aid the Soviets lavished upon him—were active in Angola and Mozambique, and leftist coups moved more established nations, like Ethiopia in 1974, into the Soviet sphere. By the end of the 1970s, a revolution in Nicaragua gave Moscow a foothold in Central America, and Afghan-

1978

APRIL. The Soviet Union's highest-ranking UN delegate, Arkady N. Shevchenko, defects to the West.

1979

JUNE. Brezhnev and President Carter meet in Vienna to sign the SALT II arms limitation treaty. The U.S. Senate fails to ratify the treaty, so it never comes into force.

JULY. Marxist Sandinista forces overthrow the regime of President Anastasio Somoza in Nicaragua.

DECEMBER. The USSR sends troops to Afghanistan to install a new Marxist government under Babrak Karmal to fight Islamic mujahedin rebels (right).

1980

JANUARY. Andrei Sakharov is sent into internal exile following his condemnation of the Soviet invasion of Afghanistan.

JULY. The United States boycotts the Moscow Olympic Games in protest against the Soviet Union's invasion of Afghanistan.

SEPTEMBER. Following labor unrest in the port of Gdańsk and elsewhere, the Polish government is forced to cede to workers the right to form an independent trade union, known as Solidarity (right) and led by Lech Walesa.

NOVEMBER. Republican Ronald Reagan (left) and his running mate George Bush defeat Jimmy Carter in the U.S. elections.

1981

MARCH. Ronald Reagan is wounded in an unsuccessful assassination attempt.

istan on the Soviet Union's vulnerable southern frontier had acquired an aggressively Communist regime. Meanwhile in Europe, Brezhnev's relentless deployment of powerful new medium-range SS-20 missiles seemed to be unnerving Western leaders and certainly encouraged an increasingly vociferous peace movement, whose outspoken anti-Americanism inhibited NATO countermeasures.

In the face of advancing Soviet power, Carter struggled on with what was left of Nixon's détente policy. But the SALT II agreement he signed in 1979, against a background of increasing public distrust, was never to be ratified by the U.S. Senate.

In fact, the Soviet Union was far weaker than its world position suggested. While the cost of the Vietnam War had done immense harm to the U.S. economy, the much smaller Soviet economy was quite incapable of bearing the strain of heavy and continued arms spending as well as the endless subsidies required by its allies. Outside the defense industries, growth was slow or even negative; Five-Year Plans were regularly unfulfilled, and agriculture remained a severe problem. For all the Brezhnev regime's expansionism abroad, at home it presided over a stagnant society. On the one hand, large-scale (and scarcely hidden) corruption among the ruling bureaucracy—the *nomenklatura*—ensured a high standard of living for party officials and their dependents; on the other, chronic shortages condemned ordinary citizens to hours standing in line for many goods. Infant mortality rose and life expectancy fell. Ideological enthusiasm had practically vanished, to be replaced by a deep cynicism of which widespread alcoholism was only the most obvious symptom.

The pattern of demographic change made grim reading for the Russian-dominated Politburo: Within the Soviet Union, the proportion of ethnic Russians was sinking toward—and in some areas below—50 percent. Only in the USSR's southern republics was the Russian population growing. And these republics were not only racially

A giant U.S. flag is a meeting place for some of the 400,000 young Americans who assembled at the Woodstock Music and Arts Festival in New York State in August 1969. The Woodstock gathering was the high point of the so-called counterculture movement that emerged in America during the 1960s, when millions of young people rejected traditional social values in favor of a lifestyle in which drugs, sex, and rock music would produce a new world of peace and love. But from the start, the hippies provoked an ill-tempered reaction from the American working class, who sourly noted the affluent, middle-class background from which they mostly came, and peace and love proved hard to attain.

different: Despite generations of persecution from officially atheist Soviet authorities, most of them still clung to their ancestral Islamic faith. With neighboring Iran in religious ferment—from 1980 it was heavily engaged in a holy war with Iraq—it was an ill omen for the Soviet future.

The Soviet Union's southern borders seemed increasingly vulnerable. Afghanistan's Communist government—hard-line even by Moscow's standards—had contrived, mainly by ignoring its people's Is-

1982

NOVEMBER. Leonid Brezhnev dies of a heart attack at the age of seventy-five. He is succeeded by the ex-head of the KGB, Yuri Andropov *(right)*.

1983

MARCH. President Reagan proposes a space-based antimissile defense system, soon dubbed the Star Wars project.

MAY. The United States publicly backs the Contra rebels fighting to overthrow Nicaragua's Sandinista government, led by Daniel Ortega *(right)*.

SEPTEMBER. A Soviet fighter plane shoots down a Korean Airlines Boeing 747 flying off-course near military installations in Siberia, killing all 269 civilians on board.

OCTOBER. U.S. troops invade the Caribbean island of Grenada to restore democracy following the overthrow and murder of its prime minister in an army coup.

lamic faith, to provoke a near-unstoppable rebellion against itself. Fearful of the consequences of such disorder on its borders, the Soviet Union in December 1979 responded with brutal efficiency: The Red Army invaded the country, murdered the existing Communist despot, and replaced him with a more compliant puppet. Brezhnev's fear of disorder thereby committed the nation to indefinite guerrilla fighting against the notoriously tough Afghans, passionate Muslims convinced that their struggle was a holy war and provided with some of the world's most rugged territory in which to fight it. Soon Soviet helicopter gunships were burning villages, and teenage Soviet conscripts were coming back home in military coffins. The Americans were not alone in finding the situation horribly reminiscent of Vietnam.

More troubles were approaching. Poland had rumbled with dissent for years: Strikes and riots in the 1970s had been partly repressed, partly bought off with economic concessions to Polish workers. By the summer of 1980, discontent had produced the Solidarity trade union, which organized waves of strikes and sought a political revolution. The union's leaders were careful in their public utterances, and the Polish government yielded as much as it dared: Both Solidarity and the Polish Communist party remembered the fate of Hungary and Czechoslovakia, and neither wanted to provoke a heavy-handed Soviet reaction.

The Soviet Union was indeed alarmed, but despite the Brezhnev Doctrine it was reluctant to intervene. The reasons were partly economic: During the 1970s détente, not only Poland but all of the Eastern European countries had borrowed heavily from Western banks. In general, the money had been spent with even less wisdom than the bankers had shown in lending it, and most of the satellites were teetering on the brink of economic failure. Even as Solidarity staged mass demonstrations, Polish government negotiators were seeking a rescheduling of their debt repayments. A Soviet intervention would undoubtedly bring Western financial sanctions, which might prove the last straw not only for Poland but for the whole of the Soviet bloc.

1984

FEBRUARY. Yuri Andropov dies of kidney disease at the age of sixty-nine. He is succeeded as Soviet leader by the seventy-two-year-old Konstantin Chernenko.

MAY. The USSR announces that it will boycott the Los Angeles Olympic Games.

NOVEMBER. Ronald Reagan is reelected U.S. president. Stalin's daughter Svetlana Alliluyeva returns to the Soviet Union after seventeen years in the West. (She will return again to the United States two years later.)

There were other reasons for Soviet hesitancy. Although *Pravda* talked of "irresponsible, anarchist, and antisocialist elements," the Kremlin was well aware that Solidarity had overwhelming popular support. An invasion would likely be met with armed resistance: Soviet prestige would plummet, and even military victory would lead to a long and expensive occupation. Brezhnev bided his time.

While they were waiting, the Americans replaced Carter with the sternly right-wing Ronald Reagan in the November 1980 elections. Détente was already dead, killed by the Russian invasion of Afghanistan: Reagan now buried it under a tirade of anti-Soviet speeches. The president rejected Brezhnev's offers of arms-reduction talks: There was no point in negotiating with what he called the "evil Empire." Instead, the United States would rearm with new and more potent weapons systems, including a new strategic defense program, which would use ultrahigh-technology laser weapons on earth and in space to shoot down Soviet missiles.

Launched in 1983, the program, soon dubbed Star Wars, was ambitious in the extreme, at the edge of America's engineering ability and perhaps beyond it. It frankly appalled the Soviets, who could not hope to keep up with it and who threatened to respond by a massive increase in missile numbers that would simply swamp Reagan's vaunted defense—although even an expansion of existing weapons systems would strain the ailing Soviet economy. Star Wars upset many of Reagan's NATO allies, too, who appreciated at least the stability of the current nuclear balance. Nevertheless, despite waves of protest from antinuclear demonstrators, the NATO countries went ahead with the installation of the U.S. cruise and Pershing missiles the alliance had agreed should counter Brezhnev's SS-20s. Once more, the Cold War grew cooler.

The situation was far from resolved when Brezhnev, long ailing, died in 1982 at the age of seventy-six. During his last years, he had been little more than a figurehead, kept in power simply to prevent a succession struggle. His replacement, Yuri Andropov, was not much younger and was almost as ill: Although he began a series of cautious reforms, they had had little effect on Soviet society by the time of his death in 1984. The economy was still dangerously weak, and agriculture, as always, was a national embarrassment. Changes could not long be delayed; yet party leaders temporized once more, entrusting the fate of the Soviet Union to a seventy-two-year-old conservative, Konstantin Chernenko. Frail and in poor health, Chernenko made his exact contemporary Reagan—the oldest president the United States had ever elected—seem a young man; Kremlin leadership had reached its nadir.

But the gerontocracy, by its very nature, could not survive indefinitely. When Chernenko, too, went to his grave, in March 1985, the Brezhnev generation could no longer keep its hold on power. To the delight of most of the Soviet people, his successor was Mikhail S. Gorbachev, at fifty-four the youngest leader since Stalin.

1985

MARCH. Mikhail Gorbachev becomes leader of the Soviet Union following the death of Konstantin Chernenko. He ushers in an era of *glasnost* and *perestroika*—openness and economic restructuring.

NOVEMBER. East-West relations grow warmer as Gorbachev and President Reagan meet in Geneva to discuss arms reduction and human rights *(left)*.

1986

JANUARY. The American space shuttle *Challenger* explodes shortly after takeoff, killing all seven crew members on board.

APRIL. A fire at the Soviet nuclear reactor at Chernobyl in the Ukraine spreads dangerous levels of radioactivity across Europe.

DECEMBER. Andrei Sakharov *(left)* is released from internal exile and returns to Moscow.

RUSSIAN SOVIET FEDERATED SOCIALIST REPUBLIC (RSFSR)

The task before the new leader was immense: The Soviet Union's political and economic problems had been avoided for decades by his predecessors, and now they had to be solved with desperate urgency. Gorbachev, surrounded by a team of young and sometimes radical advisers, set to work at once. His reform policy was twofold. Politically, he insisted on openness and public accountability: *glasnost*. Economically, the country would move away from the paralyzing system of centralized control into a new era of economic freedom: *perestroika*.

In foreign policy, too, he broke new ground. It was obvious that continued high

1987

DECEMBER. Meeting in Washington, Gorbachev and President Reagan agree to cut their countries' medium- and short-range missile arsenals.

1988

MARCH. Troops are sent to the Soviet republic of Azerbaijan to prevent violence between Azerbaijanis and Armenians.

MAY. Soviet troops are withdrawn from Afghanistan *(left)*, leaving President Najib Najibullah's government to face rebel mujahedin forces alone.

OCTOBER. Nationalist demonstrators in the Soviet republics of Latvia and Lithuania call for greater self-government.

NOVEMBER. Republican candidate George Bush—shown at right with his wife, Barbara—defeats Michael S. Dukakis in the U.S. presidential elections. The Soviet republic of Estonia adopts a constitution establishing greater autonomy.

weapons spending would cripple any possible reforms. It was equally evident that such spending had bought the Soviet Union precious little extra security. Believing the world to be increasingly interconnected and interdependent, the new Soviet leader saw little room for superpower interventionism; "neither the Soviet Union nor the United States is able to force its will on others," he wrote in his book *Perestroika*. Within months of taking office, Gorbachev was proposing to the United States a breathtaking series of arms reductions. Gone were the days when every missile and every soldier was a matter of weeks of wrangling. Gorbachev needed drastic cuts, and he wanted them at once.

Reagan was caught off balance by the turnabout. For the first time since the war, the Soviet Union had a leader who could catch the enthusiasm of Western public opinion. In visits to Western Europe and the United States, Gorbachev was mobbed by joyful crowds; the words *glasnost* and *perestroika* entered half a dozen Western languages. But despite the president's initial suspicions, he adapted quickly to the new climate. In 1987, he signed the Intermediate-range Nuclear Forces (INF) Treaty, by whose terms medium-range missiles—an entire class of weapons—were simply abolished. The Cold War, both parties publicly declared, was over. In 1988, Soviet troops started pulling out of Afghanistan.

But Gorbachev found domestic politics more difficult than foreign affairs, even though at first the new openness was a triumphant success. At the twenty-seventh Party Congress in 1986, he won a clear victory over his conservative opponents, who were all too aware that their long-held privileges would vanish rapidly in the new light of *glasnost*. The Soviet media, never in living memory anything but the mouthpiece of official policy, started acquiring the exciting skills of investigative journalism. State archives were gradually opened: Soviet citizens began to learn in detail some of the horrors of their own history. Free elections to local soviets and the Supreme Soviet itself were another innovation, and hundreds of die-hard party chieftains of the Brezhnev era found themselves ejected from their comfortable positions by the people they had claimed to serve. In early 1990, Gorbachev went even further: He pressed through a constitutional amendment that removed the Communist party's privileged status. In the future, it would have to compete for power with other parties in an open contest.

Economic reform, however, was harder to implement. The backwardness of the Soviet economy was such that attempts to improve it led in the short term to a fall, not a rise, in Soviet living standards. In the climate of rising expectations created by *glasnost*, discontent was voluble. Lines lengthened, and strikes began to become a

A patchwork of fifteen ethnically diverse republics with an eleven-hour time difference between its extremes, the USSR has never been the monolith its leaders and its enemies alike have often fondly or fearfully imagined. By 1985, the core Russian republic *(shaded yellow)* contained barely half the Soviet population, and most of the other republics chafed to go their own way. Lenin, the Soviet Union's founder, once called czarist Russia the "prison of nations"; by 1990, his heirs were contending with a rash of escape attempts. The Muslim republics in the south looked to the Islamic world; the Baltic states of Lithuania, Estonia, and Latvia sought independence and closer contact with the West, and the Ukraine, the USSR's most fertile region, bubbled with nationalism.

1989

JANUARY. The Hungarian parliament passes legislation permitting the formation of opposition political parties.

JUNE. Poland's Solidarity wins all but one of the seats in the first free election in fifty years.

NOVEMBER. East Germany opens the Berlin Wall.

DECEMBER. In the course of a summit meeting in Malta, Gorbachev and President Bush both assent to a press conference suggestion that the Cold War is over. In Czechoslovakia the Communist party relinquishes power to a multiparty cabinet. Romanian dictator Nicolae Ceauşescu is executed.

feature of industrial existence. National unrest in the non-Russian republics of the Soviet Union was another unwanted complication. By 1989, Gorbachev was faced with near civil war between Armenia and Azerbaijan in the south, while the Baltic republics of Estonia, Latvia, and Lithuania clamored to secede from the USSR.

In Eastern Europe, *glasnost* had even more dramatic effects. Hungary slowly began to transform itself into a democratic state, with multiple political parties and free elections. The barbed wire that guarded its socialist frontiers was ostentatiously taken down. In Poland, citizens were able to elect their first non-Communist president. Both countries looked eagerly to the EEC for aid—and perhaps eventual membership.

Nineteen eighty-nine was the *annus mirabilis* of Eastern European freedom. By late summer, East Germans were fleeing by the hundreds of thousands through Hungary's newly open borders to citizenship in West Germany. Mass demonstrations in East Germany's cities at first brought threats from its government, but when it became clear that Gorbachev had no intention of using the Red Army to protect the Communist apparatus, the government simply abdicated. In November, the Berlin Wall was torn down under the amused—if somewhat astonished—gaze of East German border guards. Events in Czechoslovakia ran a similar course: Dissident playwright Václav Havel began 1989 in jail and by year's end was the country's new president, while secret police headquarters were ransacked and Communist officials made themselves scarce. Gorbachev himself encouraged a quiet revolution in Bulgaria, and in December, the Romanian people and their conscript army fought bloody battles with Nicolae Ceauşescu's security police; the dictator found himself facing a firing squad before the year was out.

The message was simple, and it came from Gorbachev as well as from the streets of Europe: There could be no going back. As the 1990s began, the superpowers were making plans to withdraw troops from central Europe, and Eastern European Communist parties sought new identities in which they might compete with some hope of success in the forthcoming elections everywhere. German reunification, once the Cold War's most taboo subject, was under way.

In the Soviet Union, Gorbachev was still engaged in a race to achieve the goals of *perestroika* before the associated unrest brought not just the Soviet empire but the USSR itself down in ruins—a race whose outcome was far from certain. The Cold War of Truman and Stalin, Kennedy and Khrushchev, Nixon and Brezhnev, was certainly over, and it was hard to see how it could be revived. In a way it had been won by the United States and the nations of the Western alliance: After all, Soviet power had clearly mellowed, as George Kennan had hoped more than forty years before, and the Western nations had retained their freedom and independence. Whether the USSR had lost remained to be seen, for, although the game had been played for frighteningly high stakes, the people of the Soviet Union and its satellites seemed to have gained far more than they could ever have received from a "victory."

In fact, the concepts of victory and defeat no longer seemed meaningful. The struggle had been long and confused, marked as much by each side's blunders as by the intelligent application of strategy. But whatever the faults of the policymakers and generals who had fought the Cold War, there was one mistake none of them ever made. Despite fear, tension, and sometimes outright hatred, they had kept the nuclear peace. The missiles stayed in their silos; the human race survived.

SPACE ODYSSEYS

In July of 1969, watched by millions of television viewers throughout the world, the American astronaut Neil A. Armstrong descended from the lunar module of his *Apollo 11* spacecraft to become the first human to walk on the Moon. It was the culminating moment of the space race, an epic contest that had started twelve years earlier when the Soviet Union launched the first man-made satellite into orbit around the Earth, startling the United States into a costly and ambitious response.

In the tense atmosphere of the Cold War, the Soviet Union's success was perceived by the U.S. government as a serious threat. The technology of the Russians' orbiting sphere was unexpectedly advanced; and it was obvious that the huge rocket that had carried it into space was equally capable of delivering a nuclear weapon without being intercepted. The United States accelerated its own space program, successfully

launching a satellite just four months later. In the years that followed, other nations joined the race, but the two Great Powers always remained ahead.

While the Americans concentrated on the miniaturization of equipment and developed vehicles to carry out reconnaissance and collect scientific data, the Russians built bigger satellites and launched larger rockets. Scientists in both nations vied to dominate space, demonstrate technological superiority, and astonish the world with spectacular achievements.

The mood of the contest changed, however, after the Moon landing of 1969. During the next decade, a new spirit of cooperation emerged. The Great Powers banned nuclear weapons from space and agreed that no nation could lay claim to any territory in the universe. Although their separate programs continued, they also undertook a joint project in which manned U.S.

and Soviet spacecraft rendezvoused in orbit, and they began to share some of the data gleaned from space stations and the unmanned craft that they were sending to the planets and beyond.

The exploration of space came increasingly to be seen as an adventure of humankind as a whole, rather than of any one nation. Besides expanding man's knowledge of the cosmos, it fostered new technologies and led to the development of fresh materials and manufacturing processes. Commercial uses were found for many of its innovations, from freeze-dried food to advanced insulation and lubricants.

The long-term results of the venture into space, however, remain to be determined. It may be many years before the discoveries made even in its first decades yield all their secrets; and the future possibilities of man's journey into the cosmos are as limitless as space itself.

Sputnik 1, the first man-made object to be put into space, trails four long radio antennas. It remained in orbit around the Earth for 162 days, circling it every 96.17 minutes.

The first living creature in space, a black and white mongrel called Laika, waits to board Sputnik 2 on November 3, 1957. After more than a week in orbit, pretreated food put Laika to sleep before her oxygen supply ran out.

Soviet cosmonaut Yuri Gagarin's pioneering space flight lasted just 108 minutes. Launched in Vostok 1 on April 12, 1961, he made one orbit of the Earth at 190 miles, traveling at a speed of 18,000 miles per hour. He never went into space again, dying in a plane crash in 1968.

FIRST STEPS
INTO ORBIT

The Soviet Union achieved most of the breakthroughs in the early years of the space race, largely thanks to a superiority in rocket technology. In part, this stemmed from the Russians' earlier choice of rockets rather than airplanes as conveyors for their nuclear weapons. Their huge R-7 rocket, adapted for space use as the A-1, was capable of carrying much larger payloads than its U.S. equivalent.

The Soviets capped the triumphant launch in October 1957 of the world's first orbiting satellite, Sputnik 1, the following month by dispatching the 1,000-pound Sputnik 2 carrying a dog, the first living creature to travel in space. In April of 1961, Yuri Gagarin became the first man in space, beating his American counterpart, John Glenn, by ten months. In 1963, Soviet cosmonaut Valentina Tereshkova was the first woman space traveler.

Two years later, Soviet cosmonaut Alexei Leonov made the first spacewalk when he left his craft Voskhod 2 for eleven minutes—and almost became the first space victim. Once outside the craft, he discovered that his movements were so limited by his pressurized suit that he could not maneuver his way back in again. To reenter the craft, he had to release air from the suit, risking depressurization, and once inside reinflate it again rapidly.

Although the Russians dominated the early years of the space race, the Americans were never far behind. In the less glamorous areas of technological development, such as communications and weather satellites, American scientists led the way despite the fact that the bulk of their space budget was being spent elsewhere, on the Apollo Moon project.

Edward H. White, the first American to walk in space, floats outside his *Gemini 4* spacecraft on June 3, 1965. Once the self-maneuvering unit in his right hand ran out of fuel, he moved by tugging on the lifeline attaching him to the craft.

The rocket carrying America's first astronaut, John Glenn, into orbit blasts off from Cape Canaveral in Florida on February 20, 1962. Glenn circled the Earth three times before splashing down early as a result of a faulty instrument reading.

THE MOON MISSIONS

In 1961, after Yuri Gagarin's orbit of the Earth, U.S. President John F. Kennedy called for "any program now, regardless of its cost, which offers us hope of being pioneers in a space project." The result was a plan to put men on the Moon by the end of the decade. Known as Project Apollo, it involved more than 400,000 people and cost at least $25 billion. It also claimed lives: In 1967, the three-man crew of *Apollo 1* was asphyxiated when fire broke out during a simulated launch. But the mission was crowned with success when on July 20, 1969, Neil Armstrong descended onto the Moon's surface.

The successful *Apollo 11* mission, whose three-man team also included Edwin "Buzz" Aldrin and Michael Collins, consisted of three principal sections: a three-stage *Saturn V* launch rocket, the combined command and service modules, and the lunar module, *Eagle,* which carried Armstrong and Aldrin down to the Moon's surface. There they spent more than two hours setting up instruments, planting the American flag, and leaping in gravity only one-sixth as strong as that on Earth.

Another six missions followed before the project came to a close with the return of *Apollo 17* to Earth in December 1972. In all, it had involved eleven manned flights; a dozen astronauts had landed on the moon, and twelve more had orbited it. Televised pictures of their exploits had helped establish America's primacy in the space race. More important, the Apollo project marked the beginning of a new era in exploration; humankind had finally established a first foothold on another celestial body.

The *Apollo 11* lunar module returns to its parent vehicle after its successful landing on the Moon. Its awkward shape created no problem in the Moon's weak gravity, which precludes the need for streamlining.

Astronaut James B. Irwin salutes the American flag during a moonwalk on the 1971 *Apollo 15* mission; also pictured are the lunar module and a lunar rover. Powered by thirty-six-volt batteries driving electric motors in each wheel hub, the vehicle, which was operated by a single control between the seats, cruised at eight miles per hour.

The U.S. space shuttle *Discovery* returns to Earth after completing a mission in November 1989.

WORKSHOPS OF THE NEW AGE

In 1971, the USSR launched the first in a series of orbiting space stations designed to act as military observation platforms and laboratories. *Salyut 1* was abandoned after the first crew to visit it died when air leaked from their spacecraft during the flight home. But the program continued, reaching a new level of sophistication in 1977 with the launch of *Salyut 6,* larger, more comfortable, and provided with a second docking port to allow resupply of the station from automated cargo ships.

In 1986, the first of a new breed of Mir space stations went into orbit. Almost sixty feet long, Mir boasted advanced recycling technology, a research laboratory in a separate module, and six docking ports. Between 1987 and 1988, a crew lived in the station for a record 366 days.

The only U.S. space station, Skylab, was launched in 1973, to be abandoned the following year after playing host to only three crews. In the ensuing years, American planners turned their attention instead to the space shuttle program. These reusable craft were designed to reduce the cost of putting payloads into orbit. Launched on the side of a rocket, the shuttles returned to Earth under their own power, landing on runways like airplanes.

Between 1981 and 1986, four shuttles carried out twenty-four successful missions, many for commercial customers, before tragedy disrupted the program. On January 28, 1986, faulty seals allowed burning gases to seep out of one of the rocket boosters launching the shuttle *Challenger,* causing an explosion that killed its crew of seven. Thirty-two months of testing were to pass before a shuttle flew again.

Skylab orbits the Earth, protected by an emergency umbrella replacing a thermal shield torn away in takeoff. Power to operate the craft was generated by solar cells deployed on the folding wing extending from its side; a second, similar appendage was ripped off with the thermal shield.

American and Soviet astronauts meet in the hatch between their two spacecraft in July 1975, in the course of the first joint mission of the space superpowers.

Photographed from *Viking 2,* boulders litter the surface of Mars, its soil colored red by a heavy concentration of iron. Although U.S. missions discovered more about Mars than any other planet, they failed to settle conclusively the question of whether it could support any kind of life.

ВЕНЕРА-9   22.10.1975   ОБРАБОТКА ИППИ АН СССР ВЕНЕРА-10   25.10.1975   ОБРАБОТКА ИППИ АН СССР

Taken in 1975 by two Venera probes at points about 1,200 miles apart, these images of rocky debris on Venus were the first pictures from the surface of another planet.

This false-color view of Saturn, taken in 1980 by *Voyager 1* from a distance of 20 million miles, combines images shot through ultraviolet, violet, and green filters, interpreted and enhanced by computer.

EXPLORING THE FAR FRONTIERS

From the early 1960s, both the United States and the Soviet Union have been sending unmanned spacecraft far beyond the range of manned flights in an effort to explore the other planets of the solar system and to gain information on conditions in outer space.

The first exploration was of the planets neighboring the Earth. Soviet planners concentrated on Venus with their Venera program, while the American Mariner and Viking probes sent back data on Mars, Venus, and Mercury.

In the 1970s, the U.S. space agency, NASA, launched two ambitious series of probes designed to fly by the outer planets of the solar system. *Pioneer 10,* launched in 1972, encountered Jupiter the following year, then flew on into outer space to become, ten years later, the first man-made

object to leave the solar system. *Pioneer 11,* dispatched the following year, flew by both Jupiter and Saturn.

The follow-up program was even more successful. The two Voyager craft, blasting off within sixteen days of one another in the summer of 1977, sent back valuable data on Jupiter and Saturn. But while *Voyager 1* then continued, like the Pioneer probes, out into deep space, *Voyager 2* took advantage of an alignment of the planets that occurs only once every 175 years to complete a grand tour of the large planets of the outer solar system by also flying by Uranus and Neptune. Powered by heat from radioactive plutonium in their thermal generators, the instruments aboard *Voyager 1* and *2* are expected to continue transmitting scientific data until well into the twenty-first century.

Photographed from *Voyager 1,* twin satellites Io and Europa orbit Jupiter. Beyond Io lies the planet's famed Red Spot, a huge anticyclonic storm first observed three centuries ago but possibly a thousand times older.

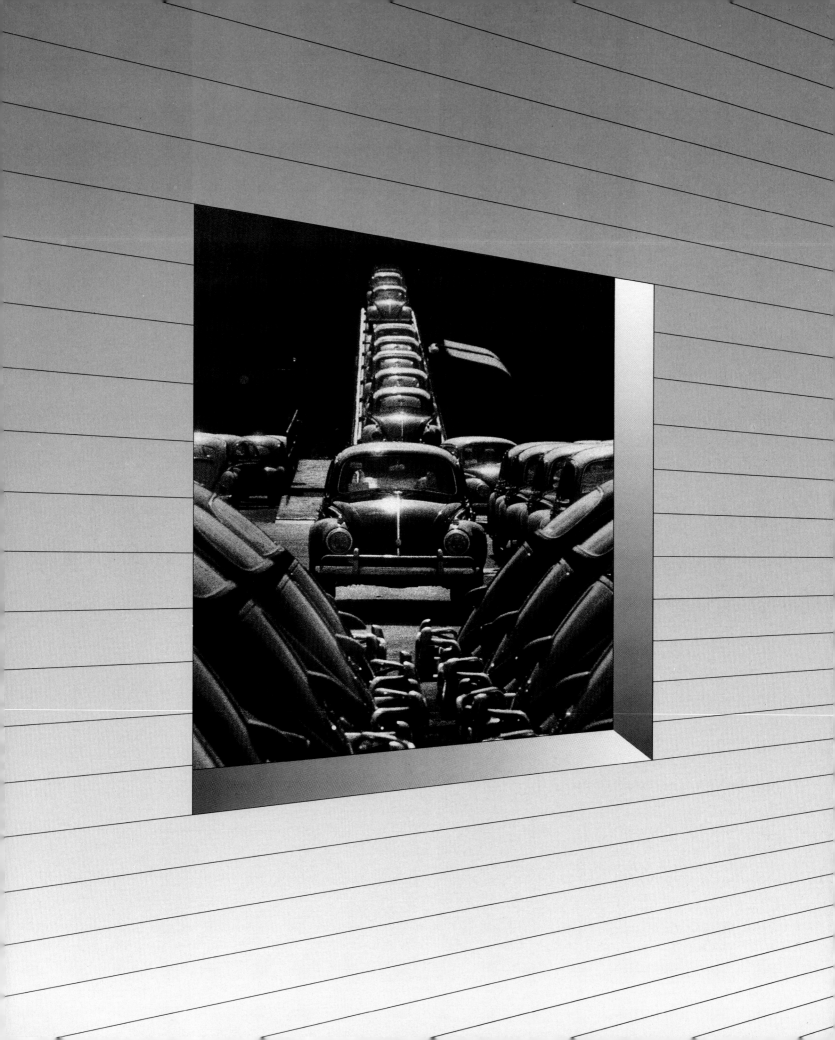

EUROPE RISES FROM THE ASHES

2 "What is Europe now?" demanded Britain's wartime leader Winston Churchill rhetorically at a political rally in 1947. He answered his own question: "A rubble heap, a charnel house, a breeding ground for pestilence and hate."

His comfortless vision was not exaggerated. Six years of global conflict had shattered the victors and vanquished of World War II alike. Much of Germany lay beaten flat. Allied bombing raids, it was estimated, had destroyed 40 percent or more of its buildings, and its great cities—Berlin, Frankfurt am Main, Düsseldorf—were uninhabitable. Britain, once banker to the world, had become the world's greatest debtor nation. Two-thirds of Europe's factories had fallen silent, and many were in ruins. Agricultural production had collapsed to 50 percent of its prewar level. France had lost half of its livestock. Damage to major roads and railways had crippled the transport of relief supplies. Only one serviceable bridge spanned the Rhine in 1945.

Peace did not bring an end to suffering. All Europeans experienced hardships, while those in areas of particular devastation faced malnutrition and disease. In parts of Germany, adults were sentenced to a slow starvation on 700 calories per day, only one-sixth of the ration allocated to occupying U.S. troops. Civilization, it seemed, had fractured beyond repair. For this apparently hopeless state, the Germans used a haunting phrase: *Stunde Null*, the zero hour.

Time may have reverted to zero, but it was hardly standing still. Out of the ruins grew a new Europe whose western half would emerge within the next quarter-century as an economic power to rival any in the world. The vehicle of growth was the EEC, founded with six members in 1957 but by 1990 embracing twelve nations and more than 300 million people. The eastern half of the continent was slower to develop, caught as it was in the shadow of the USSR. But its sudden liberation in 1989, and the prospect of increased economic integration within the EEC after 1992, left Europe poised to provide the twentieth century with an intriguing denouement.

It would have taken a determined optimist to have foreseen such a rosy future in the immediate postwar years. The Continent was not merely facing an enormous task of reconstruction. It was also politically divided by what Churchill memorably described in a 1946 speech as an iron curtain, separating the Western democracies from the Soviet satellites of Eastern Europe.

The takeover of Eastern Europe by the Russian leader Joseph Stalin had been determined and ruthless. Even before the war was over, Stalin had installed a Moscow-trained candidate in charge of newly liberated Poland. In other countries, he encouraged what one Hungarian Communist described as the "salami technique," slicing away piece by piece at any political parties that stood in the way of communism until the time was right to seize control. Czechoslovakia held out dog-

Volkswagen cars on parade in 1957 proclaim the post-World War II renaissance of German industrial might. Known as the Beetle, this distinctive Volkswagen (people's car) model was first produced under the Nazis in 1939. After the war, the impetus of U.S. financial aid revived the German auto industry, which soon began to manufacture for export as well as the domestic market. By 1979, when the Beetle was discontinued, 19 million cars had been driven off the assembly line.

gedly, but it too collapsed under Soviet pressure in 1948. Only Yugoslavia, led by the national resistance hero Marshal Josip Broz Tito, successfully defied Soviet domination, claiming the right to chose its own road to socialism.

The bitterest division was that of Germany. After its defeat in 1945, it had been split among the Allies, Britain, France, and the United States dividing the larger western region, the Soviet Union taking the east. Berlin, though 100 miles inside the eastern zone, was also partitioned. The western zones were united in 1949 to form the Federal Republic of Germany. A month later, the Soviets announced the creation in their sector of a socialist state, the German Democratic Republic (GDR).

In that same year of 1949, the growing hostility between the two blocs in Europe was formally recognized by the establishment of NATO. The alliance brought together all the democracies of Western Europe and Scandinavia, along with Canada, in a pact with the United States that guaranteed mutual assistance against aggression. In practice, NATO promised Western Europe the shelter of the American nuclear umbrella. The NATO camp was substantially reinforced in 1955 when West Germany was admitted to the organization—a move that led the Eastern-bloc countries to retaliate by setting up their own alliance, the Warsaw Pact.

By that time, the ideological divide between the two blocs had a three-dimensional

The Europe of 1950 was divided by political differences into two hostile camps. In the East, the Soviet Union and its Communist satellites fell under the totalitarian influence of Stalinism. In the West, most countries had democratically elected governments; exceptions were Spain and Portugal, which were ruled as dictatorships until the mid-1970s. Yugoslavia, though Communist in ideology, did not align itself with the Warsaw Pact countries *(shaded yellow)* when that treaty was made in 1955; Albania withdrew in 1968.

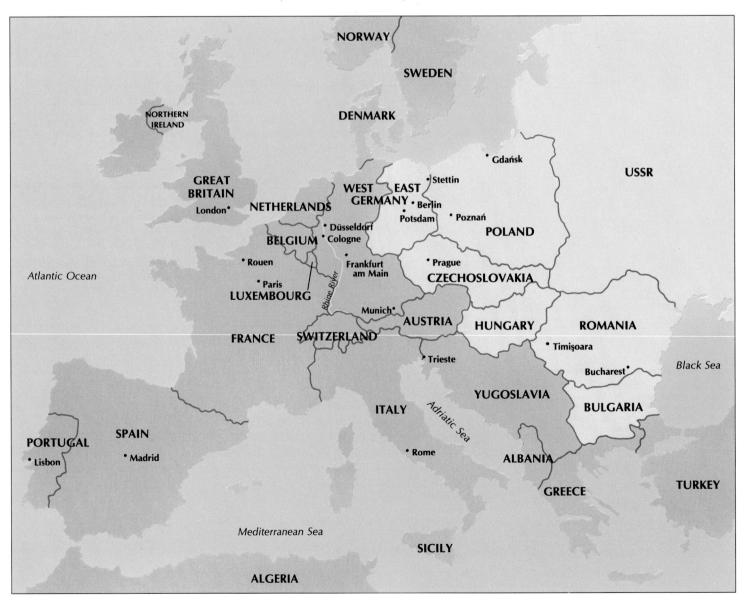

manifestation within Germany. In 1952, when it had become clear that the prospering West would prove too great a temptation for the impoverished citizens of the GDR, East Germany started to construct a barrier of barbed wire, chain-link fencing, and minefields to separate the two Germanies. The only way for Soviet-controlled East Germany to keep workers, it seemed, was to physically contain them.

While the East fell under Stalin's shadow, Western Europe for the most part vigorously adopted democracy. Spain and Portugal, spurned for their fascist sympathies, remained isolated from their neighbors until the mid-1970s. The other states of Western Europe, however, had all established parliamentary systems by 1949, dispelling widespread fears that Communists would seize power in France or Italy.

Christian Democrat parties, which promised progress and stability coupled with the reassuring morality of the Roman Catholic church, emerged as the main stabilizing force. In Italy and West Germany they provided a suitable ideology for national regeneration. In France, too, the Catholic-influenced Mouvement Républicain Populaire (MRP), sharing a similar viewpoint, was to play an important role in shaping policy throughout the twelve-year life of the Fourth Republic, established by plebiscite in 1946 to replace the provisional wartime Vichy regime.

Christian Democrats benefited from the leadership of some remarkable men. Arrested under Benito Mussolini and imprisoned in Rome's Regina Coeli prison, Italy's new prime minister, Alcide De Gasperi, had been surrendered to Pope Pius XI when the Lateran Treaty of 1929 recognized Vatican City as a sovereign state. He remained in sanctuary there through the war years, working as a librarian. "Be Catholic first, then Italian," he had pleaded in his very first speech in 1902, and he remained true to this philosophy throughout his career.

As head of Italy's first postwar government, he discarded his coalition partners, the Communists, in 1947 and presided over a vigorous, free-enterprise economy. Although De Gasperi's "government of rebirth and salvation" had to be reorganized eight times before his death in 1954, it won the invaluable support of the United States and established Italy as a stable, conservative force in postwar Europe.

West Germans reestablished their reputation as an order-loving nation by choosing Konrad Adenauer for their first postwar leader. Mayor of Cologne until ousted by the Nazis in 1933, Adenauer was already in his seventies when he became chancellor, claiming at the time that poor health would force him to retire within two years. In fact, he remained in office until 1963, leading Germany through an unparalleled era of tranquil prosperity. A conservative Catholic from the Rhineland, he looked west, especially to France and the United States, for political allies, attaching less importance than many of his compatriots to the reunification of the nation. His political insight, combined with his grandfatherly and decidedly civilian image, helped assure his new partners that Germany was at last intent upon peace.

The French found no such figure to lead them out of the chaos of war. From 1946 to 1958, under the Fourth Republic, executive power was held by a bewildering succession of more than twenty governments, while the only leader who could possibly have united the nation remained aloof. Charles de Gaulle, hero of the wartime resistance, had stalked out of mainstream politics in 1946, impatient with dissent from his coalition partners. The general's brooding presence darkened French politics for the rest of the Fourth Republic's short life; only at its demise in 1958 would he return triumphantly to power as the first president of the Fifth Republic.

For all its political problems, France nonetheless shared in the vibrant new economic life that was soon transforming the democracies of Western Europe. In May 1947, William L. Clayton, U.S. assistant secretary of state for economic affairs, had penned a memorandum calculated to send waves of alarm through his superiors: "Europe is steadily deteriorating. The political position reflects the economic. One political crisis after another merely denotes the existence of economic distress. Millions of people in the cities are slowly starving." A month later, Secretary of State George C. Marshall launched a program intended to stem this perceived tide of starvation and anarchy. The United States had already contributed more than $15 billion toward the redevelopment of Europe. Under the European Recovery Program—popularly called the Marshall Plan—another $23 billion poured across the Atlantic from 1947 to 1952.

In fact, by the time the aid began to flow, the beneficiaries of the Marshall Plan were not in half such dire need as had been expected. There were still pockets of extreme deprivation, but economic recovery was already taking Western Europe worlds away from the utter hopelessness of *Stunde Null*. Britain's industries, which

had been least affected by enemy action, were producing as much just one year after the war as they had in 1939. By 1948, France and most of its Continental neighbors had matched prewar levels of production. Only Germany, still war shattered and politically retarded by the occupying powers, lagged conspicuously behind.

Whether or not it saved the West from poverty or from communism, the Marshall Plan gave the economies of Western Europe a boost that propelled them into the next decade at a rate they had never before experienced. By the end of 1950, industrial output was one-third higher than its prewar level; in just three years, steel production had increased by 70 percent, coal by 80 percent, and the manufacture of vehicles by 150 percent. During the same period, exports nearly doubled. Agriculture, set back by the bitter winter of 1946 to 1947, was slower to respond, but increased mechanization and the availability of new fertilizers resulted in steady growth.

As with many apparent miracles, there were down-to-earth explanations for Europe's postwar recovery. A number of factories had, in fact, escaped destruction; others were rapidly restored, while those requiring complete reconstruction gained the long-term advantage of modern technology. Nor was there a shortage in the work force. Despite losing millions of lives, Western Europe had a labor surplus during the crucial postwar years. Even when the flow of refugees from the Soviet bloc was cut off, agricultural workers, displaced by rural poverty or mechanization, flocked to the industrial centers in search of jobs and higher wages. Before the war, one-third of Western Europeans had made a living from the land; by 1955, that figure had fallen to less than one-fourth and was declining rapidly.

Governments assumed an active role in their national economies. Fearful of a return to the inflation and unemployment of the 1920s and 1930s, postwar politicians accepted some need to direct their countries' burgeoning growth. At one extreme, Britain's new Labour government nationalized major industries in an attempt to reorganize production and reduce unemployment. At the other, Italy, reacting against Mussolini's stranglehold on the economy, adopted a laissez-faire attitude. Even there, however, the government maintained many of its prewar financial holdings and promoted public works in the impoverished south.

Social welfare was another policy common to the new European states. With the prewar depression still fresh in their memories, voters insisted on financial and physical security as rights rather than privileges of birth. Health insurance, pensions, unemployment benefits, and family allowances helped ensure a minimum standard of living unimagined twenty years earlier, while state-supported building projects addressed the problem of postwar homelessness. The cost of welfare rose dramatically as the average age of the population increased, and expectations continued to grow. It was not until the mid-1970s, however, that governments dared consider reducing the scale of these popular programs.

France was soon in the forefront of economic growth through the activities of the Commissariat au Plan, a government agency administered by a mere handful of senior civil servants. It was not the Commissariat's policy to impose economic solutions upon the country. Rather, it advised on industrial modernization and encouraged its favored projects by directing investment and by offering attractive tax rebates to industries willing to cooperate. Its founder, a former brandy merchant named Jean Monnet, was a short, amiable man whose passionate vision of European unity—revealed in a torrent of words—was to inspire a generation of internationally minded statesmen, winning him the title of the Father of Europe.

The fourteenth-century Church of Saint Katherine in Hamburg lies in ruins after World War II, destroyed by Allied bombing raids that also razed almost one-half of the city's homes. Much of the surrounding rubble, crushed and mixed with cement supplied by the United States, was used to erect new apartment buildings. The church itself was restored and reconsecrated in 1957.

In 1950, Monnet's program for uniting the European coal and steel industries was proposed by Robert Schuman, foreign minister of France. "It is no longer a moment for vain words," announced the Schuman Plan. "For peace to have a real chance there must first be a Europe." The next year, six nations joined the European Coal and Steel Community (ECSC): France, Germany, Italy, and the Benelux states—Belgium, the Netherlands, and Luxembourg. Britain had been expected to take the lead but balked at the diminution of sovereignty that joining the ECSC entailed.

In 1955, representatives of the six member nations of the ECSC, under the leadership of Belgium's foreign minister Paul-Henri Spaak, met in Sicily to discuss a more comprehensive economic union. With astonishing speed, they hammered out the agreement that established the EEC. In 1957, the European Economic Community, or Common Market as it became popularly known, was duly authorized with the signing of the Treaty of Rome. Its assembly met for the first time the next year.

The primary aims of the EEC were economic. They included the elimination of internal tariffs, the establishment of a common external tariff, the free movement of labor, and a common investment policy. In the minds of its founding fathers—Monnet, Spaak, Schuman, and others—however, it also held out a long-term promise of political union. Its charter reflected their views, expressing the determination "to eliminate the barriers that divide Europe." Over the ensuing decades, the EEC steadily edged toward this goal.

Charles de Gaulle   **Konrad Adenauer**   **Alcide De Gasperi**

EEC policy was to be formulated by the Commission, whose members were appointed for "general competence" and "indisputable independence." Originally, there were nine commissioners, but the number grew as the community expanded. The Council of Ministers, drawn from the cabinets of the member states and representing national interests, worked alongside the Commission, maintaining the power to oppose its recommendations. The European Parliament (at first an appointed body but directly elected after 1979) served largely as a forum for debate but also had some budgetary powers and the authority to dismiss the Commission on a two-thirds majority vote. The increased authority conferred on it by direct election made it more assertive and influential. A fourth major institution, the Court of Justice, adjudicated disputes between members, and it considered appeals from individuals and organizations on issues ranging from sexual discrimination to company takeovers.

The EEC on occasion infuriated its members. Its extravagances, its high-handed assumption of supranational power, and its army of highly paid bureaucrats were regular objects of ridicule. But few questioned its success. By the early 1960s, its six founder states already constituted the world's greatest trading bloc. Collectively, the EEC was the world's largest exporter and second-largest importer.

Not surprisingly, there was a rush to clamber aboard. Britain, which had missed the boat when the community was launched, now discovered that it had, in fact, been left behind; the industrial production of the Common Market increased nearly three times faster than Britain's during the first five years of its existence. In 1960, Prime Minister Harold Macmillan executed a smart about-face and applied for EEC membership. "Europe must unite or perish," pleaded his chief negotiator, Edward Heath.

In the end it did neither. Months of agonizing negotiations solved many of the problems of Britain's membership. (No duty, it was decided, would be levied on tea, cricket bats, or polo sticks imported to Britain from Commonwealth countries.) But Macmillan had not reckoned with the implacable opposition of President Charles de Gaulle of France. In 1963, convinced that Britain was merely the Trojan Horse for U.S. involvement in Europe, the general emphatically vetoed the British bid.

Britain remained out in the cold for another ten years. In 1973, along with Denmark and Ireland, it gained entry to the EEC. In 1981, Greece increased the membership to ten. Five years later, Spain and Portugal, whose peaceful transition from dictatorship to parliamentary democracy had been the political miracle of the 1970s, were also welcomed into the mainstream of European economic life.

National interests and rivalries did much to dull the Common Market's initial idealism. The Common Agricultural Policy (CAP), which created wine lakes and butter mountains by means of guaranteed subsidies to farmers, was a frequent cause of contention. Insisting on selling wheat to the Soviet Union on its own terms, France boycotted the Council of Ministers for seven months in 1965. Britain under Margaret Thatcher—a reluctant European—clashed noisily with other member states about overpayments to inefficient Continental farmers in the 1980s. Yet the movement toward increased political union continued, given a fresh impetus by the Single European Act of 1986. This aspired to transform the EEC in 1992 into "an area without frontiers in which the free movement of foods, persons, services, and capital is ensured," a prospect calculated to breathe new life into the Common Market as the century drew to a close.

Behind the desire to build a strong, united community lay Europe's growing aware-

New leaders for a new Europe, Charles de Gaulle of France, Konrad Adenauer of West Germany, and Alcide De Gasperi of Italy, shared in common a Roman Catholic upbringing, a record of implacable resistance to Nazism, and a determination to regain for their nations a position of respect and security. De Gaulle, one of the most charismatic figures of postwar Europe, disdained participation in the government of the Fourth Republic from 1946, but was recalled in 1958 to deal with the crisis caused by a revolt in Algeria. He established a presidential constitution and oversaw the dismantling of France's African empire, believing that strength within Europe was the means to restore his nation's former glory. The primary goal of Adenauer, who was seventy-three years old when he became the first West German chancellor in 1949, was to reconcile Germany with its neighbors and create a more unified Europe; the climax of his efforts came in 1957 with the foundation of the European Economic Community. De Gasperi, whose coalition government was beset by factionalism that mirrored bitter divisions within Italian society, piloted his country to economic recovery.

ness that it no longer played a major role on the international stage. Trapped between the postwar superpowers, the Continent risked becoming little more than the battlefield upon which the Cold War was fought, its once-powerful military might overshadowed by the vast arsenals of the United States and the Soviet Union.

Contributing to this sense of global impotence was Europe's loss of territory, as one by one, its far-flung colonies achieved independence. There was no preconceived pattern of decolonization. Some territories achieved freedom through rebellion; many more were thrust away by mother countries that had begun to find them burdensome. The first power to withdraw entirely from its colonial commitments was the Netherlands, which granted independence to its rebellious Indonesian colonies in 1949. Confronted with conflict in the Congo, Belgium abruptly withdrew from Africa in 1960, leaving the United Nations to resolve a bloody civil war. Portugal granted independence to Angola and Mozambique in 1975, a year after its own successful rebellion against a dictatorial government.

Britain and France, by far the greatest colonial powers, took longer to shed their empires. With considerable skill, Britain oversaw the peaceful transition of many colonies to full independence. The intention, as stated in a white paper of 1948, was "to guide the colonial territories to responsible self-government," but the nation's leaders were at first slow to implement this liberal policy. In the early 1950s, they looked to the colonies as an alternative to economic entanglement with their Continental neighbors, but the dramatic success of the EEC gradually convinced them that the country's future lay, after all, within Europe. The colonies had not prospered as anticipated; instead, they were proving a financial drain on the mother country. Furthermore, Britain had developed an independent nuclear arsenal that made a colonial empire largely irrelevant to strategic thinking.

In the years after 1960, new states emerged with a speed that had cartographers working overtime. The majority achieved independence peacefully, although violence erupted in countries such as Kenya and Rhodesia, where wealthy white elites attempted to cling to their privileges. Most of the emergent lands chose to become members of the Commonwealth of Nations. Britain's special trade agreements with this loosely knit association were a major stumbling block in its attempt to enter the EEC, but the Commonwealth's existence fulfilled a special need. Although the colonies may have been economically redundant, their loss still involved a blow to Britain's pride that continuing links of a voluntary nature helped assuage.

France was at first less willing than Britain to let its colonies slip away. Humiliated by its swift defeat during World War II, the French army hoped to recover its lost honor on colonial battlefields. Such ambitions were jolted in 1954 when, after eight years of combat, Communist forces overran the Vietnamese fortress of Dien Bien Phu and drove France from Indochina. Within four months, attention had shifted to Algeria, where one million French colonists—10 percent of the population—were engaged in a struggle for survival against the independence fighters of the Front de Libération Nationale, or FLN. This resistance movement, fired by hatred of a corrupt and discriminatory colonial regime, pursued a campaign of coldly calculated terror. With increasing independence and savagery, the army attempted to crush the rebellion, ignoring political directives from the mother country. By 1958, under threat of a military coup, the ailing Fourth Republic disbanded, summoning to rescue the nation the one man who still commanded the respect of both civilians and the military: General Charles de Gaulle.

"There will be no Dien Bien Phu in Algeria," de Gaulle assured his supporters. In fact, he was rapidly realizing that France could only dissipate its economic strength and corrupt its moral fiber by continuing the hopeless war against the FLN. Celebrations within the army turned to rage when it became clear that the general, now president of the newly formed Fifth Republic, intended to negotiate a settlement. In 1962, after eight years of ruthless warfare, Algeria won independence. The human cost exceeded that of any other colonial conflict. Apart from the hundreds of thousands who had died, more than one million refugees fled to France.

De Gaulle's anticolonialism did not end with Algeria. Within three years of coming to power, he had granted independence to all of France's black African colonies. "France is the light of the world" was an article of faith for this most nationalistic leader, but he was clear-sighted enough to realize that a dominant position in Europe would provide the best vehicle for French national ambitions.

The colonial age had passed, but Europe was not allowed to forget its imperial history. In the 1960s, the trickle of immigrants from the newly independent colonies became a flood. Some—such as the Algerian émigrés—were reluctant refugees;

Sporting oversize sunglasses and a trendsetting miniskirt, a sixties teenager strolls through the Bohemian Carnaby Street district of London. Miniskirts designed by the British fashion designer Mary Quant were flamboyant badges of a generation of youngsters who enjoyed greater spending power than ever before. Affluence and the availability of the contraceptive pill gave rise to a youth culture of sex, drugs, and rock and roll, which contrasted sharply with the dour atmosphere of 1950s reconstruction and bonded the young of Western Europe more to their American peers than to their Eastern European neighbors.

others were at first welcomed as cheap labor for jobs that Europeans scorned. London's public transportation system became the workplace for thousands of West Indian immigrants. North Africans repaired the potholes in Parisian boulevards.

The friendly reception soon turned sour. A chill in Europe's economic climate brought poverty and discrimination to the new ethnic minorities. In 1981, with Britain's immigrant community constituting 6.3 percent of the population, riots directed mainly against the police broke out in West Indian districts of London and other cities. Muslim Arabs in France were increasingly subject to racist abuse.

Freed from colonial commitments, Europe's leading nations turned their energies to internal development. None had greater problems to overcome than France, faced with massive dissension over the Algerian conflict. In this respect, too, de Gaulle served his country well. The Fifth Republic that he created in 1958 instituted a presidential system of government presided over by a directly elected head of state whose policies were to be carried out by the prime minister, his own appointee. As the first president, de Gaulle was at the helm of France for eleven years, steering a fiercely independent course. He saw Europe as a league of sovereign states, dependent on neither of the superpowers: "We will never descend to the level of American vassals," he declared. His enmity toward those he called the Anglo-Saxons and his desire for preeminence in Europe led him not merely to veto British entry into the EEC but also to withdraw France from the military command structure of NATO (in 1966) and insist on developing an independent French nuclear force.

De Gaulle resigned in 1969, an old man broken by the student and industrial unrest that had swept France the previous year. Subsequent French presidents have never aspired to de Gaulle's imperial manner, and France has found a less-abrasive way of

dealing with its neighbors. The nation shuddered in the 1980s at the prospect of a socialist president—François Mitterand—"cohabiting" with a conservative legislature, but the expected confrontation never took place. Mitterand turned his attention to foreign affairs, becoming a leading exponent of European unity. Along with his former finance minister Jacques Delors, president of the EEC Commission, he was a driving force behind the Single European Act, the greatest step toward political union the community had ever considered.

France's neighbor across the Channel saw fewer political crises in the postwar years but also enjoyed more limited economic growth. This would have surprised observers in 1945, who assumed that Britain was destined to take the moral and political lead in Europe. It had suffered less industrial damage than most of its Continental neighbors, its political institutions were unchallenged and vigorous, and it boasted a special relationship with the United States that apparently could only work to its advantage. Yet Britain failed economically to keep pace with its Continental competitors. Although the nation made considerable progress after the war— its gross national product (GNP) grew at an average rate of 2.5 percent between 1948 and 1962—other nations did better, and by the 1960s, its standard of living had fallen behind that of France and Germany. Ten years later, Britain was the "sick man of Europe." In the mid-1970s, inflation soared above 20 percent and the British pound fell by more than one-third in comparison to most other European currencies. Only a huge loan from the International Monetary Fund kept the economy afloat.

Failure to join the EEC at its inception was one cause of Britain's economic dawdling, but the problem had deeper roots. In fact, Britain's postwar status was far less privileged than it appeared. The country had won the war but had lost one-fourth of its net wealth. Only U.S. aid kept the nation afloat, and this was withdrawn at the

Under the slogan For Socialism—For Peace, ranks of Czechoslovaks take part in a synchronized display of gymnastic skills at the Prague Spartakiad in 1985. In common with other Eastern-bloc rulers, President Gustáv Husák of Czechoslovakia stressed "the importance of mass physical education and sports for a healthy physical and mental development of the population." The successful promotion of individual skills as well as group participation was demonstrated by the large number of medals won at successive Olympic Games by athletes from Eastern Europe.

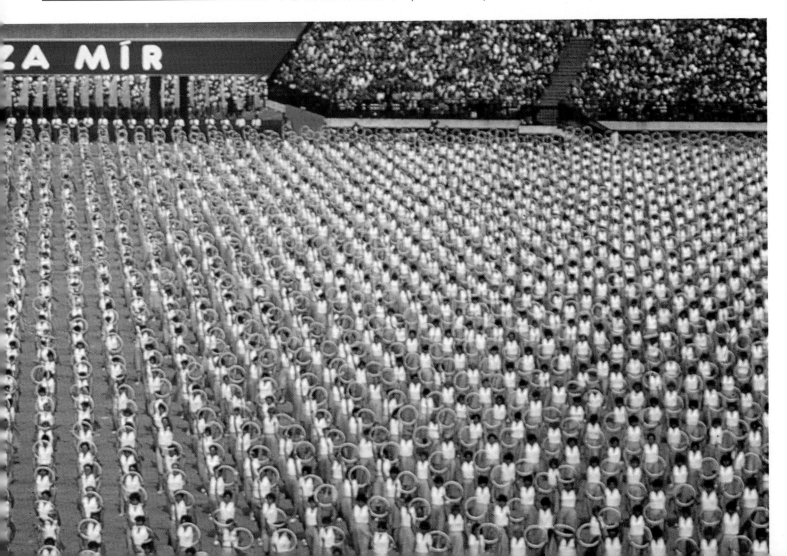

A mural in the Catholic district of Belfast, the capital of Northern Ireland, urges support for Sinn Féin, the political voice of the republican movement seeking to free the province from British rule.

Masked gunmen of ETA, the Basque separatist organization in Spain, sit beneath their people's flag, which was banned by General Franco. From 1979, the Basques had their own parliament to administer their region's internal affairs, but hardline members of ETA demanded nothing less than complete independence.

While Western Europe as a whole moved toward greater economic and political unity, some communities within individual nations became increasingly outspoken in their demands for political recognition of their separate cultural identities. In Spain and Northern Ireland, the use of violence to further separatist aims posed intractable problems for the national governments.

The Basques of northern Spain, of pre-Indo-European descent and retaining their own language, felt more affinity with their ethnic neighbors in southwest France than with their Spanish compatriots. The suppression of Basque culture during General Francisco Franco's reign led to the formation in 1959 of a paramilitary organization named Euskadi Ta Askatasuna (ETA)—Freedom for the Basque Homeland—whose terrorist attacks claimed more than 500 lives between 1959 and 1989. In Northern Ireland, the Catholic Sinn Féin (Ourselves Alone) party demanded unification with the rest of Ireland, which became independent from Britain in 1922. Between 1969 and 1989, approximately 3,000 people died as a result of sectarian violence caused by republican groups, such as the illegal Irish Republican Army (IRA), and proscribed loyalist units claiming to represent Northern Ireland's Protestant majority.

THE ANGRY MINORITIES

war's end. Reparations, a traditional source of income for the victors, were kept low to aid Germany's recovery. To make matters worse, Britain was obliged, in the killing cold of 1946, to pump $320 million into the ruins of Hitler's Third Reich to avert mass starvation. "It is a strange and ironical reward," wrote Chancellor of the Exchequer Hugh Dalton, voicing the indignation of the British people.

Another school of thought blamed Britain's archaic trade unions and inefficient managers for its poor postwar performance. Approximately 600 individual unions made British labor relations a nightmare for negotiators. Since the unions were organized by craft and not by industry (as in West Germany, where there were only sixteen such bodies), a large factory could include representatives from several labor organizations. A strike by a group of workers, perhaps over an issue as petty as the length of a tea break, could cripple an entire industry. Over this crazy quilt of crafts and trades loomed Britain's union leaders, who exercised an obstructive power unparalleled in the rest of Europe.

British management, for its part, became notorious for its class-ridden arrogance and reluctance to adapt to modern methods of production and marketing. One study indicated that the segment of industry under American management in Britain averaged 50 percent greater efficiency than the British-run sector.

In the 1980s, the vigorous Conservative government of Prime Minister Margaret Thatcher attempted to address the root causes of Britain's woes. It first successfully attacked inflation with a policy of austere monetarism, then tried to revitalize industry through aggressive union reform and the privatization of state-run enterprises. Thatcher's policies had a radical effect on Britain's economy, but whether they had succeeded in transforming it remained unclear as the 1990s began.

Britain's postwar record seemed lackluster when contrasted with that of its erstwhile adversary, Germany. Under the stewardship of Ludwig Erhard, Konrad Adenauer's economics minister, the Federal Republic's economy went from strength to strength. The Germans themselves were startled by the speed of industrial recovery—*Wirtschaftswunder* they called it, the "economic miracle." Between 1950 and 1964, West Germany's GNP tripled, and unemployment plunged from nearly 9 percent to less than 0.5 percent.

Germany's success began in 1948, when the Western Allies replaced the worthless reichsmark. The new currency was kept in such short supply that shopkeepers were forced to sell their hoards of stock, from thermos bottles to floor polish. Enter Erhard, who allowed German businesses considerable freedom, while using his office to protect small industries, discourage monopolies, and promote reinvestment. He was aided by a huge pool of refugee labor and by the fact that there were no armed forces to finance until 1955. As a result, Germany was the one European country to profit from the war in Korea, its steel industry increasing production to cope with demands of its neighbors.

Prince Juan Carlos de Bourbon and his wife pay their last respects to General Franco, the dictator who ruled Spain from 1939 to 1975. Franco had decreed that the monarchy should be fully restored and had personally prepared Juan Carlos for the succession. However, Juan Carlos and his prime minister, Adolfo Suarez, confounded expectations by leading the country through a rapid and peaceful process of liberalization. In 1978, a new constitution established Spain as a parliamentary democracy, and in 1986, Spain became a member of the European Economic Community.

During these years, Germany remained relatively free from the industrial disputes that plagued its neighbors. Its managers were highly trained and hardworking; its unions were intelligently organized by industry, not craft (a system imposed, ironically, by the British after the war). Although German unions were restricted in their power to strike, workers were represented by law on the boards of directors of all companies with twenty or more employees.

The miracle finally came to an end. A major recession in 1966, followed by the international oil crisis of 1973, set West Germany's progress back on an equal footing with its European neighbors. Growth rates between 1980 and 1987 averaged 1.6 percent, less than half the figure for the previous fifteen years. Yet West Germany remained the high-technology heartland of Europe, and the prospects for expansion after the introduction of the single European market in 1992 looked bright.

Even West Germany's reduced growth rates would have seemed beyond the highest hopes of most nations of Eastern Europe, where economic stagnation was the rule

Striking Polish workers at the Lenin Shipyard in Gdańsk kneel at a celebration of the Mass in 1980. Led by Lech Walesa *(inset)*, the two-month strike forced unprecedented concessions from the Communist government, including the right to form trade unions. Solidarity, the first independent trade union, rapidly became the focus for nationalist protest, with six million members and the open support of the Roman Catholic church. Walesa and 14,000 activists were later imprisoned, but their struggle was rewarded in 1989 when Solidarity won a free democratic national election.

after the iron curtain descended. Politically, sullen acquiescence was broken by sporadic acts of violence. On June 16, 1953, bricklayers in Berlin walked off the job to protest against the higher productivity quotas imposed by Moscow. The following day, the whole country was on strike, campaigning not for better conditions but for free elections. When the German police proved unable to suppress the rebellion, Soviet tanks rolled into action. Crushed and starved into submission, the strikers returned to work, faced with the prospect of even more punitive quotas.

Stalin's death later that year led to attempts by Soviet leaders to create better conditions for their European satellites. The immediate results were counterproductive. Nikita Khrushchev's condemnation of Stalin and the attendant thaw in Soviet attitudes led to Europe's worst violence since 1945. "Long live freedom, bread, and justice," chanted strikers from a locomotive factory in the Polish town of Poznań in 1956. Within a day, the rebellion had ended, at a cost of fifty-four lives.

A far greater tragedy occurred in Hungary that autumn. Inspired by signs of political liberation in Poland, a popular rebellion swept the land. Students and factory workers occupied public buildings and tore down statues of Stalin. For a miraculous few days, their demands for freedom appeared to be met. Then, in early November, the Soviet army made its move, crushing the rebellion with fifteen divisions and 6,000 tanks. The violence of this response, in which 25,000 Hungarians and 7,000 Soviet soldiers lost their lives, stunned Eastern Europe into reluctant submission.

It was twelve years before Czechoslovakia offered another challenge to Soviet rule. Here the revolution came from the party, in elections that swept away the inefficient leadership of Antonín Novotný. Despite growing Soviet unease, Alexander Dubček, first secretary of the Central Committee, promised "socialism with a human face."

For a few months, Czechoslovaks exulted in a freedom they had not enjoyed since before the Nazi occupation. Discovering that they were in an intolerable position, the official censors resigned. And as the Communist party looked on benignly, students, workers, farmers, and intellectuals called for sweeping changes, including free elections and the dissolution of the secret police. "We demand a Christian republic," proclaimed placards in the May Day parade. But the Prague Spring of 1968 ended that summer with an invasion by Soviet and Warsaw Pact troops. There was little resistance. Dubček was discredited and expelled from the party. Thousands of dissidents lost their jobs, while under the eye of the omnipresent police, the silence of oppression settled over Czechoslovakia for twenty-one more years.

Throughout the years of the Cold War, Westerners tended to view Eastern Europe as a single entity, its way of life drab and unvaried. In reality, although all of the Warsaw Pact countries were constrained by Soviet policies, each retained its own individual character and distinct political atmosphere.

After the tragic uprising of 1956, few could have imagined that Hungary would emerge as the freest, most "Western" state of the Soviet bloc. Stranger still, the man who led Hungarians toward the promised land of free enterprise was János Kádár, who had turned against the rebel cause and become a willing puppet of the Soviet Union. As new party leader, however, the despised Kádár began to reveal a surprisingly relaxed attitude toward communism. Peasants were allowed to profit from their own small plots of land, censorship lessened, and political amnesties granted freedom to a number of the counterrevolutionaries of 1956. Taking his reforms further still, Kádár introduced his New Economic Mechanism in 1968. This freed industry from rigorous state control. Managers were encouraged to respond to the market,

A young Romanian woman waves the national flag, its Communist emblem cut out to symbolize the popular demand for the overthrow of dictator Nicolae Ceauşescu's repressive regime. The last of the Eastern-bloc peoples to revolt against Communist rule in 1989, the Romanians paid the highest price in lives lost: Demonstrators were massacred in the city of Timişoara, while other protesters were killed by the security police after the army had sided with the people. Following several days on the run, Ceauşescu and his wife were captured, tried on charges of mass genocide and abuse of state power, and executed by firing squad.

taking responsibility for their own successes or failures.

Kádár's reforms had dramatic results. Food lines shrank as private shops flourished. By the 1980s, one out of three families owned a car. Nearly one-half the population took their vacations abroad, while thriving Budapest became a magnet for envious tourists from Hungary's eastern neighbors.

Behind the window dressing of wealth and freedom, Hungary's situation was far from ideal. Critics were quick to point out that the party had absolute rule; the apparatus of a police state was intact. And in spite of the proliferation of TV sets and haute couture, the economy began to deteriorate. Hungary had depended too heavily on trade with the West. The oil crisis of the 1970s and recession in the 1980s dried up most of that market, and the national debt soared. In 1982, Hungary nearly went bankrupt; in 1985, its standard of living was lower than that of all its eastern neighbors, barring Albania.

What saved Hungary—and kept goods in the shop windows—was a thriving black market. It was estimated in the mid-1980s that up to 30 percent of the nation's GNP was unofficial. Two-thirds of all apartments were built illicitly; eight out of ten Hungarians had an unofficial job on the side. It was a precarious way to live, but it upheld Hungary's reputation—in the words of an oft-repeated joke—as the most comfortable barracks in the concentration camp.

By far the richest barracks—though perhaps not so comfortable—was the GDR. Eclipsed by the dazzling advances of its Western neighbor, East Germany's achievements were easy to overlook. In fact, its *Wirtschaftswunder* was almost as miraculous as that of the Federal Republic.

Unlike West Germany, the GDR got off to a slow start. Determined to extract punitive war damages from its former enemy, the Soviet Union dismantled nearly 50 percent of East Germany's industry immediately after the war, then proceeded to take an average 25 percent of its annual GNP until 1953. The shortage of labor was a chronic problem. Even after building the formidable barrier between the two states, East Germany continued to lose its citizens through the border in Berlin, sometimes at the rate of thousands a day. The Berlin Wall, built in 1961, was a primitive solution to this problem, but there was no question that it worked. With a skilled and captive labor force, the economy boomed. By 1970, it was tenth among the world's industrial nations, its standard of living an estimated 50 percent higher than the Soviet Union's.

The gap between their economies had narrowed, but there was no catching the Federal Republic. Nor, for many East Germans, could their all-embracing state ever provide the freedom and variety of the West, whose television programs they eagerly watched. Only in 1989, Eastern Europe's watershed year, did the extent of East Germans' dissatisfaction become apparent to Western observers.

The remarkable series of events that transformed Eastern Europe in 1989 had their origins nine years earlier in the Polish port of Gdańsk. Poland was one of the poorest and most rebellious of the Soviet satellite states. Its economy was chronically mismanaged. Corruption, inefficiency, and an obsessive concern for heavy industry resulted in regular shortages of consumer goods. The Poles did not submit passively to these indignities. Poland's long history of occupation by foreign powers had imbued its people with a spirit of disobedience that often flared into violence. At the forefront of protest was the Catholic church, a role heightened in 1978 by the election of Karol Wojtyla, cardinal of Kraków, as Pope John Paul II.

In 1970, the announcement of a massive rise in the price of staple foods sparked strikes throughout the country. In the Baltic port of Gdańsk, protesting workers were shot and killed in front of the gates of their shipyard. A new government under Edward Gierek temporarily restored order, but the economy was plunging into crippling debt, and resentment against the recent violence had stiffened the people's resolve.

In 1980, workers in Gdańsk scored a stunning victory over the state. Under the determined leadership of Lech Walesa, an electrician at the shipyard, they forced the government to recognize their independent union Solidarność, or Solidarity, the first time a Soviet-controlled state had ever made such a concession. For sixteen months, the world held its breath while freedom and oppression contended for power, and the country teetered on the brink of anarchy. To many it came as no surprise when Poland's new leader, General Wojciech Jaruzelski, declared a state of war in December 1981 and attempted to snuff out the memory of Solidarity.

But the union would not die. As one opposition thinker put it, "The thread of helplessness was cut." Poles stubbornly refused to cooperate with the economic measures of their unelected government, and it quickly became clear that the Soviet Union's new leader, Mikhail Gorbachev, would offer no military assistance to those in power. In January 1989, after a series of pro-Solidarity strikes, General Jaruzelski agreed to negotiate. From that moment, his regime foundered. Eight extraordinary months later, Tadeusz Mazowiecki, editor of Solidarity's newspaper, became Eastern Europe's first non-Communist prime minister in forty years.

The mood of revolutionary change spread with bewildering speed through the rest of Eastern Europe. In November 1988, Hungary had already announced a plan for multiparty rule. Six months later, Hungarian soldiers began tearing down the fortified border with Austria, dismantling their section of the Iron Curtain. That autumn, the current of change became a tidal wave, sweeping away long-established regimes—buttressed no longer by Soviet might—like sandcastles in its path. East Germany, disoriented by a mass exodus of citizens through newly liberated Hungary, bulldozed holes in the Berlin Wall. Bulgaria ousted its leader of thirty-five years in a bloodless coup. In Prague, a week of astonishing demonstrations saw the Communists forced from power and a beaming Alexander Dubček greet the crowds after twenty-one years of obscurity. Only in Romania did the new forces meet with savage resistance, but there, too, the last vestiges of President Nicolae Ceauşescu's cruel regime were quickly swept away. "I must weep for joy that it happened so quickly and simply. And I must weep for wrath that it took so abysmally long," said the East German protest singer Wolf Biermann, reflecting the mood of millions.

Euphoria was mixed with doubt. There were hopes for democracy and a lurking dread of further disorders. Meanwhile, Western Europe looked on in disbelief and helpless delight. Few observers were foolish enough to attempt a prophecy. With the dawn of the 1990s, the only certainty was that the old certainties had vanished. The continent of Europe—west and east—anticipated a rare opportunity to start afresh.

No more potent symbol of the postwar division between Western and Eastern Europe could have been devised than the Berlin Wall, a barrier of concrete and barbed wire snaking twenty-eight miles through the heart of the former capital of Germany.

It was built in 1961 on the orders of the East German leader Walter Ulbricht as an "antifacist protection barrier." Unlike most defensive walls, however, this one was constructed to keep people in, not out. Berlin, like the rest of Germany, was partitioned at the end of the Second World War into four zones, controlled by Britain, France, the United States, and the Soviet Union. In 1949, when the three Western sectors of Germany combined in the Federal Republic and the Soviet sector became the German Democratic Republic (GDR), the Western zones of Berlin remained an anomalous enclave deep inside the new Communist state. As such, they provided a convenient escape route for 2.7 million citizens of the GDR who sought to improve their lot in the West—until, on August 13, 1961, the gap was plugged.

For twenty-eight years, the Wall—overlooked by watchtowers and backed up by a razed strip of land with mines and trip wires—reduced the one-way flood of humanity to a trickle. East Germans unwilling to risk being shot by border guards as they attempted to flee to the bright lights of the West had to wait until 1989, when Communist Hungary opened its borders with Austria. A new escape route was open, and once more the GDR's economy was threatened by the loss of its work force. This time, however, the solution was not to impose restrictions but to lift them: At midnight on November 9, 1989, the East German government opened the Wall, and with it, a new era of German unity.

In 1961, East German cranes maneuver prefabricated concrete blocks into position to bisect the city of Berlin *(above)*. In November 1989, after the cancellation of restrictions on travel between East and West, jubilant Berliners dance atop the Wall in celebration of their reunion *(below)*.

THE CONCRETE CURTAIN

The body of eighteen-year-old Peter Fechter—shot while trying to scale the Wall—is carried away by East German guards in 1962. By luck, daring, or ingenuity, some would-be escapees succeeded, but seventy-four shared the fate of Peter Fechter.

CHINA: MAO AND AFTER

Nineteen eighty-nine was supposed to be a year of celebration for the People's Republic of China. Forty years earlier, on October 1, 1949, in Tiananmen Square in the heart of Beijing, Mao Zedong had proclaimed the Communist republic after finally vanquishing Jiang Jieshi (Chiang Kai-shek) and the Guomindang, or Nationalist party, his opponents in a twenty-two-year struggle for control of the nation. For China's elderly leaders, the fortieth anniversary would be the last chance, perhaps, to commemorate the victory of their revolution. There were other significant dates to look forward to. On May 15, Mikhail Gorbachev, leader of the Soviet Union, was scheduled to arrive in the Chinese capital for a visit marking the formal reconciliation of the world's greatest Communist powers after thirty years of estrangement. The Sino-Soviet summit would take place about two months after a visit by George Bush, the new president of the United States. Like many Western leaders, Bush—who had served as a diplomat in Beijing—was impressed by the policy of economic reform initiated ten years earlier by China's eighty-four-year-old ruler, Deng Xiaoping.

But behind the facade of unity that China's leaders presented, the country was in a crisis. Deng's attempts to establish a market economy had created unprecedented prosperity but had also triggered inflation of nearly 30 percent, its highest level since 1949, when hyperinflation had helped turn the middle class against Jiang Jieshi's regime. Corruption—another reason for the overthrow of the Nationalists—was rife. Some of the country's more than fifty national minorities were restive under the rule of China's Han majority; in March 1989, Tibet's bid for self-determination had been bloodily suppressed and the remote autonomous region placed under martial law.

The most frightening specter to haunt China's leaders in 1989 was the growing agitation among intellectuals for a greater degree of democracy. Inevitably, the freeing of the economy had raised hopes for greater political freedom, and although Deng was the champion of economic change, he remained opposed to any reform of the political system that would undermine the power of the Chinese Communist Party (CCP). "We cannot do without dictatorship," he declared.

This conflict would dramatically manifest itself in April, as thousands of citizens took to Beijing's streets to demand democracy, freedom of speech, and an end to corruption. "This is not an ordinary student movement but turmoil, a conspiracy to negate the leadership of the Communist party," Deng said of the protests. When threats failed to disperse the demonstrators, Deng summoned the People's Liberation Army (PLA). The students held their ground, hoping that the PLA would refuse to turn their weapons on unarmed civilians. On June 3, their illusions were shattered.

From the start, the People's Republic was based on systematic control by the Communist party, but for the majority of the Chinese people, impoverished by decades of

At a mass demonstration staged during China's Cultural Revolution, youthful Red Guards recite from the "Little Red Book," a collection of Chairman Mao Zedong's thoughts. China's supreme leader since the founding of the People's Republic, Mao initiated the Cultural Revolution in 1966 to purge Chinese society and its ruling Communist party of pragmatic elements opposed to his philosophy of permanent revolution. Among the most frequently quoted of the sayings contained in the book were "All reactionaries are paper tigers" and "Every Communist must grasp the truth: Political power grows out of the barrel of a gun."

war, famine, and exploitation, the Communists' early successes in reviving the shattered economy, stamping out corruption, and tackling public health problems seemed to usher in a golden age. After the party had created a national administration, the first major step toward social and economic goals was taken in June 1950, when the CCP extended its policy of land reform across the country, a process that involved the confiscation of land and its redistribution to poor peasants. Mao Zedong, state chairman and himself the son of a peasant family, hoped thereby to increase the support of the peasants for the party, while depriving the landowning class of its power. Poor peasants were encouraged to attend "speak bitterness" meetings and denounce their landlords, who were then punished or murdered. By the time land reform was completed in 1952, an estimated two million people had been killed.

Since the CCP had few members with direct experience with industry, a more cautious approach was adopted in reforming the urban economy and society. At first, nationalization was confined to the largest enterprises, and about one-third of industry was left in private hands. However, any illusions that the CCP would permit capitalism to survive were dashed by two mass campaigns during 1951 and 1952. The Three Antis Campaign against corruption, waste, and excessive bureaucracy

The establishment of Communist rule in China in 1949 reunited the country after years of civil war and Japanese occupation. However, the world's most populous nation—with 1.1 billion inhabitants in 1989—remains characterized by geographical and cultural diversity. Ninety percent of the Chinese live on only one-sixth of the land, predominantly in fertile river valleys such as those of the Yangtze and the Yellow rivers. The vast and sparsely populated territories of the west are home to many ethnic, often nomadic, groups; prominent among them are the Tibetans, whose homeland was reincorporated into the People's Republic after declaring itself independent during the civil war.

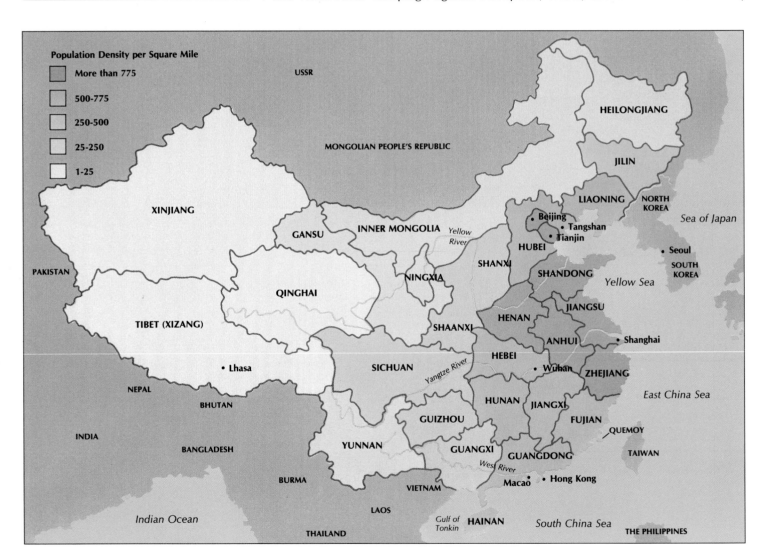

Population Density per Square Mile

- More than 775
- 500-775
- 250-500
- 25-250
- 1-25

targeted officials. The concurrent Five Antis Campaign, directed at bribery, tax evasion, theft of state property, cheating on government contracts, and stealing economic information, was waged against capitalists. People accused of such crimes often had to sell stock to the state in order to pay large fines, thus strengthening government control of industry; others were executed in a "settling of accounts." At the same time, drug trafficking, gangsterism, gambling, and prostitution were also stamped out.

In addition, a campaign was mounted to supplant the traditional loyalty to the family with unquestioning obedience to the state. Total control of the media facilitated this task, but many intellectuals and other individuals regarded as resistant to state control were subjected to a process called thought reform. Pressure was brought to bear on them by various methods, including the seizure of private papers, denunciations, social isolation, and forced confessions of deviant or bourgeois thinking. By 1955, the campaign had developed into a reign of terror. Many could not bear loss of face and committed suicide.

These campaigns against real and imagined enemies were exacerbated by tensions caused by the propaganda battle with Taiwan, where the remnants of the Guomindang had taken refuge, and by China's involvement in the Korean War. The People's Republic had been reluctant to participate, but when South Korean and UN troops advanced deep into North Korean territory, almost as far as the Sino-Korean border, PLA "volunteer" units 400,000 strong crossed the Yalu River and forced the invaders back across the 38th parallel, capturing Seoul in January 1951. A war of attrition followed, in which the Chinese forces proved that they could hold their own against the world's strongest military powers.

In addition to increasing China's prestige in the region, the Korean War pushed China deeper into the Russian camp. Under the terms of a friendship treaty signed by Mao in 1950, the Soviets pledged to come to China's aid should it be attacked by Japan or any of its allies—a reference to the United States. During the Korean conflict, the Soviet Union provided the People's Republic with substantial military assistance; more important, the alliance deterred the United States from mounting an attack directly against China. In response to the perceived Sino-Soviet threat, the Americans pledged increased support for Taiwan.

Mao himself, who had often strayed from the Soviet party line, felt the relationship one-sided and was scathing in his criticism of the economic support that he had won from Moscow—a process he likened to snatching meat from a tiger's mouth. Nevertheless, when China published its First Five-Year Plan in 1953, it was modeled almost entirely on Soviet experience and implemented with the participation of 10,000 Soviet advisers. In accordance with Soviet thinking, emphasis was placed on

An elegantly dressed officer awaits evacuation on a Shanghai dockside following the defeat of China's Guomindang, or Nationalist, army by Communist troops in 1949. Two months after Mao Zedong proclaimed the People's Republic, the Guomindang leader Jiang Jieshi fled with the remnants of his forces—along with China's gold reserves and treasures from the national museums—to the island of Taiwan, 105 miles off the Chinese coast, where he established the rival Republic of China.

the industrial sector; more than 50 percent of the state investment was devoted to industry, while less than 8 percent of investment was allocated to agriculture.

The Communist leadership, nonetheless, remained deeply concerned with rural conditions. Land reform by itself had not achieved the hoped-for increase in production, and Mao now feared that the emergence of a landowning peasantry would lead to new class divisions as the better-off peasants exploited their poorer neighbors. The solution, agreed upon by the CCP as early as 1951, was a process of collectivization, starting with the setting up of Mutual Aid Teams, in which peasants pooled their equipment, animals, and labor, and ending with the creation of agricultural producers' cooperatives, in which private ownership of land was eliminated. The only disagreement within the leadership was over the pace of change. Conservative planners argued that full collectivization should follow the development of industry and extensive mechanization, while Mao and his radical colleagues came to believe that the very process of collectivization would be so enthusiastically embraced that it would generate the surpluses necessary to support mechanization.

By the middle of 1955, some 650,000 cooperatives had been set up, accounting for approximately 15 percent of China's peasant households. According to the plan, this number was to increase to one million by October 1956, but Mao wanted to speed up the process still further, fearing that failure to maintain momentum would lead to backsliding. During a speech in July 1955, he went over the heads of his party colleagues for the first time; accusing some of them of "tottering along like a woman with bound feet," he advocated the completion of the program by 1958.

In fact, full collectivization was achieved ahead of schedule; by 1957, it had affected 96 percent of China's huge rural population. The speed with which the process had been implemented reflected both the acquiescence of the peasantry and the zealousness of local party activists. Among the well-to-do peasants there was some resistance, including outright revolt, but there was little of the violence and loss of production that had characterized Soviet collectivization in the late 1920s.

Such apparent successes boosted China's prestige abroad among socialist governments that were disenchanted with the Soviet model imposed by Stalin. The republic was also making a favorable impression in the world diplomatic arena. At a conference held in Geneva to discuss the Korean and Indochinese questions, the urbane Zhou Enlai—who held the post of foreign minister as well as that of premier—had skillfully advocated a moderate policy, in marked contrast to the hard line taken by U.S. Secretary of State John Foster Dulles, whose hostility to "monolithic atheistic" communism was so implacable that he refused to shake Zhou's proffered hand. Zhou's and China's influences in the Third World were further enhanced at the Bandung Conference in April 1955, attended by twenty-nine Asian and African countries, when Zhou declared his country's support for the Five Principles of Peaceful Coexistence, which included, besides peaceful coexistence itself, mutual respect for territorial integrity and sovereignty, nonaggression, noninterference in each other's affairs, and equality between nations.

With the Soviet Union, however, relations suffered a setback in February 1956, when Nikita Khrushchev made a speech denouncing Stalin's crimes and implicitly criticizing the cult of personality the former leader had constructed around himself. Although Mao had had serious differences with Stalin, he objected strongly to this attack, which inevitably called into question his own position. Where Stalin had erred, Mao believed, was in allowing a gulf to form between the party and the people.

Refugees fleeing southward clamber over the remains of a bridge in P'yŏngyang partially destroyed by United Nations forces as they retreated before a major Chinese offensive in the Korean War. The Chinese went on to temporarily occupy Seoul, the capital of South Korea, before they were pushed back close to the 38th parallel, where the war settled into a bloody stalemate. P'yŏngyang was heavily bombed in the ensuing months; by the war's end in 1953, only two department stores and the town hall remained standing.

Determined to fan popular support for the revolution, he launched an initiative in May 1956 urging independent thinking and free discussion, and encouraging criticism of incompetent or corrupt officials. "Let a hundred flowers blossom, and let a hundred schools of thought contend," he declared.

With the bitter lessons of thought reform still fresh in their minds, few people rushed to respond. Nor were Mao's colleagues enthusiastic about the initiative. At the Eighth Party Congress in September 1956, they gave it formal approval but at the same time took steps to curb Mao's power, creating a powerful Politburo standing committee to watch over him and deleting from the constitution a reference to Mao Zedong Thought, the body of Mao's ideas that had been enshrined as the guiding ideology of Chinese communism in 1945. One member of the standing committee, Liu Shaoqi, stated that there was no such thing as a perfect leader; and Deng Xiaoping, Mao's ultimate successor who was awarded the post of party general secretary at the congress, stressed that no individual could be without fault.

A few months later, the state chairman nonetheless again risked his colleagues' ire by renewing his call for a debate between the nation's intellectuals and the party, citing the recent uprising in Hungary as an example of what could happen if the party became isolated from the masses. This time, the flowers did bloom. Students and intellectuals pasted up posters denouncing party cadres as arrogant and insensitive to the people's needs and even demanding the abolition of one-party rule.

Shaken by the vehemence of the criticism, Mao abruptly terminated the campaign in June 1957. With the support of his colleagues, including Deng Xiaoping, he then mounted a drive against just those individuals whose opinions he had so enthusiastically invited. With all the fury of a man who had lost face, Mao demanded that all academic institutions unmask a quota of so-called rightists. More than 500,000 victims, dubbed enemies of the people, were expelled from the cities to perform menial tasks in the countryside. Mao thereafter remained vindictively opposed to intellectuals, scorning them as "poisonous weeds." As a result, a generation of Chinese youth was deprived of the country's best teachers, and China was robbed of the technical expertise needed for its future development.

If Mao's mistrust of intellectuals had been confirmed by the Hundred Flowers Campaign, his faith in the revolutionary zeal of the rural masses remained unswerving. "The outstanding thing about China's 600 million people," he stated in April 1958, "is that they are poor and blank. This may seem like a bad thing, but in reality it is a good thing. . . . On a blank piece of paper free from any marks, the freshest and most beautiful characters can be written." Having dispensed with the technological elite, Mao decided to harness people-power to achieve a Great Leap Forward—nothing less than a nationwide economic revolution aimed at achieving the Communist millennium within a few years.

With the initial support of planners such as vice chairman Liu Shaoqi, the gradualist Soviet model for the Second Five-Year Plan was scrapped. Instead, the nation was exhorted to "go all out, aim high, and achieve greater, faster, better, and more economical results"; three years of hard work, the party claimed, would be followed by 1,000 years of happiness. Agricultural production was to be doubled in 1958 and again in 1959; industrial production, it was predicted, would rise so fast that China would surpass Britain in iron and steel output within fifteen years.

The key element in the Great Leap Forward was the amalgamation of existing cooperatives into self-sufficient economic, administrative, and social units. The speed of the process was breathtaking. Between April and September 1958, fully 90 percent of the peasant population was organized into communes, each averaging about 5,000 households. Although Mao was an advocate of decentralization who argued that self-management by the community would ultimately bring about the withering away of state power, he insisted that party workers manage the communes, because ideological soundness was more important than technical expertise. "There is no unproductive land," he declared, "only unproductive thought."

Madness resulted. To reduce the importance of the family, farmworkers wasted hours trudging to communal mess halls to eat cold, unappetizing food. In a bid to achieve unrealistic steel production targets—set at 11.9 million tons for 1958, double the 1957 figure—peasants were asked to set up backyard furnaces, fueled in some cases by timber from their old houses and fed with scrap metal. To boost grain production, the population was deployed in a campaign to destroy seed-eating birds by banging pots until the airborne fowl died of exhaustion. No endeavor was spared. When a dance troupe was formed in Tianjin, the organizers boasted: "It takes seven years to train a ballerina in the West, and we have done it in seven days."

Enthusiasm and muscle power produced some achievements in water conservation, irrigation, and drainage systems, but the campaign was a fiasco. At first, the activists refused to admit failure and reported bumper harvests. In fact, thanks to unusually favorable weather, the 1958 harvest was good (though not as good as claimed), which persuaded planners to set even higher goals for 1959 and encouraged managers to divert peasants from farming to grandiose construction projects.

By the end of 1958, it was apparent to some of the leaders that the country was heading for a crisis. In June 1959, against a background of increasing tension with the Soviet Union and an armed uprising in Tibet, Peng Dehuai, the defense minister, wrote a private letter to Mao listing some of the follies of the Great Leap Forward. Interpreting the letter as a personal attack, Mao accused Peng of leading an antiparty clique. The defense minister's case was not helped by the fact that his criticisms coincided with a condemnation of the Great Leap Forward by Khrushchev, whom Peng had visited only the month before, suggesting that he was in collusion with the Soviets. Other party leaders rallied around Mao, and in September, Peng was dismissed from his post and replaced by the radical military commander Lin Biao.

Mao's chagrin was so intense that he forced an intensification of the program, with disastrous results. Drought in the north of China and floods in the south made things worse, but the fundamental cause of the problem was political; so much reliance had been placed on false estimates that a great deal of land had been left fallow in the belief that there would be insufficient storage capacity to handle the anticipated surplus. By 1960, grain production had been reduced to 75 percent of the 1958 figure, and famine stalked the land. How many died is not known for certain, but realistic estimates suggest that up to 20 million perished, making the famine the worst in the world during the twentieth century.

China's economic and human calamity was compounded by a diplomatic and political crisis, for by 1960, Sino-Soviet relations were on the verge of collapse. Cracks had been widening for some years. Although China had been a beneficiary of Soviet technical aid since 1950, including assistance in making nuclear bombs, Mao and Khrushchev had fallen out in 1957 over the strategy for resolving the conflict with capitalism. That year, the Soviets launched two sputniks, deeply impressing Mao, who thought that such a demonstration of socialist technological superiority should be used to bring pressure on the United States. "The east wind has prevailed over the west wind," he told Khrushchev who, fearful of the consequences of nuclear war, was pursuing a policy of détente with the West.

But to Mao, the bomb was a paper tiger. "We have at present no experience with atomic war," he told the second session of the Eighth Party Congress in May 1958. "We do not know how many must die. It is better if one-half are left, the second best is one-third . . . . After several Five-Year Plans, China will then develop and rise up. In place of the totally destroyed capitalism, we will obtain perpetual peace. This will not be a bad thing."

At a 1958 meeting in Beijing, the two leaders disagreed over a Soviet proposal to establish naval bases in China. For his part, Khrushchev was incensed when, soon after his visit and without his knowledge, Mao ordered the bombing of Quemoy and

As part of China's Great Leap Forward, the biggest mobilization of manpower in history, Sichuan peasants attack a hillside with hoes and mattocks to prepare it for rice growing. Launched by Mao in 1958, the Great Leap Forward was an attempt to achieve extremely rapid economic development by mobilizing the energy of the masses. It failed in its objectives; agriculture was seriously disrupted as farmers were diverted into futile backyard steel production or massive land engineering schemes, and in 1959 and 1960, the man-made chaos was compounded by disastrous weather. The resultant famine caused so many deaths that for two years China's expanding population actually fell.

other Guomindang-occupied islands between China and Taiwan. The United States sent its Seventh Fleet and Fifth Air Force to guard the Taiwan Strait, but it was only after the Chinese backed down that Moscow voiced its support, reinforcing Mao's fears that Soviet backing in any confrontation with the United States was doubtful.

Provoked by Mao's brinkmanship during the Taiwan Strait crisis, Khrushchev scrapped the nuclear weapons agreement in 1959. At the same time, the Soviet leader attacked the Great Leap Forward, ridiculing Chinese assertions that the commune system offered a shortcut to full communism. In the summer of 1960, Khrushchev decided that his country's efforts in China were being wasted, and all Soviet advisers and technicians were withdrawn, taking with them the blueprints for the projects they were helping to build. As a result, more than 200 cooperative projects were abandoned. From then on, both sides waged a war of words that culminated in 1963 in the formal scrapping of relations between the Chinese and Soviet Communist parties.

Alone and almost without friends, China faced the task of reconstruction. The disaster of the Great Leap Forward had seriously damaged Mao's prestige among the party hierarchy. In 1959, he had given up his position as state chairman to Liu Shaoqi, and although he remained chairman of the party, in charge of revolutionary strategy, he was increasingly ignored on important economic decisions. His colleagues, he complained, treated him "like a dead ancestor." Liu, in line to succeed Mao, ran domestic policy along with the pragmatic Deng Xiaoping and the veteran economic planner Chen Yun; together, they proceeded to reverse many of Mao's policies, restoring the peasants' right to farm private plots and allowing free rural markets. The new mood of pragmatism was summed up in a remark attributed to Deng: "What does it matter if the cat is white or black, so long as it catches mice?"

Mao regarded this approach as heresy. He was also affronted by articles questioning the necessity of continuing the class struggle and by a trend toward elitism, which he discerned generally in culture and particularly in education. By 1962, he was beginning to make ominous calls for a struggle against revisionism, not only in society at large but also within the party itself. Chief among his allies was the new defense minister, Lin Biao, who set about increasing revolutionary fervor in the armed forces. It was Lin, the main architect of the burgeoning cult of Mao, who published the Great Helmsman's thoughts in the "Little Red Book," which was distributed to all PLA members with the injunction to "study Chairman Mao's writing, follow his teachings, and act according to his instruction."

On the cultural front, Mao set up a five-man Cultural Revolution Group in 1964 to rectify revisionist tendencies in art and literature, but the group, headed by Peng Zhen, mayor of Beijing and head of the capital's party committee, displayed little enthusiasm for its task. Frustrated, Mao enlisted the support of his wife, Jiang Qing, a former actress who wanted to replace traditional and classical Chinese opera and other arts with proletarian works extolling the revolution. Jiang organized a clique of like-minded activists from Shanghai, including an ultraleftist literary critic, Yao Wenyuan, and a journalist and party propagandist, Zhang Chunqiao. In the succession struggle that followed Mao's death, this team made up three-fourths of the group that won notoriety as the Gang of Four.

It was Yao Wenyuan, almost certainly acting with Mao's approval, who provided the spark that detonated the Great Proletarian Cultural Revolution. In November 1965, he published a criticism of a play, *Hai Rui Dismissed from Office*, written five years earlier by Wu Han, deputy mayor of Beijing. Set in the sixteenth century, it concerned an upright official of the Ming dynasty who criticized the emperor's policies and was sentenced to death for his pains, his life being saved only by the emperor's untimely demise. Yao claimed that the play was an attack on Mao and that the sacking of Hai Rui was a thinly concealed reference to the actual dismissal of the former defense minister, Peng Dehuai.

After Yao's article was published, the attacks on critics of the Maoist line were stepped up. In April 1966, Mao forced the dismissal of Wu Han's boss, Peng Zhen. With Peng out of the way, Mao replaced the Cultural Revolution Group with his own allies, including Jiang Qing, who soon became the ruling force in Beijing. This move was trumpeted in a circular issued on May 16, in which Mao declared that the aims of the Cultural Revolution were to "expose the reactionary bourgeois stand of those so-called academic authorities who oppose the party," and to "repudiate reactionary bourgeois ideas in the spheres of academic work, education, journalism, literature, and art." To achieve this, it was necessary to clear out "those representatives of the bourgeoisie who have sneaked into the party . . . persons similar to Khrushchev, for example, who are still nestling beside us." In the closed world of Chinese politics, this was interpreted as an attack on Liu Shaoqi and Deng Xiaoping.

Ten days after the circular was published, a middle-aged philosophy lecturer at Beijing University pasted up a poster attacking the university authorities. Adopting the slogan To Rebel Is Justified, tens of thousands of students followed her example, and soon the walls were thick with messages. Radical fervor increased in June when the president of Beijing University was fired, and it was announced that schools and universities would be closed for six months so that a new system of education emphasizing ideological soundness over academic merit could be worked out.

Initially, Mao stayed out of sight, in central China, leaving Liu Shaoqi to try to contain the situation in Beijing. But then the chairman made a spectacular reappearance. On July 16, the Chinese people were astonished to see photographs of their seventy-two-year-old leader swimming fully clothed in the Yangtze River—a feat intended to prove his extraordinary vigor. Returning to Beijing in triumph, Mao convened a Central Committee meeting packed with his Shanghai supporters. Outnumbered and outmaneuvered, Liu was demoted to eighth position in the Politburo, his place as Mao's presumed successor going to Defense Minister Lin Biao.

Soon after the August meeting of the Central Committee, Mao appeared in Tiananmen Square to receive the mass adulation of young supporters, who ended the rally with cries of "Ten thousand years to Chairman Mao"—a salute formerly used only for emperors. At the meeting, Mao, wearing a PLA uniform, donned an armband of the Red Guards, a movement that had started among Beijing University students in May and was spreading to schools, colleges, and workplaces throughout the country. Allowed to travel free of charge on China's railways, some 10 million Red Guards converged on the capital to attend six mass rallies staged between August and November. Mao worship, fostered by Lin Biao, now reached fanatical proportions, with hysterical youngsters weeping, waving red flags or copies of Mao's "Little Red Book," and singing "The East Is Red"—an anthem that compared Mao with the sun.

Inspired by his call to eliminate the "four olds"—old culture, ideas, customs, and habits—Red Guards rampaged through the cities destroying anything connected with either prerevolutionary China or the West, both of which in Maoist eyes were models of an outdated social order. Targets included tight trousers, jazz records, silk clothes, mah-jongg sets, antiques, classic and foreign literature, religious objects, and even

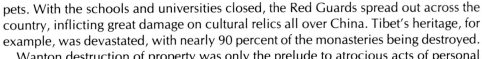

pets. With the schools and universities closed, the Red Guards spread out across the country, inflicting great damage on cultural relics all over China. Tibet's heritage, for example, was devastated, with nearly 90 percent of the monasteries being destroyed.

Wanton destruction of property was only the prelude to atrocious acts of personal cruelty, including beatings that often led to death. Before receiving their punishment, many victims were humiliated at public "struggle" sessions in which they were forced to confess their "crimes" before crowds of baying tormentors. At the trial of Mao's accomplices in 1980, it was alleged that nearly 800,000 people had been "framed and persecuted," of whom 34,900 were "persecuted to death"—a figure that does not include the many victims who committed suicide in protest or despair.

In the early stages of the Cultural Revolution, the targets were mostly intellectuals and individuals suspected of proforeign and bourgeois tendencies, among them a pianist whose fingers were broken because he played Chopin. But by late 1966, the Red Guards, incited by Jiang Qing and her allies in the Cultural Revolution Group, were selecting more overtly political targets. The most prominent were the head of state, Liu Shaoqi, and the party general secretary, Deng Xiaoping, who were denounced as traitors number one and two. After 1966, Liu was not seen in public. Stripped of his post in 1968 and accused of being a Guomindang spy, a "counter-revolutionary, renegade, traitor, and scab," he died wretchedly in prison in 1969.

On a tortuous journey to supply Chinese army garrisons, a military convoy winds through Tibet's mountainous eastern border region. Claiming Tibet as an integral part of the nation, the Chinese occupied the country in 1950, assuming control of the government but leaving the nation's traditional religious leader and ruler, the Dalai Lama, as titular head of state. Communist policies later stripped Tibetans of their lands and rights, and after a revolt in the capital of Lhasa in 1959, the Dalai Lama was forced to seek refuge in India.

Two years earlier, his American-educated wife had been "struggled" against by Red Guards, who paraded her in high heels, a tight slit dress, and a necklace of Ping-Pong balls, parodying the pearls she had worn. Deng survived, and in 1969, after making a self-criticism laced with praise for Mao, he was sent into internal exile to spend the next four years working in a tractor factory and, it was said, playing one-handed bridge. His son suffered more; an attack by Red Guards left him paralyzed from the waist down.

At the end of 1966, a call went out to workers and peasants to "seize power from below." Led by Jiang Qing's Shanghai allies, who now included a former security guard named Wang Hongwen—the fourth member of the Gang of Four—radical workers and Red Guards in Shanghai took over the government and, in February 1967, triumphantly established the Shanghai People's Commune. The event was intended to trigger an uprising of workers throughout China, but in many cities the workers resisted Red Guard invasions, setting up their own armies and battling in the streets. The Maoists met their most serious setback in Wuhan where, in July 1967, a worker-militia alliance attacked a Cultural Revolution group sent to the city. Mao apparently had second thoughts about the worth of urban communes, condemning the Shanghai version as "sheer anarchy." It was dismantled after seventeen days, but Shanghai remained an important base for Jiang Qing's clique.

As the Cultural Revolution degenerated into factional infighting, Mao began to see the looming specter of civil war. "China is now divided into 800 princely states," he com-

Dancers enact a scene from *The Red Detachment of Women*, classified as model repertory by Jiang Qing. Exercising total control over the arts during the Cultural Revolution, Jiang reduced China's repertoire of staged works to one concerto, two ballets, and six operas, all heavily propagandist in tone.

Accused of being a counterrevolutionary and a "political pickpocket," a Red Guard victim is paraded through Beijing. In 1967, China's foreign minister, Chen Yi, was humiliated in a similar fashion.

THE CULTURAL REVOLUTION

Forced to take a less active role in government after the debacle of the Great Leap Forward, Mao grew alarmed that the new, pragmatic policies adopted in its wake were eroding socialism. He was also angered by the reemergence of elitism in education and in Chinese culture in general.

Assured of the army's support, Mao went on the attack in 1966, using the idealism of China's youth to implement his radical line. Schools and colleges closed, and students joined the Red Guards, formed to protect and further the revolution. Permitted to travel anywhere in the land, they were given free rein to vent Mao's frustrations against the "enemies of socialism."

In a frenzy of violence, so-called capital-ist roaders as well as intellectuals were denounced, physically attacked, and in many cases, killed. Moderate members of the Communist party leadership were stripped of office. Soon, however, the Guards' revolutionary zeal degenerated into bloody factional warfare.

Unnerved by the chaos, Mao called in the army to disband the Red Guards and send them into the countryside. By the end of 1968, the campaign of terror was over, but Mao himself, supported by his wife Jiang Qing and her radical coterie, continued to stress the need for permanent class warfare. Only the death of Mao in 1976 ended what his successors were later to dub the "ten-year catastrophe."

plained, recalling the warlord eras that had devastated China several times during its history. Early in 1967, he had not lifted a finger to save his foreign minister, Chen Yi, when Red Guards dressed him in a dunce's cap and forced him to confess his errors. For a time, Mao tolerated the erratic policy course set by the new masters, but when the rebels, proclaiming the universality of the revolution, attacked foreign embassies in Beijing and burned down the British legation, Mao had the leader arrested and ordered the PLA to take control of the Foreign Ministry.

Months of savage fighting lay ahead, and many students died in interfactional strife before the Red Guards were disbanded and packed off to the countryside "to learn from the peasants." By the end of 1968, mob violence had been suppressed in most of China, but the political and ideological conflicts would last for years.

On April 1, 1969, the Ninth Congress of the Central Committee of the Communist party met. Although hailed as the climax of the Revolution, it in fact confirmed that the movement intended to attack all authority had ended with the PLA firmly in control. Of the 1,500 delegates, two-thirds were in military uniform, and there was virtually no representation from the radical youth. It was at this congress that Lin Biao reached the apogee of his power, being named officially as Mao's successor.

But already there were serious disagreements between Mao and Lin. One source of dissension was foreign policy. After a decade of increasing tension with the Soviet Union, polemics gave way to bullets in 1969, when Chinese and Soviet troops clashed on the disputed northeast border. Whereas Lin favored repairing relations with the old ally, Mao and Zhou Enlai began to put out feelers to the United States, believing that the reduced U.S. involvement in Vietnam made it less of a threat than China's northern neighbor. In July 1971, U.S. Secretary of State Henry Kissinger visited China to prepare the way for an official visit by President Richard Nixon in February 1972. Normalization of relations took several years, but one early result of rapprochement was the withdrawal of U.S. opposition to China's entry into the UN. The People's Republic took its place in the organization in October 1971.

One month earlier, a Trident aircraft had crashed 250 miles beyond the Chinese border in Mongolia, killing everyone on board, including—so the Chinese claimed much later—Lin Biao, his wife, his son, and leading members of the Chinese high command. The truth of the matter may never be known, but it is likely that Lin, subjected to a campaign of denigration orchestrated by Mao, tried to recover his position by organizing a coup. When it failed, he attempted to flee to Moscow and was killed when his plane ran out of fuel or was shot down.

After the convulsions of the Cultural Revolution, Mao played a less active part in government. He was enfeebled by Parkinson's disease, and as his strength dwindled, another power struggle broke out between Jiang Qing's Gang of Four and the pragmatic faction led by the prime minister, Zhou Enlai. The Gang of Four had control of the media, but it lacked sufficient party backing to take over the running of the government and the economy. Confident that he had a majority of the Politburo on his side, Zhou proposed a major economic reform program called the Four Modernizations—in agriculture, industry, defense, and science and technology. Zhou himself was dying of cancer, and in 1973, conscious that his time was short, he used his influence to have Deng Xiaoping rehabilitated and appointed vice premier. Soon the radicals were lambasting Deng for emphasizing production over class struggle and preferring imported foreign technology to self-reliance.

Zhou died in January 1976. Mao's unswerving ally since the 1930s, he had kept the party together in the chaotic days of the Cultural Revolution, and his personal charm and courtesy, together with his efforts to curb the worst excesses of the radicals, had made him greatly loved. Fearing a demonstration of popular grief for their enemy, the Gang of Four banned any mourning. Defying their instructions, the populace placed thousands of white wreaths around the Monument to the People's Heroes in Tiananmen Square at the Qing Ming festival in April, the traditional time for sweeping ancestors' graves and mourning the dead. Among the tributes were many poems denouncing the "Shanghai Mafia," who reacted by eventually having the wreaths removed. As news spread, angry crowds converged on the square, to be brutally dispersed by the police and militia. Deng Xiaoping was accused of orchestrating the protest and, at the instigation of Jiang, was again stripped of his posts.

Zhou's death presaged a disastrous year for China. In the summer, the Tangshan earthquake struck northeastern provinces, claiming an estimated 250,000 lives; while rescuers dug in the rubble, the Gang of Four exhorted the survivors to study the works of Mao. Then on September 9, the chairman, the Great Helmsman of the Chinese people for nearly three decades, died. When reports reached her opponents in the Politburo that Jiang was preparing to seize power, they had the entire Gang of Four arrested on charges of plotting a coup. Found guilty in 1981 of charges ranging from persecuting millions during the Cultural Revolution—an era officially brought to an end by her arrest—to watching imported videos including *The Sound of Music*, Jiang was sentenced to death, suspended for two years dependent on good behavior. Her codefendants were given heavy sentences in proportion to their crimes.

During her trial, Jiang claimed that she had only followed Mao's directives: "I was Chairman Mao's dog," she said. "Whomever he told me to bite, I bit." An official

Soon after Mao's death on September 9, 1976, grieving mourners file past his body as it lies in state in Beijing's Great Hall of the People. Later it was transferred to a mausoleum in Tiananmen Square. According to an official assessment of the dead leader's career published by the party five years after his death, his achievements outweighed his mistakes up to the late 1950s, when he launched the disastrous Great Leap Forward. As he grew older, the report continued, he no longer made a "correct analysis" of the situation, and by "confusing right and wrong and the people with the enemy," he unleashed the turmoil of the Cultural Revolution.

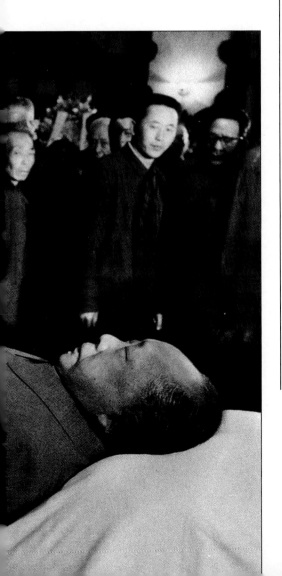

party assessment of Mao's role was finally published in 1981; while acknowledging his early great achievements, it conceded that, from 1955, he had committed errors.

Hua Guofeng, a leftist, succeeded Mao as chairman of the party, but he was unable to consolidate his position and lost the ensuing power struggle to Deng Xiaoping, who had been rehabilitated for a second time. It was Deng who, under the slogan Seek Truth from Facts, cleared the way for the analysis of Mao's career, and after he emerged as the paramount leader in 1978, the stage was set for a startling shift from class struggle to economic reform.

"The main task of socialism," Deng explained later, "is to develop the productive forces, steadily improve the life of the people, and keep increasing the material wealth of the society. Therefore, there can be no communism with pauperism, or socialism with pauperism." His views on economic reform were shared by Hu Yaobang, party general secretary from 1981, who soon demonstrated his modernist style by becoming the first senior Chinese leader to wear a Western business suit instead of a plain Mao jacket, and by declaring that "Marx and Lenin can't solve our problems"—a statement later amended to "can't solve *all* our problems."

Once more espousing pragmatism, Deng proposed to modernize China's industry by importing technology. This open-door policy went further than the mere import of machinery, however. Joint Sino-foreign ventures were permitted, the first being the construction of hotels to cater to an influx of tourists. Special economic zones were created, where foreign investment was invited and Chinese labor hired. Thousands of students were sent abroad to study not only science and technology but also business management techniques.

At home, the first impact of Deng's change of direction was felt by farmworkers, who still formed 80 percent of the population in 1980. With the adoption of the "responsibility system," individual peasant households became the unit of production. Although they were given grain quotas to fill, they were allowed to dispose of any surplus at rural markets. Later, individuals were allotted land to rent—effectively in perpetuity. At first, grain production soared, but farmers soon found that they could earn more money by diversifying into cash crops and other sideline products for which higher prices could be charged. The result was a declining grain yield when too many people abandoned their traditional crops and moved into more lucrative ventures such as fish farming and flower production.

Hand in hand with its efforts to increase food production, the government mounted a drive to limit population growth. Whereas Mao had seen China's masses as the nation's greatest asset, Deng was conscious of the growing problem of feeding 20 percent of the world's population with less than 5 percent of its arable land. Aiming to stabilize the population at 1.2 billion by the year 2000, the State Family Planning Commission established in 1981 began a campaign to restrict families to no more than one child—two in special cases—with transgressors penalized by fines or the withdrawal of educational or welfare benefits. In the cities, where housing was limited, the program proved generally successful, but in rural areas, where households relied on their children to work the land and to provide for their parents in their old age, the one-child family met with widespread opposition. One unfortunate consequence of the restriction was a rise in female infanticide; in Chinese peasant society, boy children have traditionally been valued more highly than girls, because daughters leave home upon marriage, thus depriving their families of their labor.

After the agricultural reforms had been implemented, attention was turned to industry. The new policy for the large state-owned enterprises was intended to make "socialist producers and managers wholly and truly independent, self-managing, and solely responsible for their own profits," according to Premier Zhao Ziyang; in practice, party interference in the day-to-day running of factories was reduced. Managers were allowed to pay bonuses and were given limited powers to hire and fire—a departure from the established system, in which jobs were guaranteed for life and sometimes passed down from parent to child.

Small businesses could now be leased outright by their managers; one such manager in Liaoning province took advantage of the new rules to lease eight stores that soon dominated local food sales. Other entrepreneurs sprang up to satisfy the demand for clothes, shoes, workshops, and quality consumer goods.

But by the late 1980s, the reforms had run into all kinds of trouble. Rapid growth

In Fujian province, citizens read posters denouncing the Gang of Four, the radical clique led by Jiang Qing that tried to seize power after Mao's death. In a society practicing heavy censorship of the news, such hand-lettered messages became important for the expression of political opinions, often providing the only clues to power struggles within the ruling Communist party.

and unchecked capital expenditure fueled inflation, while wage increases and across-the-board bonuses led to a consumption boom, which placed an increased financial burden on the state because in China most raw materials and commodities are heavily subsidized. People on fixed salaries, including teachers, doctors, academics, and government functionaries, suffered from the inflation without benefiting from the liberalization, building up resentment at their own economic plight. Uncontrolled development led to serious pollution problems and a shortage of raw materials, which were often converted into products that could not be moved to markets on China's antiquated transport system, or into shoddy goods that no one wanted. When news spread that the government intended to rectify the situation by increasing prices, the public went on a panic buying spree, hoarding goods as a hedge against the price rises, and thus causing acute shortages. In 1988, when price ceilings on some products were reimposed, the farmers simply withdrew their produce from the markets and sold it at higher, "backdoor" prices.

Another serious problem was corruption—private and official—at every level and sometimes on a grand scale. Managers found ways to sell goods made from state-subsidized raw materials on the open market at nonsubsidized prices, cheating both the consumer and the state. Party officials often turned a blind eye to such crimes, or actively participated in them, abusing their power by demanding bribes, by appointing family and friends to jobs, and by evading taxes. Even when caught, few were harshly punished. In one flagrant case of the party's protecting its own, a man who was both a senior army officer and a local party secretary escaped with nothing more

83

than a reprimand and salary cut after being found guilty of misappropriating funds totaling more than $20 million. "Such things will certainly cause popular indignation and disgust," warned a veteran Communist in 1987. "As a popular saying goes: 'A piece of rotten meat may ruin the whole pot of soup.' "

Demoralized by the spreading atmosphere of graft, many Chinese increasingly came to believe that the economic reforms would accomplish little unless the party made itself accountable to the people. As early as 1978, posters demanding greater freedom of expression had begun appearing on a wall in Beijing. "Can the Four Modernizations be achieved in a society governed by overlords and worked by professional and amateur slaves?" demanded Wei Jingsheng, a Red Guard turned dissident. No, he said—not unless China adopted a Fifth Modernization, democracy.

Rising almost 3,300 feet from the valley floor, hills *(right)* in the southern province of Guangxi have been cut into terraces so narrow that they can only be worked by hand. The scene is a vivid reminder of China's most difficult problem—how to feed its huge and rapidly expanding population. By the 1980s, the Communist regime had largely succeeded in making famine a thing of the past, but although agricultural output had more than doubled since 1949, so had the population. In the first three decades of the People's Republic, the state tolerated and even encouraged demographic growth, because Mao saw China's masses as its greatest strength in the event of a war. Later, however, the government tried to slow the increase by persuading families to have no more than one child. Ideal families such as the one below were given financial incentives, while couples who ignored the restriction were threatened with reduced pay and food allowances. The campaign succeeded in cutting the birth rate from 2.2 percent between 1965 and 1980 to 1.2 percent between 1980 and 1987; even so, China's population was expected to reach almost 1.3 billion by the year 2000.

Initially, Deng Xiaoping tolerated the protests on the so-called Democracy Wall because they provided ammunition against opponents of his economic program, but his magnanimity evaporated when he himself became a target. In 1979, soon after publishing an article calling for a general election to ensure that "Deng Xiaoping does not degenerate into a dictator," Wei was arrested on charges of betraying state secrets and jailed for fifteen years.

Student dissent swelled again in 1986. This time most complaints addressed concrete issues, particularly high prices, poor teaching, and student accommodations. For a while, the authorities exercised restraint, but in 1987, there was a clampdown. Fang Lizhi, a world-renowned astrophysicist who had supported the students, was removed from his university post. The most prominent victim, however, was Hu Yaobang, the outspoken party general secretary and a critic of China's education system, who was accused of encouraging the students in their demands. At the beginning of 1987, Hu was forced to resign, and the protests temporarily subsided. One of the last posters was an anonymous attack on the leadership. "I had no idea that in their eyes the people counted for nothing—nothing at all. . . . They carry out their 'reforms.' But if you want to participate, and if those reforms develop to the point where their interests are in danger, what do they give you?" The Chinese democracy movement would find out in June 1989, in Tiananmen Square.

The crisis began on April 15, with the death of Hu Yaobang. Although he had been forced from office, he remained a member of the Politburo, and on April 8, he had suffered a heart attack during a meeting to discuss a policy document on education. Soon after the announcement of his death, posters began to appear at Beijing University and elsewhere in the city bearing messages that were as much indictments of Deng as tributes to Hu. "A true man has died. False men are still living," said one.

Protest mounted in the days that followed. The crowd of students was swelled by workers, journalists, even policemen and party workers. On April 22, the day of Hu's funeral, 100,000 demonstrators occupied Tiananmen Square, forcing Deng and other members of the party elite to enter the Great Hall of the People through side entrances. After the demonstrations of 1986 and 1987, marches without prior approval from the police had been declared illegal. But on this day, the security forces that ringed the square stood by and did nothing. Although only one month previously the leadership had authorized the brutal suppression of civil rights demonstrations in Lhasa, the capital of Tibet, now they seemed to be paralyzed. Hard-liners such as Prime Minister Li Peng wanted the protests crushed, but a faction led by Zhao Ziyang, Hu's successor as party general secretary, advised restraint; Deng kept his own counsel. Another reason for the party's hesitant behavior was the impending Sino-Soviet summit, the first for three decades. An attack on protesters demanding democratic freedoms would have struck a jarring note on the eve of the visit by Mikhail Gorbachev, the Soviet Union's reforming leader.

In fact, Gorbachev's visit was a farce that caused the Chinese leadership massive loss of face. Three days before the Soviet leader's arrival, the students decided to stage a hunger strike—a form of protest new to China—in the middle of Tiananmen Square, the site designated for Gorbachev's official welcome. The spectacle of several hundred young men and women in a makeshift encampment vowing to fast to the death made a powerful impression, bringing more than a million sympathizers from all walks of life into the square. A tearful appeal from one of Zhao Ziyang's associates to clear the square was ignored: Gorbachev's welcoming ceremony was hastily switched to Beijing airport, and he made his journey to the Great Hall of the People by back streets. Other trips had to be canceled because of the protests, which crippled transport and brought normal urban life to a standstill.

On the second day of the summit, Zhao Ziyang used a meeting with Gorbachev to pay a barbed tribute to Deng Xiaoping, making clear that he, not Zhao, was the party's helmsman. To those who understood the subtle codes of Chinese power plays, this was not an endorsement of Deng's leadership but a signal that he alone was responsible for the crisis. "Xiaoping, thank you and goodbye," jeered the posters. "Xiaoping go back to Sichuan: Your health may be good, but your brain is addled . . . Xiaoping take a break." Rumors spread that Deng had indeed resigned.

The truth was very different. On May 17, Gorbachev's last full day in China, Deng had summoned the Politburo to approve his decision to call in the army; units had already been ordered to move on the capital. Outvoted, Zhao threatened to resign, but the next night Deng's decision was confirmed. At dawn on May 19, Zhao made a last attempt to avert tragedy, going in person to visit the hunger strikers in Tiananmen Square. "We have come too late," he apologized. "No matter how you have criticized us, I think you have been right to do so. You are not like us," he continued. "We are already old. It really doesn't matter."

His appeal to clear the square nearly worked. Rumors of an imminent crackdown had already unsettled the protesters, and later that day, the threat was confirmed by news that a contingent of the People's Liberation Army had reached the outskirts of Beijing. Instead of fleeing, however, the demonstrators formed a human chain around Tiananmen to deny entry to the troops. They never arrived. All around the city, thousands of ordinary citizens had flooded onto the streets, blocking the PLA's advance. Apparently the soldiers had no orders to use their weapons and could only sit bemusedly in their trucks while the citizens of Beijing appealed to them to retire.

On the morning of May 20, loudspeakers around Tiananmen boomed out the announcement that martial law had been declared, banning the right of assembly and granting the security forces the right to use "any means to handle matters forcefully." But the army was still stalled in the suburbs, held up by the crowds in their path. By Tuesday, May 23, the units had returned to their barracks, and for two weeks, a stalemate ensued while Zhao and his supporters fought a rearguard battle to revoke the martial law decree and thus discredit the hard-liners who had supported its imposition. During the lull, the enthusiasm of the protesters waned. Many left Tiananmen, returning briefly on May 30 to stare with wonder at a statue of the "Goddess of Democracy," which the students had erected in front of the giant portrait of Mao Zedong that dominates the square. More than thirty feet high and strongly resembling the Statue of Liberty, the image was a gross provocation to the leadership.

Within the party hierarchy, the struggle had gone against Zhao. Some of his supporters had defected to the opposition; his closest adviser had been arrested. "We can no longer retreat," warned the state president. "We must launch an offensive."

Once again, however, the PLA's attempt to reach Tiananmen Square failed dismally. Late on the night of June 2, a column of about 5,000 unarmed soldiers came jogging toward the square, only to be halted within sight of their goal by a crowd of civilians. The soldiers were unarmed and clearly bewildered. Some of them burst into tears when harangued by the crowds. Elsewhere in the city, an armed PLA contingent was surrounded and stripped of its weapons without putting up any resistance. The protesters began to say that the People's Liberation Army would never turn on them.

Within twenty-four hours they were proved wrong. At 8:00 p.m. on June 3, the Martial Law Enforcement Headquarters issued a final warning that the army would take "strong and effective measures" against the "thugs" in Tiananmen Square. Half an hour later, the sound of automatic gunfire signaled the beginning of a coordinated assault on the center of Beijing. At Muxidi, west of Tiananmen, civilians behind barricades repelled troops in riot gear, but as these soldiers fell back, their place was taken by soldiers carrying AK-47s who stormed the barricades, fired fusillades into the unarmed crowds, and then advanced toward Tiananmen, shooting as they went. At midnight, two armored personnel carriers smashed into Tiananmen Square; youths crippled one of them with firebombs, and a crew member who escaped from the wreck was lynched. Troops soon took up a position at one corner of the square.

All the while, more troops were closing in. Defiantly ignoring the approaching sound of gunfire, the students waited, some appealing for calm, others demanding weapons with which to fight back. Another troop carrier that roared into the square stranded itself on a barrier and was set on fire. At about 3:30 a.m., the column advancing from Muxidi reached the northern end of the square and opened fire on the crowd. As the remaining students around the Monument to the People's Heroes debated whether to flee or die where they stood, the lights went out. When they came back on again, the students saw that they were surrounded by troops. "Your time is up," a political commissar insisted, agreeing that the students could withdraw un-

A police launch cuts across the bow of a traditional Chinese junk in Hong Kong's harbor. A British colony partly leased, partly seized from the Chinese in the nineteenth century, Hong Kong will revert to China in 1997. But by the terms of an agreement reached in 1984, the People's Republic, which derived most of its foreign currency from Hong Kong trade, promised that the territory would continue to be run on capitalist lines for at least fifty years. Such concessions were designed to reassure Hong Kong's predominantly Chinese population, many of them refugees from communism.

harmed. Shortly before dawn, the evacuation began, and by 5:30 a.m. on June 4, the square had been, in the words of Beijing's mayor, "handed back to the people."

Clearly, the leadership had had qualms about ordering the slaughter of unarmed civilians on the most sacred site in revolutionary China; afterward, in fact, they repeatedly insisted that no one had been killed in the square itself. But once the retreating students were well clear of it, armored personnel carriers roared into the tail of the column, leaving eleven bodies mangled amid the wreckage of a bicycle rack. Another army column shot at bystanders watching its advance on Tiananmen. Soon after 10:00 a.m., troops at a corner of the square turned their weapons on crowds gathered in front of the Beijing Hotel; others were killed or injured on the approach roads and in assaults on barricades elsewhere in the city. All that day and the next, army units patrolled central Beijing, firing randomly at civilians, obviously following orders to cow the populace. But no one knew precisely what was happening, for television news had been suspended, and the party leadership issued no statements throughout the violence. It was rumored that civil war was imminent; it was claimed, wrongly, that rival army units were fighting each other.

When official news reappeared on television, the footage of the violence was edited so that only scenes of crowds attacking soldiers were shown. Grim pictures of dead soldiers were screened repeatedly, but not a single image of a civilian corpse. Officials finally admitted that 200 civilians had died and 3,000 had been injured, but the true figure for fatalities was closer to 500, possibly higher. Nor did the official casualty figures include the victims of the unrest that swept most of China's provincial cities; in Chengdu, capital of Deng's home province of Sichuan, for example, there were reports of hundreds killed after crowds staged arson attacks on public buildings.

In the weeks and months that followed, it was announced that more than 2,000 counterrevolutionaries had been arrested, of whom twenty had been executed by a bullet in the back of the head. Most of these were workers rather than students, reflecting the government line that the latter—many of them the children of party officials—had been the innocent dupes of subversives. Praise was heaped on the PLA—China's "Great Wall of iron and steel," Deng Xiaoping called it, when he broke his long silence on June 9.

This time the wall had held, but the political costs were incalculable. Deng and his venerable cronies had alienated an entire generation of educated youth—China's future—and in the eyes of many Chinese of all classes, the party had lost the last vestiges of credibility. Deng had kept his paramount position in the hierarchy, but only by forming an uneasy alliance with the selfsame hard-liners who opposed his economic reforms. For fifty years, the party had cultivated the belief that the PLA and the people were inextricably bound in friendship—"like the fish and the sea," according to Mao—but after Tiananmen, the people were faced with the truth of a different adage, that political power flows from the barrel of a gun. At the same time, however, reports that many commanders were not happy with the PLA's role indicated that the morale and future conduct of the army were uncertain.

Outside China, the massacre shocked world opinion and compelled governments and business leaders to review diplomatic and trade agreements. In Hong Kong, scheduled to be handed back to China by its British rulers in 1997, half a million people took to the streets to condemn the killings, and many of the wealthy colony's Chinese merchants and administrators prepared to emigrate. The chance of reconciliation with Taiwan, which the People's Republic hoped ultimately to woo back into a united China, was postponed indefinitely.

When questioned about the Tiananmen massacre, party spokesmen offered no expression of regret, saying that the military action was purely an internal response to turmoil orchestrated by hostile overseas powers. After decades of self-imposed isolation, the People's Republic had seemed set on adopting a more open policy toward the world, but the events of 1989 shifted power back into the hands of a xenophobic old guard, confirming them in their belief that contact with the West brought "spiritual pollution." For these heroes of the Communist revolution, the idea that the Chinese might be rejecting party ideology in favor of democracy was unthinkable. In a year during which the bastions of communism fell one by one, the spasm of totalitarian tyranny seen at Tiananmen showed that Deng Xiaoping and his veteran party men were out of step not only with the world but also with their own long-suffering people. The radical modernizers, who knew that economic and intellectual reform are inextricably linked, had lost a round in the unending battle to pull China out of poverty and isolation.

Alone and unarmed, a young man confronts a column of tanks before the suppression of the Tiananmen Square protests in June 1989, when Chinese soldiers gunned down protesters demanding greater political freedom and an end to party corruption. Despite the party leaders' assertions that they had triumphantly "braved a storm," the massacre and the events leading up to it represented a loss of face for the Chinese old guard, who were exposed as dithering factionalists concerned, ultimately, only with holding onto power.

AFRICA'S WINDS OF CHANGE

In October 1945, a conference of black politicians meeting in Manchester, England, issued a ringing declaration: "We affirm the rights of all colonial peoples to control their own destiny. . . . The long, long night is over. . . . Colonial and subject peoples of the world—UNITE!" Such talk had been commonplace from Communist powers for decades; but these men, forming the Fifth Pan-African Congress, were claiming to speak for black Africa.

Few British officials took the words seriously. Less than a century before, most of Africa south of the Sahara had been regarded as the Dark Continent by Europeans, and only a generation or so previously, the subcontinent had been divided among European powers; now, all at once, a few hotheads were talking of independence.

Yet their message proved to be prophetic. Within two decades, Britain and France, two of the principal colonizing powers, would be gone, to be followed a few years later by the third, the Portuguese. But independence was not to be the end of the story. The hasty departure of the Europeans would unleash a wholly new set of events and problems, largely unforeseen at mid-century, when no one had a clear idea of what independence might involve.

Complex crosscurrents shaped the process of decolonization. The British, French, and Portuguese empires each dissolved differently. Colonies with few European residents achieved independence far more easily than those with established communities of white settlers. Varying geographical patterns emerged in the east, west, and center of the continent; while in the south, the Republic of South Africa, economically powerful and intransigently white-ruled, held out stubbornly, affecting the attitude of all the emergent nations and dominating the evolution of the whole southern half of Africa. The search for genuine nationhood—the struggle to unite disparate peoples, languages, and traditions within largely artificial frontiers inherited from the colonial past—would pose intractable problems that were still unresolved as the century drew to a close.

In 1945, few Britons had even heard of the Manchester declaration's principal author, a thirty-six-year-old activist from the West African colony of the Gold Coast called Kwame Nkrumah. Equally unfamiliar was another speaker, Nnamdi Azikiwe of Nigeria, who set a deadline for independence in British Africa: fifteen years. Nor was the British empire the only one to be targeted. The conference also demanded independence for all the other white-ruled territories: the French colonies (which meant most of the west and center of the continent), the Belgian Congo, Portuguese Guinea-Bissau, Mozambique, and Angola, self-governing white-ruled South Africa with its black majority, and South Africa's own virtual colony, South-West Africa.

The African nationalists were appealing to principles long accepted in the West.

At a political rally in Accra, a woman's dress doubles as an electioneering poster. Under the leadership of Kwame Nkrumah, Ghana was the first sub-Saharan African nation to win independence in the post-World War II wave of decolonization. Proclaimed independent within the British Commonwealth in 1957, it became a republic three years later. President Nkrumah subsequently became the subject of a personality cult; his supporters took to calling him the Redeemer. Deposed after a military coup in 1966, he died in exile.

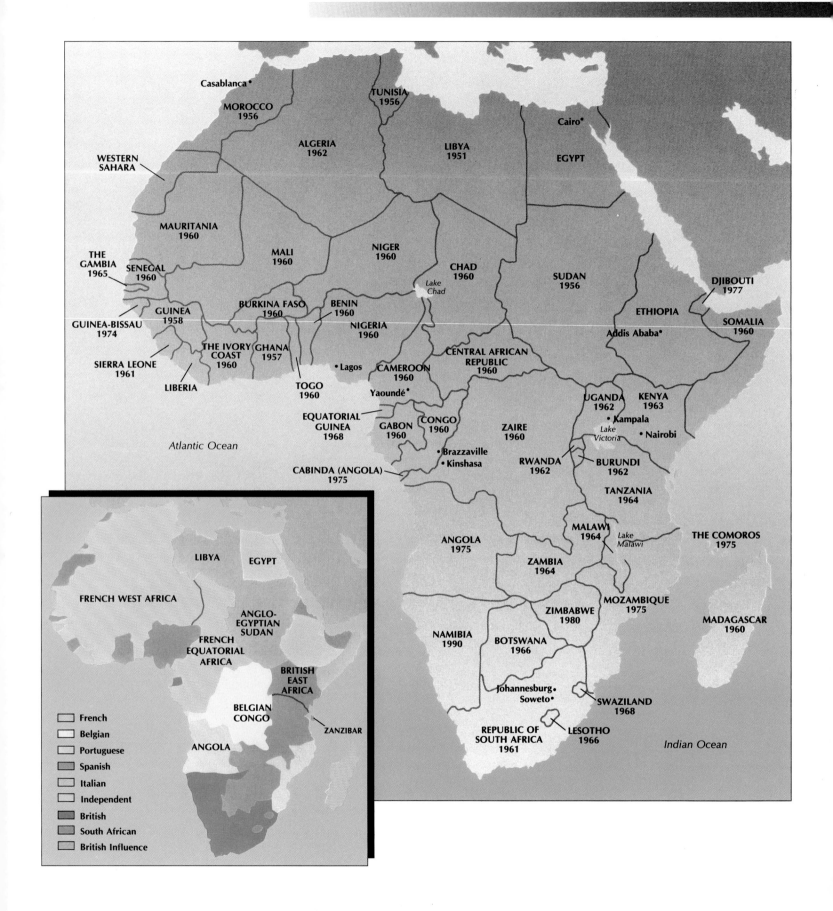

Casablanca •

MOROCCO
1956

TUNISIA
1956

Cairo •

ALGERIA
1962

LIBYA
1951

EGYPT

WESTERN
SAHARA

MAURITANIA
1960

THE
GAMBIA   SENEGAL
1965   1960

MALI
1960

NIGER
1960

CHAD
1960

SUDAN
1956

DJIBOUTI
1977

Lake
Chad

GUINEA-BISSAU
1974

GUINEA
1958

BURKINA FASO
1960

BENIN
1960

ETHIOPIA

SOMALIA
1960

SIERRA LEONE
1961

THE IVORY
COAST
1960

GHANA
1957

NIGERIA
1960

Addis Ababa •

LIBERIA

TOGO
1960

• Lagos

CAMEROON
1960

CENTRAL AFRICAN
REPUBLIC
1960

Yaoundé •

EQUATORIAL
GUINEA
1968

GABON
1960

CONGO
1960

ZAIRE
1960

UGANDA
1962

KENYA
1963

• Kampala

Lake
Victoria

• Nairobi

Atlantic Ocean

• Brazzaville
• Kinshasa

RWANDA
1962

BURUNDI
1962

CABINDA (ANGOLA)
1975

TANZANIA
1964

MALAWI
1964

Lake
Malawi

THE COMOROS
1975

ANGOLA
1975

ZAMBIA
1964

MOZAMBIQUE
1975

MADAGASCAR
1960

NAMIBIA
1990

ZIMBABWE
1980

BOTSWANA
1966

Johannesburg •
Soweto •

SWAZILAND
1968

REPUBLIC OF
SOUTH AFRICA
1961

LESOTHO
1966

Indian Ocean

LIBYA   EGYPT

FRENCH WEST AFRICA

ANGLO-
EGYPTIAN
SUDAN

FRENCH
EQUATORIAL
AFRICA

BRITISH
EAST
AFRICA

BELGIAN
CONGO

ZANZIBAR

ANGOLA

☐ French
☐ Belgian
☐ Portuguese
☐ Spanish
☐ Italian
☐ Independent
☐ British
☐ South African
☐ British Influence

The Great Powers themselves had affirmed the right to national self-determination in the 1918 peace settlements, and again in 1945, in the Charter of the United Nations. By then, India was already en route to independence, and in the Far East, new nations were emerging from the chaos of war. It was hardly surprising, then, that black leaders should also seek nationhood for their peoples, expecting sovereignty to bring in its wake all the benefits of European civilization: industrialization, economic growth, international standing.

Conditions in post-World War II Africa seemed propitious for revolutionary change. Two world wars had shown the vulnerability of the colonial rulers; in 1945, winners and losers alike were crippled by war debts and faced with awesome tasks of reconstruction at home.

The economic situation of the colonies themselves was more complex, but it also encouraged hopes of independence. On the one hand, the Second World War had ushered in an era of booming commodity prices that was to endure throughout the 1940s and 1950s. African economies geared to the export of raw materials benefited accordingly, and economic expectations rose. But so too did the level of social discontent. In colonies with a substantial white presence, such as Kenya, the settlers had taken advantage of the home government's distraction to advance their own role in local politics; and the growth in such European-dominated businesses as mining and intensive farming was seen to have helped the immigrant rather than the native population. Even in West Africa, whose independent peasant farmers gained most from the boom, the British government had organized monopoly-purchase schemes that eventually caused resentment.

Anticolonial sentiment was reinforced after the war when a fresh wave of settlers descended on the continent. Many of the newcomers were technical specialists sent with the best of intentions by colonial governments to work on veterinary medicine, crop development, road building, health improvement, and other welfare projects. Nonetheless, their arrival made the white presence on the continent more pervasive.

Discontent was most forcefully expressed in Nkrumah's homeland, the Gold Coast. In this, Britain's richest and best-educated colony, the colonial presence had always been small. The British had depended instead on a system of government dominated by traditional chiefs. In 1946, a new constitution granted Africans a majority on the ruling legislative council. But economic and political resentment continued, and in Nkrumah, who returned to the country in 1947, it found a powerful voice.

In 1948, there were riots and looting in the principal towns. In response, the British authorities appointed a new, all-African committee to rewrite the constitution. To keep up the momentum of change, a general strike was called in 1950, when Nkrumah led demands for immediate self-government. Although he was jailed for his part in organizing the strike, the following year saw the introduction of a new constitution that firmly established political power in African hands, with African ministers responsible for much of the business of government answering to an African assembly. In the ensuing election, Nkrumah's Convention People's party won easily. He was released from prison to form a government, establishing a pattern that would be followed by nationalist leaders in other countries over the ensuing years.

Under Nkrumah's guidance, the future of the country looked rosy; besides its colonial inheritance of schools, it had rich agricultural resources, mainly cocoa, and abundant mineral deposits, including gold, bauxite, and manganese. Set on the path to self-government, it emerged in 1957 as the first newly independent country south

A complex jigsaw of more than fifty nations, this map of Africa shows the 1990 borders of each country and the years in which they achieved independence. In the decades after 1950, at which time almost the entire continent was ruled by or under the influence of the colonial powers of Europe *(inset map)*, the people of Africa were compelled to resort to armed struggle as well as peaceful negotiation in their progress toward self-rule.

of the Sahara, taking the name of a medieval West African kingdom: Ghana.

Ghana's passage to independence could not have been so smooth without a considerable change of heart on the part of the colonial power. Faced with the realities of diminished economic resources in the postwar years, successive British governments came to realize the impossibility of maintaining the burden of empire. Instead, they sought increasingly to preserve the benefits of trading links through the Commonwealth, a voluntary association of formerly British territories that by 1957 included recently independent India and Pakistan in its ranks, alongside such established members as Australia, Canada, and New Zealand. Although a section of British public opinion, strongly represented in the ruling Conservative party, remained nostalgic for empire, their influence was to decline sharply after the fiasco of the English intervention at Suez in 1956.

Prime Minister Harold Macmillan, who came to power in the wake of that crisis, gave expression to the new realities of Africa's situation when, in an address to the South African Parliament in 1960, he spoke of a "wind of change" that was sweeping across the continent. The speech tacitly acknowledged that Ghana was not an exceptional case and that its example held good for the continent as a whole. Independence could no longer be confined to the relatively prosperous lands of West Africa, but must soon affect Central and East Africa also.

By that time, France's rulers had come to a similar conclusion. In the French-speaking colonies, the goal of aspiring leaders had at first not been to sever links with the imperial power, but to use those links for the greater benefit of Africans. This policy was encouraged by the French themselves. In 1944, senior members of Charles de Gaulle's Free French government-in-exile had met in Brazzaville, in the French Congo, to draw up a blueprint for the future of the continent. Their declaration, devised without consulting any African leaders, stated that Africans should be partners in a French union, with their own seats in the National Assembly in Paris, but also noted that "the establishment of self-government in the colonies, however far off, cannot be contemplated."

One of the most notable newcomers in the postwar Constituent Assembly was Félix Houphouët of the Ivory Coast, who later added to his surname the sobriquet Boigny—meaning "immovable object" in his own Baule language, a suitable nickname for this short, stocky, forceful man. A doctor by training, he was also an experienced administrator, having run his family's plantation for several years. In 1946, he helped to found the Rassemblement Démocratique Africain, an umbrella organization linking parties in several French-speaking African countries, and as one of its deputies won election to the newly restored National Assembly in Paris. Ten years later, with a seat in the French cabinet, he helped draft the Loi Cadre (Framework Law), which gave the vote to all Africans.

By then, France had passed through the trauma of a bloodstained withdrawal from Indochina and was deeply enmeshed in the struggle for Algeria. Coming to power at the height of the Algerian crisis, General de Gaulle offered France's twelve colonies

south of the Sahara the choice between independence and membership in a new French Community, in which each nation would enjoy internal autonomy. Only one country—Guinea, under the leadership of Ahmed Sekou Touré—opted for full independence. De Gaulle's response was immediate. He ordered the instant withdrawal of French financial and economic aid. Within two weeks, some 4,000 doctors, teachers, lawyers, and civil servants had left. Records were taken, generators removed, and telephones ripped out, leaving the land nearly ruined.

If these actions were intended to discourage other countries from following Guinea's example, they failed. Sekou Touré became a hero in black Africa. Ghana provided a substantial loan, helping avert economic collapse in the short term, and the Soviet Union promised long-term aid. Like Ghana before it, Guinea soon had the prestige of its own seat in the United Nations. Other French-speaking countries were emboldened by Sekou Touré's example to request formal independence, first within, then outside the community. By 1960, all of the French-speaking African nations except French Somaliland, a small enclave on the Horn of Africa, were technically independent, and the idea of a unified French community was dead.

Despite the rush to independence—seventeen new nations emerged in 1960, and another eleven were to follow in the years from 1961 to 1965—there was still no generally accepted concept of what independence would mean. Kwame Nkrumah promoted the goal of a continent united by the ideals of socialist internationalism and its own black identity, and in the beginning, many leaders were sufficiently attracted by his ideas at least to explore the option of linking their new nations in larger economic units. Mali teamed up briefly with Senegal in 1959; in 1963, Kenya, Tanganyika, and Uganda experimented with a customs union. Neither plan worked in practice, however. African nations were already too wedded to their borders, too committed to the concept of the nation-state, to abandon even a little of their newly won sovereignty.

Rejecting schemes for economic union, the new nations' leaders showed more

Suspected guerrillas are led away by guards for questioning in November 1952 in the course of the Mau Mau revolt in Kenya. Responding to a wave of assassinations and sabotage, the British authorities imprisoned more than 20,000 suspects and turned rebel strongholds into proscribed areas where Africans could be shot on sight. The Kikuyu heartland of the rebellion was eventually sealed off from the rest of the country, and another 30,000 of its inhabitants were interned.

enthusiasm for the creation of political blocs. At Casablanca in January 1961, Nkrumah brought together half a dozen nations dedicated to his own radical socialist vision. Four months later in Monrovia, a second, much larger group came together under the banner of political moderation, seeking economic and political stability through collaboration with the former colonial powers. The incipient split was healed two years later by the formation of the thirty-nation Organization of African Unity in Addis Ababa, which brought together states from both of the earlier blocs.

By that time, the winds of change had also blown through British East Africa. The transition had been surprisingly smooth considering the fact that Kenya's influential white community at first firmly opposed any form of majority rule. As late as 1945, there were still influential British voices seeking to build up the settler population, which was centered in the capital, Nairobi, and in the area known as the White Highlands, rich farmland adjoining the Rift Valley.

Although some Africans were subsequently brought into Kenya's Legislative Council, the change was not enough to satisfy black politicians. One man provided a focus for their discontent: Jomo Kenyatta, a tall, gregarious Kikuyu, who had spent seventeen years in England, where he had married (and later left) an English wife and, among other activities, had played an African chief in the film *Sanders of the River*. His return to Kenya in 1946 coincided with a growing nationalism among the black peoples of Kenya. Nationalism found its voice in the Kenya African Union, of which Kenyatta became president in 1947.

In the 1950s, Kenyatta was held responsible by the colonial authorities for masterminding the Mau Mau uprising, a bloody terrorist campaign directed against the white presence and those blacks thought to be collaborating with it. Although he denied having any part in the violence, his subsequent detention only confirmed his popularity with the black population. He spent more than five years in prison and under house arrest—years that saw a profound change in the attitudes of the British authorities. The Mau Mau troubles, and the experience of West Africa, persuaded them of the impossibility of staying on. Kenyatta—now revered by his fellow countrymen as *mzee,* or the "grand old man"—was released from house arrest to lead his country to independence in 1963. He subsequently surprised many people by taking a conciliatory line toward both white settlers and rival tribes, thereby laying the basis, at least initially, for a stable and successful government.

By then the three other British East African territories—Tanganyika, Zanzibar, and Uganda—had also won their freedom. Tanganyika and Zanzibar were linked in the United Republic of Tanzania under Julius Nyerere, a mild-mannered schoolteacher of socialist convictions. Uganda, a patchwork of rival kingdoms and tribal areas bound unwillingly together by British rule, achieved independence under the leadership of Milton Obote.

Throughout these transformations, one assumption was shared by all black Africa: that African self-rule would eventually become continent wide, spreading inexorably southward into the very heart of white supremacy, South Africa. Since 1910, this nation had been a self-governing dominion within the British Commonwealth, but in fact, the independence South Africa had won had benefited only its 2.5 million whites; on a national level, the much larger black population had no say in the running of the country. Political power had fallen increasingly into the hands of the

Clad in leopard-skin robes, Jomo Kenyatta, president of Kenya from 1964 to 1978, holds aloft a fly whisk, a traditional African symbol of authority. After seventeen years of voluntary exile and eight years in detention, Kenyatta led his country to independence in 1963. By asking the British police officer who had arrested him to stay on, Kenyatta demonstrated the pragmatism and tolerance that characterized the early years of his rule.

Afrikaners, white Africans of Dutch origin who zealously asserted their patriarchal, rural, Calvinistic, white-supremacist identity.

Segregation became formally entrenched after the Afrikaner-dominated National party came to power in 1948 on a platform of apartheid, the formal separation of the races. Thereafter, black resistance and white oppression fed on each other. When in 1952 the African National Congress (ANC), the principal mouthpiece of black opposition, advocated passive resistance by occupying public amenities reserved for whites, the government responded with emergency legislation giving it dictatorial powers. In 1955, when the opposition drafted the Freedom Charter calling for majority rule and equal rights for all races, 156 people were indicted for treason. (They were eventually acquitted, but the process took six years, during which time they were effectively muzzled.)

The apartheid system was not established without some soul-searching. As conscientious Christians, the Afrikaners faced a dilemma. They tried to find a formula that would allow them to preserve the white-dominated society they sought without giving the appearance of denying the black population (referred to as Bantu) its human rights. Prime Minister Hendrik Verwoerd attempted to resolve the problem in 1959 with the Promotion of Bantu Self-Government Act, which granted the black community full citizenship in assigned areas of the country. These Bantustans, or "homelands," were to be prepared for nominal independence, a move that could be presented to the world as decolonization.

In fact, the Bantustan policy won few supporters outside South Africa. The designated regions contained less than 13 percent of the geographical area of South Africa, including some of its poorest land. Yet they were supposed to house the bulk of a black population that outnumbered the white by four to one. For this, black people were expected to give up all political rights in South Africa itself, even though their labor remained essential to the economy of the country. Humiliating pass laws substantially restricted their freedom of movement in white areas. Urban blacks were compelled to live in vast, impoverished townships, which were easily surrounded in times of insurrection. In standards of legal protection, education, and health, the two societies were worlds apart.

Oppression and violence grew. The government equated opposition to apartheid with communism, a term of abuse that in its turn was used to justify ever more repressive measures. In 1959, radicals of the Pan-Africanist Congress (PAC), an offshoot of the ANC, advocated demonstrations against the pass laws. At one such protest, in the village of Sharpeville on March 21, 1960, the police opened fire, killing 69 people and wounding 178. Two-thirds of the dead, it was later discovered, had been shot in the back.

Further clampdowns followed. A referendum on republican status gave Prime Minister Verwoerd a small majority, and criticism of apartheid by other Commonwealth countries gave him the justification he needed to quit the organization. Those who objected were arrested, or they fled. A law allowing detention for ninety days without trial—detention that could be renewed indefinitely—was used to silence enemies of the government. Black opposition parties were banned. Nelson Mandela, an ANC leader who had left a Johannesburg law practice to devote himself to the cause of black advancement, was imprisoned in 1962. In despair, opponents of apartheid saw no alternative but armed struggle.

Their position was the more bitter in that apartheid proved to be economically successful. Its introduction coincided with a period of economic expansion, buoyed by an influx of foreign capital. Through the 1950s, more funds flowed into South African industry and the Johannesburg stock market than into the whole of the rest

Hungry Baluba women jostle for food rations in a refugee camp in the province of Katanga in 1961. After the Congo was granted independence by Belgium in 1960, ethnic rivalries erupted into civil war, and Prime Minister Patrice Lumumba called in UN troops to restore order. Fighting continued until 1965, when Colonel Joseph-Désiré Mobutu of the Congolese army staged a military coup and declared himself president.

of the continent. Although overseas investment dropped sharply in the wake of the Sharpeville massacre, South Africa could still count on its primary resources, which included six-sevenths of the world's platinum, almost two-thirds of its chromium, and nearly one-half of its gold and manganese, to underpin its wealth. In addition, 90 percent of Europe's imported oil passed along its coasts. One result was that black workers were better paid in South Africa than anywhere else on the continent, and black immigrants flowed in from neighboring states.

In these circumstances, the moral opprobrium of the world had little influence on South Africa's rulers. The international community discussed the use of economic sanctions, but took no effective action. Liberals within the country, like the prominent opposition leader Helen Suzman and Harry Oppenheimer, head of the massive Anglo-American Corporation, had little appeal to the white electorate. Implacable and self-righteous, Afrikaner hegemony seemed immovably entrenched.

In the 1960s, there seemed little prospect of help for South African blacks from the countries across the nation's borders. These were in part shared with landlocked British protectorates that were soon to become the new nations of Botswana and Swaziland; a third protectorate, the future Lesotho, was entirely surrounded by South Africa. All these territories were economically dependent on South Africa and had in effect little more freedom of action than the Bantustans. South Africa's other neighbors, Rhodesia, Angola, and Mozambique, were all firmly under white rule.

Yet changes were in motion, particularly in Rhodesia. After World War II, the British government had established the Federation of Rhodesia and Nyasaland incorporating Northern and Southern Rhodesia—separate colonies since 1923—and Nyasaland, hoping thereby to pool the economic resources of the countries to the mutual benefit of all three. Almost at once, tensions had arisen between the white minority, used to exercising political and economic power, and the black majority. African nationalists were incensed by a grossly disproportionate allocation of resources—the federation's 220,000 whites, for instance, received twenty-five times more per capita in educational spending than the 11 million blacks. Demands for independence became increasingly vociferous.

Protests in Southern Rhodesia, which had the largest and most powerful white minority, were contained by police action; but Northern Rhodesia and Nyasaland proved harder to control. The recommendations of a British commission in 1960 increased African political representation and gave each territory the right of secession. Africans duly exercised that right, and the federation was dissolved on December 31, 1963. Nyasaland gained independence under the autocratic Dr. Hastings Banda as Malawi, and Northern Rhodesia, led by Kenneth Kaunda, became the independent state of Zambia.

Southern Rhodesia's white rulers were left with the expectation that they too would be granted full independence. They could point out that, in comparison with South Africa, their legislative treatment of the black population had been benign. Black people even had a limited vote: The 1961 constitution created a second electoral roll for Africans, giving them fifteen seats out of sixty-five, with the right to amend the constitution if they could achieve a two-thirds majority. For the whites, this was liberality enough. Happy to conserve the concessions they had made and eager to stand on their own feet, they were appalled when Britain refused to allow independence without further progress toward majority rule. After increasingly bitter disputes with Britain and within the country itself, Prime Minister Ian Smith on November 11, 1965, unilaterally proclaimed his country to be the independent state of Rhodesia, justifying his defiance of the letter of the law by appealing to its spirit, and ending his statement by loyally declaring "God Save the Queen!"

Britain was placed in an embarrassing dilemma. Military action against "British" settlers would have been difficult and unpopular. Negotiating vainly with the increasingly intransigent Rhodesians and oppressed by demands for action from other African nations, Britain opted for economic sanctions, to be imposed internationally. The UN concurred. Rhodesia, said British Prime Minister Harold Wilson, would collapse "in weeks rather than months."

His optimism proved unfounded. The economic blockade was frustrated by Mozambique and South Africa, which provided corridors for Rhodesian exports and imports. Rhodesian intransigence hardened. Liberals fled. Hard-line white supremacist farmers moved in from South Africa. Weeks became months, and months years.

Yet the white regime, lacking the support of the majority of the population, was never securely based. Its position became much less secure in 1974, when a revolution in Portugal set in place a new "government of national salvation," one of whose earliest acts was to announce an abrupt retreat from empire. As a result, both Angola and Mozambique achieved independence in 1975.

Under President Samora Machel, the Marxist government of Mozambique was soon providing bases for guerrilla raids into Rhodesia. Faced with the prospect of an unwinnable civil war, Smith agreed in 1977 to accept the principle of majority rule, paving the way for a peaceful transfer of power to blacks. In 1980, Robert Mugabe became the first president of a legally independent nation, renamed Zimbabwe.

Fortress South Africa was by now under siege. Although it sought with some success to destabilize the governments of Mozambique and Angola by financing guerrilla armies within their territories, it too felt the sting of guerrilla raids. These had limited impact in the home country, but in the colony of South-West Africa, referred to as Namibia by the United Nations and supposedly destined for independence, a long-running guerrilla struggle took its toll. South Africa bowed to the inevitable in 1989, when Namibia joined the ranks of independent African nations, depriving the Afrikaners of one more buffer to the north.

By then, however, there had been dramatic changes within their own country. The cycle of protest and repression had continued through the 1970s and early 1980s on a rising note of anger. Violence had flared in 1976 in all the black townships outside Natal, most memorably in Johannesburg's southwestern township, Soweto, where several hundred demonstrators died. As Sharpeville had done before it, the Soweto massacre aroused the conscience of the international community, which hardened further the following year after the death of a young black nationalist leader, Steve Biko, in police custody. The threat of international sanctions, combined with a substantial amount of divestiture by international corporations, seemed to menace the economic well-being of the nation.

Seeking to counter the threat, the government chose to abandon some aspects of the apartheid system and to adopt more liberal policies in the hope of conciliating public opinion worldwide. Black labor unions were legalized, and the notorious prohibition on sexual relationships between members of different races was scrapped, as was segregation on public transportation. While the risk of racial conflict continued to loom over the country, there was now at least a possibility that a less

Marshal Jean-Bédel Bokassa, a former sergeant in the French army, sits in gaudy splendor on the imperial throne of the Central African Empire, formerly the French-ruled equatorial territory of Ubangi-Shari. After seizing power in a military coup, his Napoleonic dreams of empire culminated in 1977 in a coronation ceremony that reputedly cost $20 million; the annual per capita income of his subjects was about $250. Two years later, following allegations of atrocities, he was overthrown in a French-organized coup and replaced as head of state by David Dacko, under whom the Central African Republic had first gained independence in 1960.

bloody solution to the nation's problems could eventually be found through some still-to-be-defined system of power-sharing.

The satisfaction felt by black Africa at South Africa's discomfiture was tempered by a growing awareness of its own failure to realize the dreams that the "wind of change" had inspired. The heady ideals of independence had begun to erode as economies faltered and national, regional, and ideological differences emerged among the new nations. Ghana again paved the way, this time for disillusionment. Nkrumah's rule became increasingly authoritarian as living standards fell and his frustration at failing to realize his ideals grew. "Even a system based on social justice may need backing by emergency measures of a totalitarian kind," he wrote. He encouraged a cult of personality, and in 1964, after a referendum that drew a suspect 93 percent support, Ghana became a one-party state in which opposition was, in effect, treasonable. By the time he was deposed in February 1966, Nkrumah had lost much of the international respect he had won as an architect of the new Africa.

By then, events elsewhere in Africa had revealed how naive it was to think that independence of itself might be a panacea for all ills. In the Congo, postwar changes

In a forest clearing in Portuguese Guinea, an officer of a clandestine liberation army addresses his well-armed troops. Amilcar Cabral, the leader of the independence movement in Guinea, believed that the rural population must be taught how to "break the bonds of the village universe, and integrate progressively with their country and with the world." To this end, he sought to improve health care and education and to oust the Portuguese. Independence came in 1974, after a coup in Lisbon that overthrew the Portuguese dictator Marcello Caetano.

Reduced to the limits of survival, a woman cradles her starving child in a refugee camp in Ethiopia. In the mid-1970s, more than 100,000 Africans died of starvation and related diseases in the semiarid Sahel region south of the Sahara and in the Horn of Africa. The effects of renewed famine in the 1980s in the Sudan and Ethiopia were exacerbated by civil wars between government forces and breakaway liberation movements, which impeded the distribution of relief supplies. In early 1990, the UN estimated that 3.4 million people were at risk of famine and death.

had intensified the problems of a colony in which imperial control had been particularly oppressive. In the 1960s, there were still those alive who could remember the brutal methods (including the amputation of limbs) adopted in the early years of the century when the area was the personal fiefdom of King Leopold of Belgium.

Now new problems had arisen in this huge country, twice the size of any other black African nation. The white population had more than tripled in the postwar years, as newcomers flocked to the mineral-rich Katanga province, the center of economic activity. A decade of rapid economic growth in the 1950s brought mixed results for the black majority, with rising unemployment and urban discontent.

Yet the Belgians showed no signs of relinquishing power. There was little pressure on them to do so, for the black population had no qualified elite to promote its cause. Although primary education was highly developed, and almost half the country was literate, there was reportedly only one black graduate in the entire land until 1957, when the country's first university was opened. Such African organizations as existed were largely regional or tribal, divided by local rivalries or religious belief.

Only one man had more than a local following. He was the ebullient Patrice Lumumba, once a postal worker and now the leader of the radical Congolese National Movement. His main rivals were two regional leaders: Moise Tshombe, the strongman of Katanga province, and Joseph Kasavubu, whose support was centered on the capital, Leopoldville (later renamed Kinshasa).

In January 1959, discontent boiled over into rioting in Leopoldville. The unrest triggered an astonishing response: Belgium quite unexpectedly announced imminent territorial and communal elections intended to lead directly to independence. The process went ahead on schedule, and within eighteen months, Lumumba had become premier and Kasavubu president of a country that was in no way prepared for the responsibilities and burdens of self-administration.

The suddenness of the change brought chaos. The new nation was still entirely dependent on its Belgian civil service and military establishment for its day-to-day management. The independence ceremony itself revealed the underlying tensions; in the presence of King Baudouin, Lumumba delivered a diatribe against Belgian colonial excesses, confirming the belief shared by Europeans and Africans alike that neither side could trust the other.

Two weeks later, young Congolese officers mutinied against their white superiors and went on the rampage, paralyzing the government and creating a situation of anarchy in which local loyalties rapidly overwhelmed national ones. Region was set against region, while other African nations looked on in dismay. Katanga was declared independent by Tshombe, with the encouragement of a section of the European community. Lumumba and Kasavubu then appealed to the UN, which sent troops under the personal direction of the organization's secretary-general, Dag Hammarskjöld, into the rebel province to force it back into the Congo.

Confusion reigned in government circles. In September, Lumumba was arrested by his former aide, the army chief Joseph-Désiré Mobutu, at the same time that the Parliament in Leopoldville was voting him "special powers." The UN, after passionate debate, decided to continue to recognize him as the legitimate ruler. It did Lumumba little good. He was spirited away to Katanga and shot, possibly on the orders of his own president, Joseph Kasavubu.

By then, Lumumba had become a potent symbol of African independence, and his death caused riots and protests around the world. In Cairo, the Belgian embassy was burned to the ground. At the UN, members disputed the morality of interfering in the internal affairs of independent nations, and the USSR accused Hammarskjöld of complicity in Lumumba's murder. In the Congo itself, drama succeeded drama. Tshombe was arrested by Kasavubu's men and accused of treason, then released. Dag Hammarskjöld, flying into Katanga to negotiate with Tshombe, was killed in a mysterious plane crash. In early 1963, UN forces finally asserted their authority by overturning Katangan independence. Tshombe fled into exile.

But it was not the end of his career. In July 1964, backed by Belgian forces and his own thuggish band of white mercenaries, he returned as the last UN forces were

The insolent assumption of generations of European colonists that the white races were superior to all others reached its logical and absurd conclusion in the policies of apartheid pursued by the Afrikaner National party of South Africa from 1948. Apartheid—meaning "separateness" in Afrikaans—had been the unwritten rule of the game at least since the formation of the Union of South Africa in 1910, after which blacks were denied the right to own land on 87 percent of the union's territory. With the enactment of laws enforcing segregation in every aspect of public and private life, prejudice became creed and dogma.

In 1950, all South Africans were placed in a racial category: black, white, colored, or Asian. The government proceeded to strip each nonwhite group of political rights, with the aim of maintaining absolute white dominance. Blacks—outnumbering whites by four to one—were eventually permitted full citizenship in designated "homelands," but remained subject to white economic and military control. Segregation laws were applied to education, churches, job opportunities, and sports. Marriage and sexual relations between whites and nonwhites were forbidden. Casual contact was prohibited on beaches, on public transportation, and even—as shown at the left—on railroad bridges.

For four decades, economic might enabled the white government of South Africa to withstand the tidal wave of independence movements that swept through the rest of the continent. During the 1980s, however, the continued pressure of international denunciation and internal opposition forced the dismantling of some petty apparatus of apartheid. The release of black nationalist leader Nelson Mandela in early 1990, after twenty-seven years' imprisonment, appeared to create new opportunities for the system to be changed by dialogue rather than by revolution.

leaving the country. Such was his power that he was made premier to prevent him from once more leading Katanga into secession. He held the position for more than a year, while the country dissolved into civil war around him. Eventually, he was dismissed by President Kasavubu, shortly before Kasavubu himself was deposed by General Mobutu in a bloodless army coup. Military rule subsequently enforced a precarious peace on the country, now named Zaire.

Tshombe fled again, this time to Spain. Sentenced to death *in absentia,* he was hijacked in his private plane over the Mediterranean and flown to Algeria, where he was held, awaiting extradition, until his death—possibly by murder—in 1969.

This chaotic sequence of events had a powerful influence on subsequent political attitudes in Africa. The crisis forced the countries newly linked by the Organization of African Unity to assert the primacy of the nation-state, however artificial its origins, over the secessionist demands of regions. No nation wanted to risk suffering the Congo's brutal excesses.

That sentiment was reinforced by events in Nigeria that in some ways paralleled the Congo tragedy. On attaining nationhood in 1960, the country had high hopes for the future. With its ancient, productive cultures and more than 50 million people, it seemed set to become the economic giant of Africa.

Yet internal divisions came to the fore almost immediately. Tensions developed between the largely Muslim north and the more developed and primarily Christian south and east of the country, home of the Ibo and Yoruba peoples. The north was the more populous region, and it tended to dominate the government. In January 1966, some Ibo officers mutinied, assassinating the country's prime minister as well as the political leaders of the western and northern regions.

Their action lighted the fuse for civil war. The imposition of martial law failed to prevent northerners from responding to the atrocity by killing hundreds of Ibos, thereby inducing thousands more to flee to their home region to seek the protection of the local military governor, Colonel Chukwuemeka Odumegwu-Ojukwu.

In Lagos, the nation's military ruler, General Yakubu Gowon, took action to hold the federation together, but his efforts at national reconciliation on a basis of regional autonomy failed. On May 30, 1967, Ojukwu declared his region independent under the name of Biafra. Gowon proclaimed the declaration an act of rebellion, and announced that there would be a "short, surgical strike" to crush the rebels.

The war that followed was nothing of the kind. As in the Congo, a newly formed nation found itself fighting against a recalcitrant region. Both sides had their sympathizers. The United States, the Soviet Union, Britain, and the Organization of African Unity sided with General Gowon and the interests of the nation; Tanzania, the Ivory Coast, Portugal, South Africa, and the Roman Catholic church, which had many missions in Biafra, stood behind Ojukwu.

In the first three months of the fighting, the federal troops advanced on Biafra from the northwest, while also repelling a Biafran counteroffensive. By October, they had taken the capital, Enugu. Seven months later, the Nigerian army took Port Harcourt, winning the oil-rich coastal district and cutting the Biafrans off from the sea. But Biafra continued to receive foreign aid by air, and it took twenty more months to reduce the remaining opposition, during which time the Biafran civilian population was exposed to extreme poverty and eventual starvation. Ojukwu fled in January 1970; two days later, Biafra surrendered, pledging loyalty to the federal government.

In the ensuing years, a different danger was to engulf Uganda: the threat of arbitrary one-man rule. Like most of the new nations, it had no natural unity as a political entity: The British had created it out of a patchwork of rival kingdoms and tribal areas, some of which overlapped into neighboring Zaire, Sudan, Kenya, Tanzania, and Rwanda. So diverse was the nation that at one stage the state radio service was broadcasting in twenty-four different languages. The dominant Buganda people, under their king, the kabaka, were always an unwilling partner in the coalition. Nilotic tribes opposed Bantu; Christians opposed Muslims; a large Asian minority coexisted with the black majority in mutual suspicion.

In 1966, President Obote turned on Buganda, attacking the kabaka's palace and forcing him into exile. His action unwittingly sowed the seeds for future violence, repression, and economic collapse. The attack on the kabaka's palace, in which some 400 people died, was commanded by a man who had already amassed a fortune by aiding Congolese rebels. He was Idi Amin, and he was soon to win global notoriety.

At the time, it would have taken a great deal of foresight to have seen Amin as a serious threat. A former heavyweight boxing champion, he had made his reputation serving with the King's African Rifles in Kenya in the wake of the Mau Mau uprising, where he had won a reputation for brutality, extracting information from detainees by threatening—and sometimes performing—castration. At the time of independence, he was one of only two African officers in the Ugandan army. Barely literate, he had the advantage of belonging to none of the major Bantu or Nilotic ethnic groups. When Obote named him army commander a month before the attack on Buganda, therefore, his appointment roused little hostility. Obote had, however, set the stage for his own downfall; in 1971, General Amin took advantage of President

A child's gaze wanders as adult heads are bowed in a literacy class in Mozambique. Education in Africa, vital for socioeconomic development, struggled to overcome the problems of rapidly increasing populations and the lack of resources and trained teachers. In 1990, literacy rates in most African nations were still less than 50 percent. Another challenge was the need to devise locally appropriate courses, rather than copying the educational systems of the ex-colonial powers.

Obote's absence at a Commonwealth conference in Singapore to have himself proclaimed head of state in Obote's place.

Supreme power soon revealed Amin's true nature. Knowing little of politics or economics, he ruled by personal decree, often announcing major decisions over the radio. Seeking a popular cause, he turned on the country's 50,000 Asians, ordering their expulsion within a month's time and thereby dealing a devastating blow to the national economy. He loved publicity, and courted it by playing the effusively generous "Big Daddy." But he acted ruthlessly against those he distrusted, allowing free rein to his secret police, the dreaded State Research Bureau. Soon they chose their own victims. The dead included several cabinet ministers, two American journalists who tried to investigate the killings, and the country's Anglican archbishop, Janani Luwum, who was shot; the body was subsequently disposed of in a faked car crash in central Kampala. Political prisoners were shot, battered to death, or run over

Emergency supplies of Canadian wheat are unloaded in the Ethiopian town of Asmara *(above)*. In the same year of 1987, Soviet rockets are paraded in Addis Ababa, the Ethiopian capital *(right)*. In the postcolonial era, political and commercial self-interest as well as humanitarian concern continued to be motives for the involvement of the developed nations in African affairs.

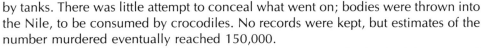

by tanks. There was little attempt to conceal what went on; bodies were thrown into the Nile, to be consumed by crocodiles. No records were kept, but estimates of the number murdered eventually reached 150,000.

Amin was finally toppled in 1979 by Tanzanian troops, who backed the return of the deposed president, Milton Obote. By then, however, the country was dissolving into civil war. Obote struggled vainly to restore his authority over the country until 1985, when for the second time he was deposed by the army. In 1986, the National Resistance Army, one of the guerrilla groups fighting for control of the country, took Kampala, and its leader, General Yoweri Musevani, inherited the task of trying to reconstruct a country whose ethnic groups were hopelessly divided and whose economy was in ruins.

The traumas of the Congo, Nigeria, and Uganda were exceptional, yet other countries too, in less spectacular ways, suffered their own forms of postindependence depression. By the end of the 1980s, most black African nations had escaped from the shackles of colonialism, yet few had fulfilled the expectations raised by the ending of foreign rule. Despite tremendous potential, they remained for the most part desperately poor. Only one small nation achieved and retained a per capita income higher than $1,000 a year: Gabon, a coastal state of west central Africa rich in minerals and oil. Other countries had great mineral wealth—oil in Nigeria, bauxite in Guinea, uranium in Niger, copper and cobalt in Zaire—but saw the money earned absorbed all too quickly by rising import bills and by growing populations.

Africa remained undercapitalized. Increased investment might have been obtained from abroad had African leaders been more responsive to foreign businesses; but men who had devoted their careers to resisting foreign domination often found it hard to change their views and welcome back their former oppressors, albeit in more benign guise. Indeed, the anti-imperialist rhetoric of decolonization tended to scare away potential investors. As a result, industrialization languished. Serious attempts were made across the continent to raise levels of production in agriculture, often with the aid of Western specialists; but no country in the first three decades of the independence era succeeded in reorganizing rural workers—traditionally the bulk of the population—to become efficient food producers on a national scale.

With some exceptions, the French-speaking countries fared slightly better than the rest. By the Convention of Yaounde in 1964, eighteen former French colonies were granted preferential trading terms with the European Economic Community. Furthermore, French troops stood ready to prop up weak regimes or to remove bad rulers. (In the Central African Republic they did both with the same man. They first backed Jean-Bédel Bokassa after he seized power in 1966; then in 1979, after Bokassa had become an African Caligula, declaring himself emperor and murdering hundreds of his subjects, the French backed the coup that removed him.)

One relative success in the early years of independence was the Ivory Coast, under the urbane Félix Houphouët-Boigny, which attained an average annual growth rate of almost seven percent in the years from 1965 to 1980. It had many assets. Its population of eight million was large enough for growth but small and unified enough for effective communication. It was rich in diverse crops—palm oil, cocoa, coffee, timber, and fruit. In those early years, Houphouët-Boigny avoided ostentatious projects and massive military spending. In particular, he retained such a close relationship with France that in many ways the economy remained a colonial one.

109

In pursuit of the elusive goal of economic success, most of the new countries quickly discarded the democratic trappings bequeathed to them at independence by their former colonial masters. Party politics were seen as a distraction, reducing national unity of purpose in the drive for development. In losing their democratic structure, however, the countries also lost any orderly way of transferring political power, and intervention by the armed forces became commonplace. In the six years from 1969 to 1975, there were twenty-five coups in seventeen different countries.

The economic and political woes of Africa were intensified in the years after 1970 by several strokes of bad luck. A disastrous drought struck the Sahel region, bordering the Sahara on the south. Studies suggested that the drought, which returned in the 1980s, formed part of a fundamental climatic shift that could make much of the area uninhabitable by the end of the century.

At the same time, the quadrupling of oil prices by the Organization of Petroleum Exporting Countries (OPEC) in 1973 had a disastrous effect on most African economies. Although it brought windfall profits to such oil-rich nations as Nigeria, Angola, and Gabon, it meant a vastly enlarged foreign-currency import commitment for the majority of the new states, which did not have their own oil. In addition, it triggered spiraling inflation in the West, raising prices for such goods as fertilizers, agricultural machinery, and industrial parts, all essential for development. As a result, African countries were forced to borrow ever-increasing sums, only to find their debt repayments rising astronomically as worldwide inflation in turn pushed up interest rates.

The vicious spiral of rising import bills, growing debt, and surging interest rates was compounded by a fall in the real value of the basic commodities that were Africa's principal source of wealth. In the early 1980s, such goods as coffee, tea, sugar, cotton, and sisal all fetched less on the world market, allowing for the effects of inflation, than they had ten years before.

To compound the problems of its politicians, the continent was experiencing a population explosion of an unprecedented kind. Medical advances, and the new availability of clinics, increased life expectancy in virtually all the countries while at the same time vastly reducing infant mortality rates; more babies survived into a longer adulthood. The result was national populations growing typically at rates of more than three percent a year—enough to double a country's inhabitants in a single generation. The more successful countries expanded even faster; relative prosperity encouraged figures of over four percent annually in Gabon, the Ivory Coast, and Kenya in the years from 1980 to 1987. Only in the late 1980s did fears of a continent-wide AIDS epidemic suggest a possible check to the ever-growing life expectancy figures—and the surging population numbers.

Traditionally the main source of employment, agriculture could not absorb all the new labor, so more and more teenagers flocked to the cities, putting an impossible strain on the infrastructure of urban services. There, most were compelled to eke out a miserable living, at best through day labor, at worst through crime and prostitution.

In some cases, political leaders compounded the problems by ill-judged policies. Many nations, including relatively successful ones such as Kenya, allowed state bureaucracies to expand into inefficient and unwieldy revenue swallowers, as ruling parties paid off their political debts by rewarding their supporters with comfortable, state-salaried jobs. And even the shrewdest of leaders could show an inopportune taste for self-aggrandizing projects, as the Ivory Coast's Félix Houphouët-Boigny

Drums of Kenyan coffee berries are carried on the heads of workers toward a pulping machine that will strip the flesh from the husks, from which the beans will be extracted. Although most Africans in 1990 still earned a living from some form of agriculture, a large proportion of their produce—including coffee, tea, cocoa, and peanuts—was exported, while fertilizers and machinery were generally imported. With the goal of increased self-sufficiency, some governments promoted agricultural programs, hoping to make their economies less dependent on fluctuations in the world market.

demonstrated when he commissioned the building of a cathedral only slightly smaller than Saint Peter's Basilica in Rome to grace the scrubland village of Yamoussoukro in which he had been born. Straightforward corruptión played a part in such countries as Zaire, whose rulers had racked up a foreign debt of some seven billion dollars by 1987 without much evident benefit to Zaire's population, one of Africa's poorest.

Yet despite internal strife, economic woes, and venal leadership, there were, as the 1990s began, two major causes for optimism. One was the continent's immense potential wealth in natural resources; a substantial and lasting rise in commodity prices could quickly break the spiral of dependency and set Africa on the path of development and growth. The other was a dawning realism among African leaders themselves about the extent of the task confronting them. There was a growing realization that if the dreams and expectations of the 1960s were finally to be met, it would be not so much by means of grandiose schemes of social engineering as through small-scale, grass-roots projects, drawing wherever possible on the experience and wishes of their intended beneficiaries. It was a hard lesson for leaders to learn, but the political time bomb of the population explosion lent it urgency.

THE SCOURGE
OF TERRORISM

On May 30, 1972, after landing at Tel Aviv's Lod Airport, three passengers collected their suitcases from the conveyor belt, removed rifles and grenades, and then opened fire indiscriminately on travelers in the crowded baggage hall. Twenty-four people—mainly Puerto Rican Christian pilgrims—were murdered, and seventy-two others wounded. In the ensuing police action, one terrorist was killed. Another took his own life. The third was captured and later made a full confession.

It emerged that the gunmen were well-educated young members of the neo-Marxist Japanese Red Army. They had trained as urban guerrillas in Japan, North Korea, and Lebanon and were chosen for the suicide mission by the Popular Front for the Liberation of Palestine (PFLP). They had flown via Paris to Frankfurt, where they received forged passports; had gone by train to Rome, where they obtained Czech rifles and explosives; and had then boarded an Air France jet to carry out an attack designed to deter travel to Israel. The action, involving support in at least five nations, had been coordinated from headquarters in Lebanon.

The Lod Airport massacre was not unique; similar outrages would follow in the years to come. At the time, however, its impact was exceptional, for it provided the first composite picture of modern terrorism, operated with total callousness on an international scale.

Not that there was anything new about the use of terror in support of political, military, or religious aims. The Zealots, Jewish rebels opposing Roman rule in Palestine in the first century AD, included fanatics known as Sicarii, or "dagger-men," who struck down individuals, Jewish or otherwise, thought friendly to Rome. In the eleventh century, the political murders carried out by a Persia-based Islamic group gave rise to the word *assassin*—a corruption of *hashishin,* or "hashish-eaters"—because it was believed that the killers were given the drug as a foretaste of the pleasures they would enjoy in heavenly gardens after they had completed their missions.

Modern terrorism, however, can be traced to the nineteenth century. In the wake of the upheaval of the French Revolution, educated young people in many European countries, but particularly in Germany and Russia, concluded that the social injustices they saw around them justified any means to remedy them. Dedicating their lives to a future of humanity and justice whose outlines they could barely imagine, they chose, in the absence of legal means of political action, the bomb and the bullet as the vehicles of change. Doomed to live in times they considered unbearable, they found a romantic apotheosis in the denial of self demanded of them by the Revolution. Sergey Nechayev, a Russian nihilist who, having killed a doubting comrade, was to die in prison, expressed this group's despairing creed: "The revolutionary is a man condemned in advance. He must have neither romantic relationships nor any object to engage his feelings. He should even cast off his own name. Every part of him should be concentrated in one single passion: the revolution."

The nineteenth-century campaign of direct action climaxed in the four decades before World War I. In 1878, there were two attempts on the life of the German emperor. Czar Alexander II was killed by a bomb in 1881. In 1893, a bomb went off in France's Chamber of Deputies; the next year, the nation's president was stabbed to death. In 1898, Empress Elizabeth of Austria was murdered, and in 1901, an anarchist shot dead President William McKinley of the United States.

These were the incidents that history remembers, but they were by no means the whole story. In 1892 alone, there were more than 1,000 dynamitings in Europe, and almost 500 in the United States. These figures compare closely with their equivalents for recent times; in the 1980s, there were some 17,500 international or major domestic terrorist outrages worldwide, an average of about 1,750 a year.

What was new about terrorism after 1950 was not its frequency or the prominence of its victims. If anything, improved security made society's leaders less likely to be targeted, although it

A jet explodes in Jordan during a Palestinian terrorist operation in 1970. Three aircraft hijacked over Europe were diverted to the airstrip, then blown up; the passengers were released unharmed.

A terrorist looks out from the balcony of Israeli team quarters at the Munich Olympic Games in 1972. Palestinians seized the building, killing two athletes; in an ensuing gun battle with police, nine more hostages died.

could not protect against attack by their own bodyguards, as in the case of Indian Prime Minister Indira Gandhi in 1984, or by members of their military, such as those who shot Egypt's President Anwar Sadat in 1981. In general, the postwar years saw a democratization of terror, with victims chosen for their ordinariness.

What was extraordinary was the multiplication of groups willing to use terrorist methods to achieve their goals. A sample could include urban guerrilla groups, variously labeled Marxist, Maoist, Trotskyite, or Castroite, in countries throughout Latin America; black militants and white right-wingers in South Africa; Basque, Tamil, Corsican, Québecois, and Kurdish separatists; Sikh zealots demanding their own state of Khalistan; Muslims demanding Kashmir's independence from India; Armenians retaliating for the massacres by Turkey in 1915; Islamic fundamentalists campaigning against Western influence in the Middle East; and an array of groups dedicated to the liberation of Palestine.

No country, it seemed, was remote enough to escape the scourge. Previously, with few exceptions, extremist groups had conducted their campaigns of violence within their own territories or in those of their declared enemies. Now there were no recognized borders for the pursuit of political aims, and the most vulnerable targets tended to be the countries that allowed freedom of movement to all.

Terrorism without frontiers was a natural, maybe an inevitable reflection of the technological advances of the age. With the introduction of jet travel in the 1950s, later followed by the development of intercontinental television communications, the Earth became an infinitely smaller place. Terrorists were high-profile residents of what the Canadian theorist Marshall McLuhan named the "global village."

They were also children of the media age. Terrorism thrived on what Britain's Prime Minister Margaret Thatcher called the "oxygen of publicity"—practitioners of violence could now command a worldwide audience. Newspapers and television vied to report the news, and no one could deny that sieges and hostage-taking made headline material. Terrorists conducting press conferences while holding civilians at gunpoint became a familiar and disquieting event.

In 1972, by murdering eleven Israeli athletes at the Munich Olympic Games, members of the Palestinian Black September group gained access to almost every television channel in the world—an audience of more than 500 million people. Minor terrorist groups were no less alert to the value of media coverage. Few people, for instance, had heard of the south Moluccas until 1975, when rebel islanders hijacked a Dutch train, holding some fifty passengers hostage to publicize their demands for independence from Indonesia.

Yet if publicity provided the rationale for the upsurge, it could not be described as its cause. Many of the bitterest campaigns had roots deep in history, drawing inspiration from real or perceived grievances that appeared to some people to be resolvable only by force.

Some were spawned from the traumas of decolonization: in Kenya, where assassinations and sabotage were features of the Mau Mau revolt against British rule; in Cyprus, where the EOKA dedicated itself to winning union with Greece; in Algeria, where the struggle for independence was darkened by particularly brutal atrocities. Other movements, among them the Basque separatists' fight for an independent homeland and the seemingly endless war waged by the Provisional wing of the Irish Republican Army against the British presence in Ireland, had their origins even further in the past.

The seeds of the most relentless of all the campaigns, however, were sown as recently as 1949 when, following Israel's victorious war of independence against its Arab neighbors, homeless Palestinian refugees were gathered in more than fifty United Nations Relief Works Agency (UNRWA) camps in Jordan, Syria, Gaza, and Lebanon. The camps were to be the prime recruiting grounds for a rising nationalist group, first called the National Liberation Movement and subsequently the Palestinian Liberation Organization (PLO). By 1959, one of its leaders, Yasser Arafat, was preaching that Palestinians should rely only on themselves for the liberation of their country, and that their weapons should be guerrilla warfare—and terror.

The picture was complicated after 1967, which saw another Israeli victory, this time in the Six Day War. The Arab defeat deprived Palestinian guerrillas of nearly all their land bases on Israel's borders. As a result, there emerged among militant Palestinians groups of extremists who, lacking clearly defined territory of their own, chose to make the whole world their battlefield. The PFLP, the PFLP-General Command, Black September, the Abu Nidal group—the organizations remained shadowy, but the names became feared everywhere.

The splintering of the Palestinian movement coincided in the crucial year of 1967 with an entirely new phenomenon. From the European and U.S. student protests of the late 1960s emerged a generation of politicized young people who rejected the materialistic values of the consumer society. By far the greater part of the New Left, as it was styled, was committed to nonviolence in its pursuit of social change; but on the fringes of the movement small groups impatient with the slow processes of democracy dedicated themselves to direct action. Among them were Uruguay's Tupamaros, the American Weathermen, Britain's Angry Brigade, and the French Action Directe.

It was in Germany and Italy, however, that the new revolutionary sensibilities found their most sanguinary expression. In Italy, the violence rumbled on throughout the 1970s, climaxing in 1978, which saw nearly 2,500 attacks by disparate terrorist groups and most sensationally the kidnapping and murder of ex-Prime Minister Aldo Moro. Germany's notorious Baader-Meinhof gang drew headlines in the years after 1970, surviving the capture of its two leaders in 1972 to spawn another, equally lethal terror group, the Red Army Faction.

The Red Army Faction survived throughout the 1980s, carrying out the murder of a leading banker in 1989, but by that time, its membership was reduced to about twenty and it was beginnning to seem anachronistic. The fact was that there had been a shift in attitudes among Europe's youth, who were now less concerned with political ideology and more with the issues of environment and lifestyle.

Partly as a result, the focus of terrorism in the 1980s swung back to the Middle East, where a major source of violence had emerged: Islamic fundamentalism. The upsurge drew its inspiration from the Iranian revolution of 1979. The Islamic revolutionaries, devoted to a holy war against the secularizing influence of the West, often pursued their targets with suicidal fervor. In 1988, fundamentalists hijacking a Kuwaiti airliner in Iran wore white sheets emblazoned: "We are in love with martyrdom." That attitude had found expression five years earlier when members of Hezbollah, the Iran-backed "Party of God," drove explosives-laden trucks into the headquarters of U.S. and French peacekeeping forces in Lebanon. The ensuing blasts killed the drivers, along with almost 300 servicemen, creating in the words of one survivor "a carnage I have not seen since Vietnam."

The rise in terrorist activity in the 1970s and 1980s caused governments to take increasingly severe countermeasures. Stricter security was introduced at frontiers, airports, and seaports. In some countries, laws were introduced to increase the power of the police to detain suspects, or to restrict media coverage of known terrorists. Security around heads of state and public figures was increased to the point that it sometimes seriously incommoded other citizens.

Most spectacular, counterterrorist units were set up. One of the best known was Britain's 22d Special Air Service Regiment—the SAS. On May 5, 1980, this crack commando force staged with deadly efficiency the most public of all the major antiterrorist operations when, in the glare of television cameras, SAS men in black balaclavas and carrying submachine guns climbed onto the balconies of the Iranian Embassy in London and overcame anti-Khomeini rebels who had seized twenty-six hostages six days earlier. Five of the six terrorists were killed; all but one of the surviving hostages were saved.

So far as the United States and Europe were concerned, there were signs in the late 1980s that improved countermeasures, including the pooling of information about terrorists and their financial backers, were proving effective. The epidemic, it seemed, could be contained. Yet the threat of violence remained. It was hard to visualize any foolproof way of preventing attacks on so-called soft targets— private citizens—designed to destabilize governments by creating panic. In the long run, hope seemed to lie in the creation of societies in which grievances could be addressed through legitimate channels. Even in that ideal world, there would no doubt be a ruthless minority lethally aware of the attention-getting effects of individual acts of violence. And so the cycle of random terror and state repression seemed destined to go on. Bombs would explode; relatives would mourn; TV cameras would whir.

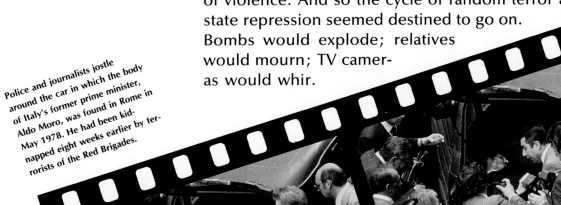

Police and journalists jostle around the car in which the body of Italy's former prime minister, Aldo Moro, was found in Rome in May 1978. He had been kidnapped eight weeks earlier by terrorists of the Red Brigades.

Egypt's King Farouk I was a monarch with few admirers. Ascending the throne in May 1936 as a handsome and smiling teenager, he had pledged himself to work for the welfare and happiness of his people. Farouk, however, had shown himself to be more interested in feasting, womanizing, and gambling than in the problems of the poverty-stricken Egyptians, and the once-bright hope had become an object of scorn and ridicule. "A man who can lose $120,000 in a night can lose anything," reflected one courtier, and so it was. On July 23, 1952, Farouk was ousted in an army coup. Three days later, he sailed out of Alexandria harbor for the last time, his yacht loaded with gold ingots and erotica. He was to die, thirteen years of lonely exile later, following a heart attack in a Rome restaurant.

On the evening of the coup, jubilant crowds surged through the streets of Cairo and other Egyptian cities to celebrate its success. It was the first in a series of volcanic eruptions that were to change the political topography not only of Egypt but of the entire Middle East and beyond. The new force in the region was nationalism, and its chief exponent, Gamal Abdel Nasser, was to become one of the most revered—and reviled—leaders of the post-World War II years.

Born in 1918, the son of a minor post office official in Alexandria, Nasser was an early recruit to the cause of Egyptian nationalism. Like most of the Arab world, Egypt had been ruled for centuries by the Ottoman Turks—a situation that had changed in 1882, when the British had taken over the country. The Egyptians had finally won their independence in 1922, but with Britain retaining control of such matters as defense and communications, it was an independence that most regarded as little more than a sham. Although the Anglo-Egyptian Treaty of 1936 drastically reduced British influence, it confirmed Britain's right to station troops in the Suez Canal zone—which aroused the indignation of the extreme nationalists, including Nasser.

In 1937, the future leader entered Egypt's Royal Military Academy in Cairo, where he graduated from simple street-corner agitation to underground conspiracy against the government. His military duties appear to have been undemanding, and as he wrote later, life at that time was "like a thrilling detective story. We had dark secrets and passwords. We lurked in the shadows; we had caches of pistols and hand grenades, and firing bullets was our cherished hope." But the thrills were sometimes outweighed by the horror. On one occasion, having helped to shoot a political opponent, Nasser was haunted by the wailing and screaming of the victim's wife and child. "I reached home," he recalled, "and threw myself on my bed. All night I lay awake, chain-smoking in the darkness trying to collect my thoughts. But those sounds kept ringing in my ears." He subsequently avoided bloodshed whenever possible; even after the 1952 coup, Farouk, the chief target of the plotters' hatred, was exiled, rather than executed by hanging.

Swathed in the traditional Islamic veil, the chador, and shouldering automatic rifles, female supporters of Iran's fundamentalist regime parade through the streets of the capital, Tehran. Under the pro-American shah, Iranian women were among the most emancipated in the Middle East, but with his ousting in 1979 by the militant Muslim cleric Ayatollah Khomeini, they faced an increasing number of constraints. Western fashions and makeup were denounced, mixing with men outside the immediate family was deplored, and admission to higher education and the professions was restricted.

The king had always been unpopular with nationalists, who regarded him as being more interested in clinging to his throne than in opposing the British. His position was further undermined in 1948, when the armies of Egypt, Syria, Lebanon, Iraq, and Jordan attempted to crush Israel, the Jewish state that had just been proclaimed in Palestine. The result was an unmitigated disaster for the Arabs, and it was Farouk who was held primarily responsible. Among the Egyptian troops, food and medicine were in short supply, arms and equipment were obsolete, and senior officers were often incompetent and sometimes cowardly. Nasser, who was wounded in the fighting, wrote later that he and his comrades had been "thrust treacherously into a battle for which we were ill prepared, unarmed, and under fire, our lives at the mercy of greed, conspiracy, and lust."

The regime in Cairo attempted to divert attention from its own shortcomings by whipping up a popular campaign against the British. It announced the unilateral abrogation of the 1936 Anglo-Egyptian Treaty and encouraged "liberation" squads to carry out sabotage and guerrilla attacks against the 80,000 British troops in the Suez Canal zone. In January of 1952, after an incident in which a police station

Embraced by a common culture and united in their opposition to the state of Israel, founded in 1948 as a Jewish homeland, the Islamic nations of the Middle East were rent by constant political and military strife after World War II. Revolutions toppled monarchies in Egypt, Iraq, Iran, and Libya; civil wars erupted in the Sudan, Yemen, and Lebanon; and nationalist ideologies caused conflicts between neighboring countries—most notable was a war lasting eight years between Iran and Iraq. In addition, the oil wealth of Saudi Arabia and of the Persian Gulf sheikdoms made the region vital to the world economy, and both the United States and the Soviet Union tried to build a network of alliances.

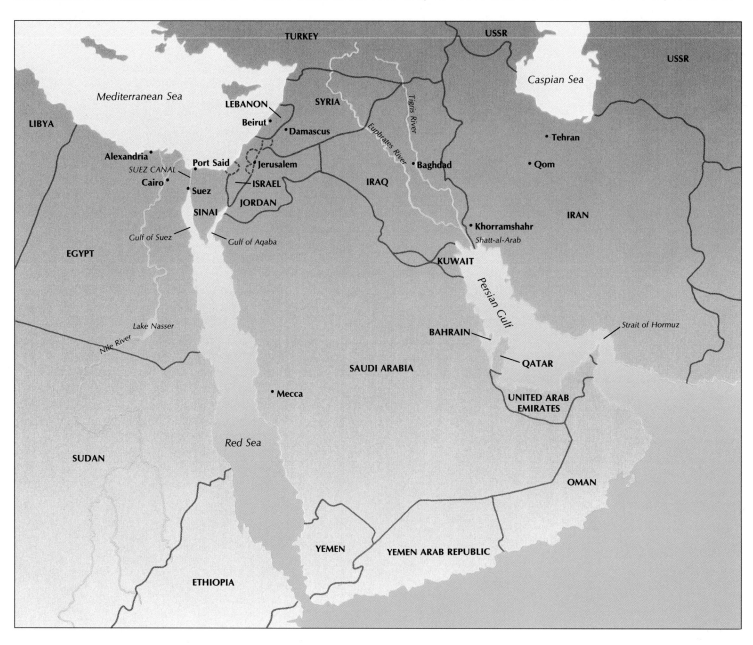

suspected of harboring guerrillas was stormed by the British and some fifty Egyptian armed police were shot dead, a frenzied mob rampaged through the capital, attacking buildings with British and other foreign connections. It was not until the evening that the government took any action to restore order, by which time twenty-six foreigners, mostly British citizens, had been killed and much of the city's center had been reduced to smoking rubble.

Six months later, with the country sliding into increasing chaos, the underground army organization that Nasser had founded, the so-called Free Officers, decided to strike. Although Nasser, by now a colonel, inspired and masterminded the coup, its nominal leader was another veteran of the fighting in Palestine, General Muhammad Naguib. Amiable, avuncular, and reassuring, he was the ideal figurehead for a regime devoted to radical change. However, when Naguib tried to play more than a purely decorative role, Nasser swept him aside and took over the government himself. In July 1954, only three months after assuming the premiership, he scored his first big success—a new treaty with the British. Under the treaty terms, Britain agreed to withdraw all of its troops from Egypt within twenty months; Egypt accorded Britain the right of reoccupation in the event of war; and both Britain and Egypt pledged themselves to uphold the 1888 Constantinople Convention guaranteeing free passage through the Suez Canal to the ships of all nations.

On February 20, 1955, Nasser, recently installed as president of Egypt, met the British foreign secretary, Sir Anthony Eden (later the Earl of Avon), as he passed through Cairo on his way to a conference in the Far East. Grabbing Eden warmly by the hand, he announced the dawning of a new era of friendly relations with Britain and the West. "The ugly page in Anglo-Egyptian relations has been turned," he declared, "and another page is being written." But the public cordiality was misleading, for the two men were about to plunge into one of the most extraordinary political feuds of modern times. Although regarding him as a great improvement over King Farouk, Eden developed an instinctive dislike for Nasser, and according to Nasser's later account, he gave the Egyptian leader the impression that "he was talking to a junior official who could not be expected to understand international politics."

However, the real issue that divided them was whether or not the Middle East should be involved in the Cold War. Nasser, for his part, was looking toward the creation of a nonaligned bloc of Arab states, led by Egypt and closely linked to other neutralist countries such as India and Yugoslavia. Eden, on the other hand, believed that the Middle East, with its sensitive

Former King Farouk of Egypt, stylishly clad in a trilby hat and gold-rimmed sunglasses, takes in the chilly winter air of Italy in 1952. His reign blighted by greed and corruption, Farouk was forced into exile in 1952. Freed from the few constraints he had observed as monarch, he plunged into a frantic round of gambling, gourmandizing, and woman-chasing. But such excesses took their toll, and in October 1965, the 280-pound Farouk suffered a fatal heart attack. Two days later, his body was flown back to Egypt—a country that, although it had reviled him in life, gave him a resting place in death.

strategic location and its abundance of oil, should be tied firmly to the West. On February 24, only four days after Eden's visit to Cairo, Iraq and Turkey signed the Baghdad Pact, a military alliance that the foreign secretary hoped would be the first step toward "a NATO for the Middle East." (Britain, Iran, and Pakistan were to join later that year.) According to one observer, Nasser, on learning of this development, became so angry that he fainted. Immediately, Cairo's newly established Voice of the Arabs radio station began pouring out a stream of anti-British invective.

The final breach came in March 1956, when young King Hussein I of Jordan dismissed the British officer who commanded his army, General Sir John Glubb. Hussein was merely getting rid of a man he had long found irksome, but Eden, now prime minister, was convinced that Nasser was behind the firing. The minister of state at the Foreign Office, Anthony Nutting, recalled that "on that fateful day, he decided that the world was not big enough to hold both him and Nasser. The 'Egyptian dictator' had to be eliminated somehow or other, else he would destroy Britain's position in the Middle East and Eden's position as prime minister of Britain." A few days later, when Nutting tried to persuade the prime minister to moderate his attitude, Eden shouted back, "But what's all this nonsense about isolating Nasser, or 'neutralizing' him, as you call it? I want him destroyed, can't you understand?"

The opportunity was soon to be provided. In July 1956, having provisionally agreed to lend Egypt $270 million for the building of a huge dam on the Nile River, near Aswān, the British and Americans withdrew the offer. The official reason given for this about-face was the instability of the Egyptian economy, but it was Nasser's apparent drift toward the Soviets (the previous September he had arranged to reequip the Egyptian army with Soviet arms) together with Eden's determination to teach the Egyptian leader a lesson, that had really put an end to the deal.

Instead of meekly accepting the rebuff, Nasser decided to retaliate. On July 26—the fourth anniversary of King Farouk's abdication—he told a cheering crowd in Alexandria that the Suez Canal would be nationalized. Egypt would build the Aswān Dam with revenues from the canal, and if the imperialist powers did not like it, they could "choke on their rage." Although the canal was owned by foreign stockholders—mainly French and British—Nasser's takeover could hardly be faulted under international law, since he proposed to pay them full compensation. However, it was not the legal implications of the seizure that preoccupied the British prime minister. More than half of Britain's annual oil imports were carried along the 100-mile-long waterway, and Eden had no intention of allowing a man he regarded as a mortal enemy to remain, in his own words, with a "thumb on our windpipe."

At first, Britain appeared to be working for a peaceful solution of the crisis, inviting representatives from the principal canal-using countries to attend a conference in London. The Egyptians were also invited, but a few days before the conference was due to open, Eden made a television broadcast in which he referred to the Egyptian leader as a "man who cannot be trusted to keep an agreement. We all know this is how Fascist governments behave." Predictably, the Egyptians refused to attend the gathering, and equally predictably, the conference's subsequent proposal for an international board to operate the canal was flatly rejected by Nasser.

In his book *Spycatcher,* former British intelligence officer Peter Wright claimed that it was around this time that a plan was drawn up to assassinate the Egyptian leader by having an agent place canisters of nerve gas inside the ventilation system of one of the presidential headquarters. However, when it was pointed out that the gas would kill not only Nasser himself, but also many of his staff, Eden vetoed the plan.

A much more promising option was the one that the prime minister had had in mind from the beginning—an Anglo-French invasion of Egypt that would topple Nasser and restore the canal to Western hands. The French, who saw Nasser fanning the flames of revolt against their rule in Algeria, proved to be willing accomplices. However, since the other users of the canal, including the United States, were totally opposed to military action, Eden and the French premier, Guy Mollet, had to devise a pretext for intervening.

This was when the Israelis entered the game. Officially at war with their Arab neighbors since 1948, they had good reasons of their own for wishing to see the Egyptian leader destroyed. Following a 1955 raid by the Israelis into the Gaza Strip, Arab guerrillas had begun raiding across the border from the Sinai Peninsula; and Egyptian vessels were blockading the Gulf of Aqaba, Israel's only outlet to the Red Sea. The collaboration among the three powers was sealed at a secret meeting at Sèvres, near Paris, between October 22 and 24; and the plan they had agreed on began to unfurl in the early hours of October 29, when Israeli paratroopers were dropped into the Sinai, and hostilities began in earnest.

The next day, Britain and France, assuming the role of spontaneous peacemakers, issued a joint ultimatum that called on Israel and Egypt to stop fighting. It also demanded that the Egyptians move their troops ten miles west and the Israelis ten miles east of the canal, thus preserving it from possible damage or disruption. However, since the fighting was still about 125 miles east of the canal, the Israelis were being given a virtual carte blanche to advance another 115 miles, while the Egyptians were being asked to retire 135 miles into their own country. When the Egyptians, as expected, refused the terms, the Israelis continued their drive toward the canal. On October 31, British and French bombers went into action, knocking out Egyptian airfields and radio stations, and destroying much of the nation's air force while it was still on the ground. Five days later, an Anglo-French invasion force landed near Port Said, and after capturing the city, pushed south along the canal.

Although by now the world was holding its breath over an emerging crisis far to the north—the uprising of the Hungarians against their Soviet-controlled government—it was not about to ignore events in Egypt. Few were deceived by the protestations of the British and French that they had launched their invasion simply in order to protect the canal, and hostility toward the two allies reached fever pitch. Condemned by the United Nations, threatened with nuclear attack by the Soviets, and with their Middle Eastern oil supplies at risk, they soon realized that the cost of their Egyptian adventure was likely to be far higher than they had imagined.

But it was the intervention of the United States that proved decisive. The fighting had sparked a drastic slump in the value of sterling, and it was estimated that Britain

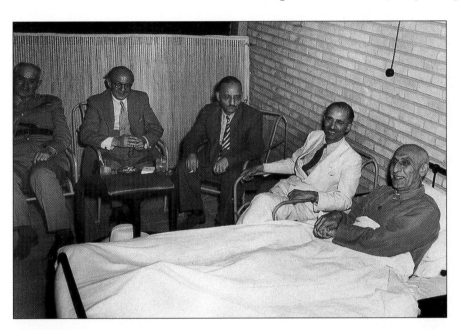

Members of the Iranian cabinet gather at the bedside of Muhammad Mussadeq in July 1951, a few months after his nationalization of the British-owned Anglo-Iranian Oil Company. A highly emotional speaker, whose orations often ended in weeping and fainting—his bed was regularly brought into the Iranian Parliament—Mussadeq was widely respected in Iran. However, with his takeover of Britain's oil holdings, he became an object of contempt and ridicule in the West. While Britain organized an international boycott of Iranian oil, Mussadeq's supporters marched through the streets of Tehran and other cities chanting "Kill the British!" The crisis ended in August 1953, when Mussadeq was overthrown in a coup backed by the British and American intelligence organizations. The shah, who had briefly fled the country, was restored, and a new oil agreement was signed under which Britain became a stockholder in an international consortium.

would need a loan of $300 million to stave off financial disaster. However, on November 6, President Dwight D. Eisenhower warned that Britain could expect no help from the United States unless it ordered an immediate cease-fire and agreed to quit Egypt completely. The British, despite serious misgivings, felt obliged to comply, and the French and Israelis could do little but follow suit.

Later that day, Britain and France voted at the United Nations for the establishment of a UN Emergency Force (UNEF) to supervise the cease-fire and withdrawal, and the units racing down the canal road ground to a halt at El Cap, one-quarter of the way to Suez. By December 23, all British and French troops had been evacuated, and a month later, the last of the Israeli forces left the Sinai. Another withdrawal was the one by Sir Anthony Eden, who, worn out by the strains of the preceding months, resigned as prime minister on January 9, 1957. (Despite admissions by other leading partic-

Ecstatic Egyptians mob their leader, Colonel Gamal Abdel Nasser, at the Cairo railroad station on October 28, 1954, two days after an abortive attempt on his life. A tall, imposing figure, with a dazzling smile and an unrivaled command of rhetoric, Nasser exercised an almost hypnotic hold over his people. But the charm hid a darker side to his character. He could be utterly ruthless toward political opponents—a number of whom were imprisoned, tortured, and executed—and as he grew older, he became increasingly paranoid, suspecting even his closest colleagues of conspiracy.

ipants, Eden would continue to deny until his death, in 1977, that the Anglo-French invasion of Egypt had been carried out in collusion with Israel.)

For Britain, the Suez conflict was a costly and humiliating fiasco, which, far from destroying Nasser, made him a hero from Morocco to the Persian Gulf—the leader who had upheld the dignity and independence of the Arabs against the machinations of the ''imperialist bloodsuckers.'' It was a role that was all the easier for him to fulfill because the region had long been starved for heroes, and its political development was still in a state of flux. Most of the area had formed part of the Ottoman Empire until its dismemberment after World War I; and when the Turks had gone, the British and French had moved in, accepting League of Nations mandates to rule, in Britain's case, Palestine and Iraq, and in France's, Syria and Lebanon. Along with independence, each of these countries had inherited the governmental systems of the re-

Scuttled ships litter the Suez Canal in the wake of the abortive 1956 Anglo-French invasion. A humiliating disaster for the two powers, Suez had a costly coda. Thousands of French and British residents in Egypt were expelled; French and British property was seized, including schools and hospitals; and Western prestige and influence in the region were irreparably damaged.

spective mandated powers; thus Syria and Lebanon became republics, while monarchies were established in Iraq and Transjordan, as the section of Palestine not incorporated into Israel was called at that time.

In this rootless and fragmented political world, Nasser's vision of Arab power and unity was a shining ray of hope. One of the fruits of his popularity was the proclamation, in February of 1958, of the United Arab Republic (UAR)—a union between Egypt and Syria, which was declared in the official communiqué to be a ''preliminary step toward the realization of complete Arab unity.'' Since attaining independence in 1941, Syria had been beset by a succession of military coups and countercoups, and it was hoped by the Syrian leaders, who were now dominated by the left-wing

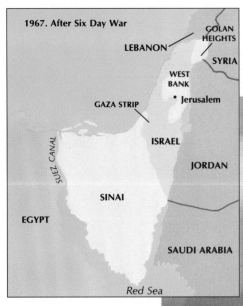

1967. After Six Day War

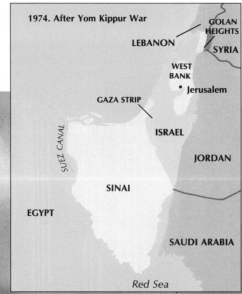

1974. After Yom Kippur War

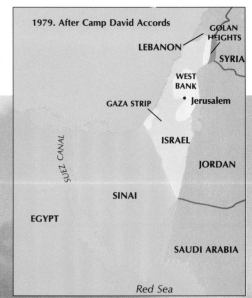

1979. After Camp David Accords

Israel

Israeli occupied

Egyptian territory

Demilitarized zone

In the forty years after 1948, Israel's borders fluctuated wildly *(maps, above)*. The fighting of 1948 and 1949 left the Jewish state in possession of most of Palestine—a total of almost 8,000 square miles. The 1967 Six Day War saw Israeli forces occupy the Sinai, the Gaza Strip, the West Bank, East Jerusalem, and the Golan Heights—an extra 27,000 square miles. After the 1973 Yom Kippur War with Egypt and Syria, Israel withdrew from the west bank of the Suez Canal and allowed captured Syrian territory east of the Golan Heights to become a UN demilitarized zone. Five years later, the Camp David Accords led to Israel's gradual withdrawal from the Sinai—but left Israel in control of 2,700 square miles of occupied territory.

From the moment of its inception, on May 14, 1948, Israel has been a nation under siege. Carved out of the British territory of Palestine, with its predominantly Arab population, the new state was seen by the Arabs as both an insult and a menace.

But every attempt to defeat Israel on the battlefield—there were three major Middle East wars between 1948 and 1989—was unsuccessful. The reason for this tenacious survival may be attributed to the Israel Defense Forces (IDF).

Compulsory military service begins at the age of eighteen and applies to men and women alike. Certain groups are exempt: Arab citizens of Israel and ultra-Orthodox Jews, for example. But regular reserve training—up to the age of fifty-five for men—has meant that the army dominates life in Israel.

Nor is the IDF's role confined to soldiering. The Defense Service Law of 1949 mandated the army to teach its conscripts Hebrew, geography, science, history, and other disciplines. The praying troops at left, for example, come from a unit that combines religious studies with military service.

Despite its successes both on and off the battlefield, however, Israel's omnipresent defense program has not been without its problems. As conquerors of the West Bank and the Gaza Strip, the Israelis found themselves ruling over almost one million disaffected Palestinians. In December 1987, after years of mounting unrest, Palestinian resentment culminated in the *intifada,* or uprising, a campaign of violent protest against the occupying forces.

The IDF's response was an "iron fist" policy of mass arrests, curfews, deportations, and shootings. According to U.S. State Department figures, the grim score after two years was 366 Palestinians dead and more than 20,000 injured, compared with 11 Israelis killed and 1,100 wounded.

Pan-Arabists of the Baath (Renaissance) party, that the merger with Egypt would help to keep them in power.

Nasser himself was less than enthusiastic about the union—he regarded the Baathists as too hotheaded and dogmatic—but to other regimes in the Middle East, still mainly conservative and pro-Western, it was yet further proof of the Egyptian president's expansionist ambitions. Encouraged by Britain and the United States, the kingdoms of Iraq and Jordan formed a federation of their own as a counterweight to the UAR. (Since winning independence from Britain, both countries had been ruled by members of the Hashimite family, which had led the Arab revolt against Turkey during World War I.)

But the radical tide was now in full flood. A pro-Nasser government briefly held sway in Jordan, but King Hussein, who had seen his grandfather, King Abdullah, fall victim to an assassin's bullet, had no intention of suffering the same fate, and he used military force to crush his opponents. His cousin, King Faisal II of Iraq, was less fortunate. In July 1958, republican army officers seized power in a coup, killing him and his prime minister. The new rulers subsequently declared their intention to ''stand together as one nation'' with the UAR.

Elsewhere in the Middle East, although the Nasserite gospel was advanced with undiminished vigor—through propaganda and subversion in Libya, Saudi Arabia, and the oil-rich states of the Persian Gulf; through terrorism and armed revolt in Lebanon, Yemen, and the British-protected emirates of South Arabia—it yielded meager fruit. Even the radical regimes in Syria and Iraq proved in practice unwilling to follow Nasser's lead. The Iraqi strongman, General Abdul Karim Kassem, came to view Nasser as a rival for the leadership of the Arab world; while a faction of the Syrian army became so resentful of Egyptian domination that, in 1961, it staged a coup and took Syria out of the UAR. The situation became more hopeful for Nasser in 1963, when fresh coups occurred in both Iraq and Syria. Nevertheless, despite the avowed friendliness of the latest Iraqi and Syrian regimes, talks held in Cairo about the formation of a new, tripartite federation were soon abandoned.

Another problem for Nasser was his increasing dependence on the Soviet Union. This had begun in the climactic spring of 1956, when Soviet leader Nikita Khrushchev had offered to finance the building of the Aswān Dam in place of the British and Americans. As Nasser's rift with the West had deepened, so the flow of aid from Moscow had increased. By 1960, Egypt had come to rely on the Soviet Union for grain, weapons, economic aid, and technical expertise. Soviet warships docked at ports once reserved for the Royal Navy, and Soviet advisers strolled down streets formerly thronged with British troops. Even the ramshackle Egyptian economy was refashioned in the Soviet style, with centralized planning, wholesale nationalization, and widespread expropriation of private property. Although Nasser was no mere puppet of the Soviet Union, many Egyptians, as followers of Islam, were affronted by his flirtation with the atheistic Communists. As Nasser's eventual successor, Anwar Sadat, was later to write, ''With the end of the 1950s and the beginning of the sixties, the revolution entered an era of painful experiences, defeats, setbacks, and some of our gravest mistakes.''

By far the most disastrous error was Nasser's decision to challenge Israel. Arab leaders spent a great deal of time and energy calling for the annihilation of the ''Zionist aggressors,'' none more loudly or persistently than the Egyptian president. However,

A Palestinian family treads through the rubbish and debris of Chatila refugee camp in Lebanon—one among dozens of such settlements scattered through the Arab world. Displaced by the wars between Israel and the Arab states, thousands of terrified Palestinians fled their homes to settle in makeshift camps in Syria, Jordan, Lebanon, and the Gaza Strip. By the late 1980s, almost half of the four million Palestinians in the world were living amid the hopeless squalor of the camps. In their frustration, many turned to the Palestine Liberation Organization (PLO), set up in 1964 to campaign for an independent Palestinian homeland. After 1969, the PLO, led by former engineering student Yasser Arafat *(inset)*, employed tactics that have ranged from the hijacking of airplanes to attacks on Israeli settlements. However, despite winning widespread international recognition as the legitimate representative of the Palestinian people, the PLO failed to wring any concessions from Israel. And even front-line Arab states, fearing Israeli retaliation, sought to control, expel, or eliminate the organization.

the rout of the Egyptian forces in the Sinai in 1956 had instilled in Nasser a healthy respect for the Israeli army, and he had been careful to avoid provoking another conflict. Nor was his enthusiasm for a renewed war with Israel increased by the fact that more than 50,000 of his best troops were tied down in far-off Yemen, helping the embattled republican regime against its royalist opponents.

Unfortunately for Nasser and, indeed, for most of the Arab world, Syria, in 1966, experienced yet another political upheaval, and this brought to power a faction of the Baath party that believed that the key to recovering Palestine was a "war of popular liberation." To this group, Palestine was another Vietnam, with the Israelis playing the role of the Americans and the Arabs that of the Vietcong. Inspired by its own fierce rhetoric, and well supplied with Soviet arms and equipment, the faction encouraged various Palestinian guerrilla organizations, notably Al Fatah (an Arabic acronym for the Palestine National Liberation Movement), to carry out sabotage attacks inside Israel. Syrian gunners on the Golan Heights also began the regular shelling of Israeli settlements. The Israelis struck back with artillery and warplanes, and they made it clear that they would retaliate even more fiercely if the raids continued.

Nasser tried to play down the crisis, but by the spring of 1967, with both Damascus and Moscow warning him that a full-scale Israeli attack on Syria was imminent, he felt compelled to take action. On May 18, Nasser asked the UN secretary-general, U Thant, to withdraw the UNEF from the Sinai, where it had been providing a buffer between Egypt and Israel since the end of the Suez conflict in 1956. While the UN force had remained in the area, Israeli shipping had been assured free passage through the Gulf of Aqaba. But once it was out of the way, Nasser, if he was to maintain his prestige, had little choice but to reimpose the blockade. This he did on May 23, while at the same time moving large concentrations of troops and armor into the Sinai. The following week, King Hussein, who up until then had been one of Nasser's bitterest enemies, flew to Cairo to sign a Jordanian-Egyptian defense pact.

Soaring skyward, like the minarets of a giant mosque, the Kuwaiti Towers, built in 1977 as part of an ambitious water-storage project, symbolize the prosperity that oil has brought to the Persian Gulf sheikdom. Petrodollars first began to flow into Kuwait during the 1950s, transforming its ancient, mud-walled port into a booming city of glass and concrete. In common with their princely neighbors, Kuwait's rulers devoted much of their oil revenues to improving social services and the economy. Poverty was virtually abolished, and by 1985, Kuwait's 1.71 million citizens were enjoying the fourth-highest per capita income in the world.

The idea that the final showdown with Israel was about to occur caused a tremor of excitement throughout the Arab world, and whatever misgivings Nasser may have had were swept away by the general euphoria. His confidence was boosted by the Egyptian commander in chief, Field Marshal Abdel Hakim Amer, who, in answer to a question about the readiness of the armed forces, pointed to his neck and said: "On my own head be it, boss! Everything's in tiptop shape."

A few days later, on the morning of June 5, Israeli warplanes attacked seventeen Egyptian airfields, destroying most of Nasser's air force before it could get off the ground. Having won command of the sky, the Israelis went on to capture not only the whole Sinai Peninsula, but also the Gaza Strip, the Golan Heights, and the West Bank of the Jordan River, including the old city of Jerusalem. By the afternoon of June 10, what would become known as the Six Day War was over.

Nasser's immediate explanation for the disaster was that aircraft from British and U.S. carriers had intervened on Israel's behalf. Although it triggered a great wave of anti-Western feeling in the Arab world, the charge was groundless. Nor could it alter the fact that Nasser, by allowing his judgment to be overcome by emotion, had made an Israeli attack virtually certain. He decided that his only course was to resign, and on June 9, shortly after Egypt had accepted the UN demand for a cease-fire, he went on radio and television to inform the Egyptian people of his intention.

To Nasser's friends, the broadcast was a genuine expression of his feelings; to his critics, it was no more than a cynical ploy to win popular sympathy. Either way, its impact on the Egyptians was electrifying. "The minute Nasser ended his short statement," Sadat later wrote, "the streets of Cairo were crammed with people—men, women, and children from all classes and walks of life, united by their sense of crisis into one solid mass, moving in unison, and speaking with the same tongue, calling on Nasser to stay on." Similar scenes occurred in other Egyptian towns, and in many Arab cities outside Egypt as well. The following day, the Egyptian National Assembly rejected Nasser's resignation and voted instead to give him full powers for the "military and political rebuilding of the country."

Despite the public adulation, however, Nasser was no longer the spotless hero of Suez. He had led the Arabs into their most fateful confrontation in a generation—and lost. The years ahead were to bring further disappointments. Although he was able to welcome two more allies into the radical Arab camp—Libya and Sudan—and hail the withdrawal of the British from their bases and dependencies in the Persian Gulf, he faced increasing problems in Egypt itself. In August 1967, he initiated a purge of the armed forces; many senior officers were imprisoned, and the disgraced commander in chief, Field Marshal Amer, was persuaded to commit suicide. There was serious rioting in the country during both 1968 and 1969, when food shortages led to discontent among students and industrial workers.

Nasser's health was also a cause of concern. Since 1956, he had suffered from diabetes—an illness that grew steadily worse following the Six Day War. The climax came in September 1970, at the end of an Arab summit meeting that he had been hosting in Cairo. Returning from the airport after seeing off the ruler of Kuwait, he had a heart attack and died a few hours later, at the age of fifty-two. If his successor is to be believed, his death must have come almost as a relief. "Those who knew Nasser well," wrote Sadat, "realized that he did not die on September 28, 1970, but on June 5, 1967, exactly one hour after the war broke out. That was how he looked at the time, and for a long time afterward—a living corpse. The pallor of death was evident

Dense clouds of smoke billow over Beirut in July 1982, as Israeli aircraft and artillery bombard PLO positions in the western section of the city.

Beirut CITY OF 1000 AND 1 NIGHT

RAMLET-EL-BAIDA BEACH

WONDERFUL BEIRUT

THE LEBANESE RIVIERA

For thirty years after the departure of the French in 1945, Lebanon was an oasis of relative stability and prosperity in the Middle East. Indeed, postcards such as those at left promoted its capital, Beirut, as the playground of the Mediterranean. But that image was shattered in 1975, when growing antagonism between Lebanon's Muslim and Christian populations flared into civil war.

As right-wing Christian militiamen joined battle with a left-wing Muslim alliance, the once-elegant capital was turned into a pockmarked and cratered killing ground. With its commercial center destroyed and its luxury waterfront hotels gutted, Beirut's dominating feature became the incongruously named Green Line, a strip of ravaged wasteland separating the predominantly Muslim west from the largely Christian east.

But nothing in Lebanon was straightforward. The intensifying conflict soon brought intervention from outside powers—invasion on the part of Syria and Israel; the sponsoring of local proxies by Iran, Iraq, and Libya—and internecine strife erupted on both sides of the religious divide. While the Syrian-backed Shiite Amal (Hope) militia clashed with its more radical offshoot, the pro-Iranian Hezbollah (Party of God), Christian paramilitary units fought regular Lebanese army units loyal to anti-Syrian hard-liner General Michel Aoun.

By the late 1980s, after a countless succession of cease-fires and stillborn peace initiatives, the Lebanese war had left an estimated 150,000 people dead, 300,000 injured, and one million uprooted from their homes. More than one-sixth of Beirut's 1.5 million residents had fled the city, while the capital had become notorious in the West as the world's kidnap center.

BATTLEGROUND BEIRUT

on his face and hands, although he still moved and walked, listened and talked."

Installed as the new president of Egypt, Sadat seemed an unlikely candidate for international acclaim. As a young army officer, he had flirted with both nazism—the British had arrested him for his pro-German activities—and Islamic fundamentalism before finally throwing in his lot with Nasser. Since then, he had served as a loyal but colorless acolyte, completely dominated by his overbearing and tempestuous leader. However, invested now with supreme power, he was to display a political style as dramatic and flamboyant as that of Nasser himself.

The first of his gestures to capture world headlines came in 1972, when he expelled all Soviet military advisers from the country. The Russian presence had long been a thorn in the side of most Egyptians, and Sadat's action in removing it won enthusiastic approval. But he was prompted by more than a desire for popularity. Indeed, his main concern was to win the favor of the United States, which he believed to be the one power capable of breaking the deadlock with Israel—a deadlock that operated very much at Egypt's expense. At that time, the whole of the Sinai, including its oil fields, was still in the hands of the Israelis; moreover, the constant artillery duels across the Suez Canal had devastated the canal zone towns, forcing approximately 700,000 refugees to flock into the already desperately overcrowded cities of the mainland.

It was Sadat's hope that, in response to his ejection of the Russians, Washington

Egypt's President Anwar Sadat *(left)* and Israel's Prime Minister Menachem Begin *(right)* clasp hands with President Jimmy Carter at Camp David in September 1978. The result of the U.S.-sponsored summit was the signing, early the following year, of an Israeli-Egyptian peace treaty—the first ever between the Jewish state and one of its Arab neighbors. Despite its fruitful outcome, the meeting was conducted in an atmosphere of polite wariness: When Rosalynn Carter suggested that all three leaders join in a prayer for success, Begin insisted on first seeing the text.

would put pressure on Israel to withdraw its forces. The Americans, however, remained coolly aloof, and Sadat decided that he had no alternative but to break the deadlock by force. The new Syrian leader, the ruthless and formidable General Hafez al-Assad, pledged his support, and on October 6, 1973, the two allies launched their attack. While Egyptian troops stormed across the Suez Canal, Syrian tanks and infantry advanced on the Golan Heights. At the same time, a significant part of the Israeli air force was destroyed by Soviet-made ground-to-air missiles.

The Israelis, who had been celebrating Yom Kippur, the holiest day in the Jewish calendar, were completely unprepared for the attack. So grim was the situation that the defense minister, General Moshe Dayan, who had been the prime architect of Israel's victory in 1967, broke down and wept in front of dozens of foreign press correspondents. The prime minister, Golda Meir, a woman not normally given to faintheartedness, later gave an account of her own gloomy reaction to the crisis: "The circumstances could not possibly have been worse. In the first two or three days of the war, only a thin line of brave young men stood between us and disaster," she wrote. "They fought, and fell, like lions, but at the start they had no chance. What those days were like for me I shall not even try to describe. It is enough, I think, to say that I couldn't even cry when I was alone."

The tide turned on October 8, when the Israelis counterattacked. By the time a cease-fire was arranged on October 24, they had driven the Syrians back to within twenty-five miles of Damascus, entrenched themselves on the western side of the Suez Canal only sixty miles from Cairo, and captured thousands of Syrian and Egyptian prisoners. The Egyptians, for their part, had retained a small strip of territory

Islamic fundamentalist troops attack President Sadat and other members of the Egyptian government during a military parade in Cairo on October 6, 1981. Although the conspirators did not incite an uprising, they succeeded in killing the president *(bareheaded and in uniform, inset)* and ten members of his entourage, as well as wounding thirty-eight others. The assassination came at a time when Sadat's popularity was at an all-time low—a month before, he had ordered the arrest of dissident students, politicians, and religious leaders—and few in Egypt mourned his passing.

on the eastern side of the canal, and this, together with the success of their opening attack, enabled Sadat to declare the war a great Arab victory.

A more effective blow was struck by the Middle East oil producers, a majority of whom—Algeria, Libya, Iran, Saudi Arabia, and the smaller Persian Gulf States—placed an embargo on oil shipments to all nations that supported Israel. A similar embargo had been imposed in 1967, only to fizzle out after a few days for lack of support. This time the oil states showed more determination, and the industrial nations of the West were soon searching desperately for supplies. The crisis was intensified by the Organization of Petroleum Exporting Countries (OPEC), whose members—Arab and non-Arab alike—subsequently quadrupled the price of crude oil in less than a year.

So drastic was the effect of the oil sanction that many pundits predicted the collapse of the world economy—a catastrophe that would have engulfed the Middle East no less than Europe and the United States. Early in 1974, therefore, the embargo was lifted. With the threat of economic disaster hanging over them, however, the Western powers had been desperately searching for a solution to the Arab-Israeli dispute. The task of peacemaking was taken on by the U.S. secretary of state, Henry Kissinger, whose "shuttle diplomacy" brought about military disengagement agreements both in the Sinai and on the Syrian border. By June 1975, Egypt was able to

reopen the Suez Canal zone, allowing the refugees to return to its deserted cities. But a deteriorating economy and mounting unrest (in January 1977, riots sparked by an announcement that bread subsidies were to be cut claimed 79 dead and 1,000 injured) made Sadat impatient for a more dramatic achievement.

On November 9, 1977, Sadat astonished the world by announcing that he was ready to negotiate directly with Israel. The Israeli prime minister, Menachem Begin, immediately responded, and ten days later Sadat flew to Jerusalem to address the Knesset, the Israeli Parliament. This was the first time in its twenty-nine-year history that an Arab leader had visited the state, and Israelis were unprepared for such an eventuality. "Disbelief prevailed and people were practically stunned," Sadat recalled. Among those waiting to greet him as he stepped off the plane were familiar foes such as Golda Meir, Moshe Dayan, and General Ariel Sharon, who had led the counterattack across the Suez Canal in 1973. "If you attempt to cross to the West Bank again," Sadat joked, "I'll put you in jail!" "Oh no," Sharon retorted, "I'm minister of culture now!"

Sadat's visit was the start of a negotiating process that culminated, in September 1978, in a make-or-break summit at the U.S. presidential retreat at Camp David. Urged on by President Jimmy Carter, Sadat agreed to recognize the existence of Israel, Begin agreed to hand back the Sinai to Egypt, and both agreed that self-determination should be granted eventually to Palestinians living under occupation in the West Bank and the Gaza Strip. The following March, an Egypt-Israel peace treaty finally brought to an end the state of war that had existed between the two countries since 1948.

Most of the non-Arab world was thrilled by the reconciliation of two ancient enemies, and both Sadat and Begin were showered with accolades, including the Nobel Peace Prize. Arab reaction, on the other hand, was bitterly hostile. Sadat, in the view of his critics, had sacrificed the Palestinians, the West Bank, the Gaza Strip, the Golan Heights, and Jerusalem simply in order to regain control of the Sinai.

The Palestinians of the occupied territories felt especially aggrieved, since Sadat, despite repeated promises to safeguard their future, had signed a treaty that left the future an open question. Although talks between Egypt and Israel about self-determination for the Palestinians were to drag on for another twelve months, no one really believed that they would produce a solution. Denounced by the Palestine Liberation Organization (PLO), the main Palestinian nationalist movement, as a traitor to the Arab cause, Sadat closed down the group's offices and radio station in Cairo. As a sign of their opposition, the other Arab states decided on a total political and economic boycott of Egypt. Diplomatic relations were broken by all but Sudan and Oman, and the headquarters of the Arab League was moved from Cairo to Tunis. Sadat responded in characteristically robust fashion, dismissing his critics as "dwarfs" and "paralytics," who were sunk in medieval backwardness.

In Egypt, relief at the coming of peace was mixed with apprehension about the country's isolation from the rest of the Arab world. In addition, a substantial body of opinion, particularly among Muslims, opposed the whole idea of détente with Israel. Sadat attempted to subdue the resulting

Resplendent in white uniform and glittering medals, Muhammad Reza Pahlavi, the shah of Iran, returns a salute at an army parade in Tehran. At his accession in 1941, he had ushered in a new era of democratic change for his people. But over the years, he became increasingly autocratic, surrounding himself with pomp and grandeur—one celebration, held in 1971 to mark 2,500 years of Iranian monarchy, cost $120 million. He ruthlessly suppressed opposition. Newspapers, for example, were forbidden to use red ink because it was the color of communism and revolution.

discontent by force, which served only to swell the ranks of his opponents.

Of these, the most dangerous were the militant fundamentalists of the Muslim Brotherhood. Founded in 1928 by an Egyptian schoolteacher, and transplanted to various other parts of the Middle East, it had campaigned consistently for the establishment of a new order based on strict adherence to the Koran and Islamic law. Although the main body of the movement aimed for peaceful change, a minority of its members advocated violence. In Egypt, they had played a prominent, and bloody, role in the struggle against both the British and the monarchy, and had given enthusiastic support to the 1952 revolution of the Free Officers. But Nasser, unwilling to tolerate a rival source of power, had suppressed the movement. Its offices had been seized, its funds confiscated, and more than 500 of its supporters arrested. The Brotherhood, in turn, had denounced Nasser as an apostate, and a few months later one of its members had tried to shoot him as he was addressing a rally in Alexandria.

In 1940, Sadat had himself joined the Brotherhood, and, on becoming president, had at first encouraged the movement as a counterweight to the left-wing Nasserites whom he regarded as his real enemies. To this end, he released hundreds of the brothers from jail, paid compensation to the families of those who had been executed, and permitted the movement to relaunch its publications. However, Sadat's peace talks with Israel put an end to the rapprochement with his former confreres, and extreme fundamentalist groups soon had his name at the top of their death lists.

It was while the Arab world was still reeling from the shock of the Camp David Accords that Sadat welcomed to Egypt another leader who had provoked the condemnation of the fundamentalists—Muhammad Reza Pahlavi, shah of Iran. Ascending the Peacock Throne in 1941, after Britain and the Soviet Union had forced the abdication of his pro-German father, he had managed to steer his oil-rich country firmly into the Western embrace. The West had been duly grateful, liberally supplying him with arms, money, and protection. When an ultranationalist prime minister, Muhammad Mussadeq, took over the British-controlled Iranian oil industry in 1951, thereby attracting more supporters than the monarchy, London and Washington later helped to overthrow him.

A few years later, with his authority fully restored, the shah launched his so-called White Revolution—a grandiose modernization scheme intended to transform Iran from a backward agricultural country into a leading industrial power. But corruption, inflation, and repression tended to offset whatever benefits were gained, and the shah's ubiquitous secret police force, SAVAK, was kept increasingly busy.

The opposition ranged from left-wing students to conservative peasants, but its most effective voice was that of the Muslim clergy, who deplored the influence of Western, and especially American, culture on Iranian society. Protest riots broke out in Tehran and other cities, and hundreds were arrested—among them a former theology teacher in the holy city of Qom, Ayatollah Ruhollah Khomeini. In 1964, Khomeini was ordered into exile, traveling first to Turkey, and then to Iraq, where his oldest son was murdered, almost certainly by SAVAK agents. In 1978, the ayatollah moved to France.

A powerful and charismatic figure, Khomeini had by now established himself as the undisputed leader of the Iranian opposition. Events began to turn in his favor in January 1978, when one of the Tehran newspapers published a direct personal attack on him. This was believed to have been instigated by the shah himself, and the result was a violent clash between the police and pro-Khomeini supporters in Qom. Police opened fire on the crowds, and an untold number were killed. Khomeini immediately called for further demonstrations, and these led to yet more bloodshed—a grim cycle, which was to be played out many times in the days ahead.

The shah, wavering between appeasement and repression, tried desperately to stem the tide, but eventually, after twelve months of constant upheaval, he departed for what was officially described as a "period of rest and holiday." He left the country on January 16, 1979, never to return. He was to die in Egypt in July of the following year, ravaged by cancer.

Three weeks after the shah's departure from Iran, the ayatollah returned. Arriving at Tehran's airport, he was greeted by three million rapturous supporters. Up to that point, the Iranian revolution had been peaceful; now fierce fighting broke out between the elite Imperial Guard and thousands of civilian revolutionaries. Within two days, the issue was decided, and a government nominated by the ayatollah took office. Although Khomeini, who was by now almost eighty years old, held no official title, his was to be the dominating influence in the Islamic Republic of Iran, which he proclaimed on April 1, 1979.

The new regime began immediately to root out the "enemies of Allah." Within two years, it had executed more than 8,000 people and imprisoned or driven into exile thousands more. At first, it concentrated on Iranians who had been connected with the old regime, but the net was gradually widened to cover liberal and left-wing groups—former allies in the anti-shah coalition whose secular views were no more welcome to the ayatollah than those of the shah himself. Other victims included Jews, Christians, and Baha'is—followers of a religion founded in Iran in the nineteenth century that stresses the spiritual unity of mankind. The Baha'is came in for particularly harsh treatment, with large numbers being tortured and killed.

Many others outside Iran also attracted the ayatollah's fury, including the rulers of virtually all the Arab states, who were condemned as enemies of Islam and allies of America, the "Great Satan." It was essential, Khomeini declared, for Islam to purge itself of Western influence, and he urged the Arabs to follow Iran's example and join in a jihad, or holy war, against the ungodly. Such appeals inflamed fundamentalist passions throughout the Middle East, especially among the Shiite Muslims, who predominate in Iran and form sizable communities in several of the neighboring countries. The Shiite Muslims differ from the larger, Sunni branch of Islam over the line of spiritual authority descending from the Prophet Muhammad. Often persecuted by the Sunnis, they have over the centuries attracted messianic and revolutionary elements of just the kind that now found in Khomeini a focus and an inspiration.

In the eyes of the outside world, the jihad was ushered in on November 4, 1979, when revolutionary guards seized control of the U.S. embassy in Tehran and held fifty-two of its inhabitants hostage, initiating a captivity that was to last for more than a year. Later that month, a revolutionary Sunni group inspired by Khomeini occupied the Great Mosque in Mecca, with the hope of causing an uprising against the Saudi royal family, and were expelled only after violent fighting that claimed more than 300 lives. In October of 1981, holy-war warriors struck an even more spectacular blow. During a military parade in Cairo, a band of soldiers ran up to the reviewing platform and opened fire at close range on President Sadat and his guests. The president himself was mortally wounded.

The Iranian revolutionaries, although gratified by the demise of one of their leading

Devoted followers press forward to kiss the hand of Iran's new leader, Ayatollah Ruhollah Khomeini, shortly after his accession to power in 1979. Born in 1902, he was only five months old when his father, the senior town cleric, was killed for provoking a local landlord. Brought up by his mother and older brother, Khomeini studied theology from the age of six and was eventually acclaimed in the 1950s as an ayatollah, or major religious leader—the name means "sign of God." An early and vociferous critic of secularism, he became the chief focus of opposition to Iran's monarchy and spent fifteen years in exile before the shah's downfall. A man of uncompromising beliefs, who set his country at odds not only with its Arab neighbors but also with the United States and the Soviet Union, he was nonetheless venerated by millions. After his funeral in 1989, the grave had to be covered with concrete slabs to prevent frantic mourners from disinterring the body.

antagonists, were by now involved in a life-or-death struggle of their own—against a rich, well-armed, and ruthlessly regimented Iraq. Like most other Middle Eastern leaders, the Iraqi president, Saddam Hussein, had been repeatedly condemned and excoriated by the ayatollah. In addition, Khomeini had called for an uprising of the Iraqi Shiite Muslims—a majority of the population, but dominated politically by the Sunnis. Hussein concluded that the threat from Tehran was too great to be ignored.

On September 21, 1980, Iraqi forces advanced along a 300-mile front deep into Iranian territory. Iraq sought justification for the attack in a longstanding dispute over the Shatt-al-Arab waterway, which controls Iraqi access to the Persian Gulf—a fact that soon led the conflict to be known as the Gulf War. But its principal objective remained the overthrow of Khomeini and the fundamentalists. According to most assessments, the revolution had left the Iranian armed forces weakened and demoralized, and Hussein looked forward to a quick victory.

What he had not bargained for was the religious and patriotic fervor of the Iranians. In March 1982, they launched a ferocious counterattack, driving the Iraqis back to the border and recapturing the port of Khorramshahr. Although most of the Arab

A convicted criminal, his trousers stained with yellow antiseptic, is publicly flogged in Karachi in 1987. Under the "Islamization" program of Pakistan's President Muhammad Zia-ul-Haq, corporal punishment could be administered with a cane, a leather whip, or a tree branch. The practice was finally abolished in 1989, following Zia's death.

In 1989, English Muslims, outraged by what they see as its insulting reference to Islam, burn copies of the book *The Satanic Verses*, by Indian-born novelist Salman Rushdie. Protests also erupted in other countries, and when Khomeini condemned Rushdie to death, the author was forced into hiding under the protection of Britain's antiterrorist squad.

A group of Afghan guerrillas, or mujahedin, keep their rifles within reach as they pray toward Mecca in 1984. The declaration of a jihad, or holy war, against the Soviet invaders was a potent force that bound the disparate threads of Afghan resistance.

THE MILITANT VOICE OF ISLAM

Ranged behind a religious poster, traditionally clad Iranian women join in a demonstration of support for Ayatollah Khomeini at the Tehran stadium in 1987. The removal of Western-style rights for women was just one aspect of fundamentalism's popularity that outsiders found surprising.

Long a powerful undercurrent in Middle Eastern life, Islamic fundamentalism came to the world's attention with the Iranian revolution of 1979. Using Iran's tremendous oil revenues, Ayatollah Khomeini set up the Office for Exporting the Islamic Revolution, and by 1982, thousands of young militants from approximately sixty countries were being trained to carry his inflammatory message abroad.

Although Khomeini and his colleagues belonged to the minority Shiite branch of Islam, their call for strict adherence to the Koran and total rejection of Western values had an appeal that went beyond sectarian boundaries. To many Muslims—poor, oppressed, and resentful—fundamentalism was the key to a better society.

One reflection of the new militancy was the amendment of some Western-style legal systems to permit the introduction of controversial Islamic punishments, such as stoning for adultery, flogging for rape, and amputation for theft. But the West was not the only target. In the demonology of the fundamentalists, the Soviet Union was just as bad—a view confirmed when the Red Army invaded Muslim Afghanistan in 1979. The result was a savage guerrilla war, which ended with the humiliating withdrawal of the Soviet troops ten years later.

By 1990, Muslim governments had learned that they ignored fundamentalism at their own peril. And even outside the Islamic heartland, in China, Europe, the United States, and the Soviet Union, fundamentalist groups had become a force to be reckoned with.

leaders gave their support to Iraq—the two exceptions were President Assad of Syria, who loathed the rival Baathist regime in Baghdad, and the radically inclined Colonel Muammar Gaddafi of Libya—the war now developed into a bloody slugging match, with neither Iran nor Iraq able to achieve a decisive advantage. In an attempt to end the stalemate, each side launched air raids on the other's cities and struck at tankers traveling to and from the other's oil terminals. Iran also threatened to close the Strait of Hormuz—and, in effect, the Persian Gulf—to all shipping, which provoked a stern warning from the United States and brought a U.S. Navy task force steaming into the Mediterranean Sea.

While the Iranians battled it out in the Gulf, other followers of the fundamentalist cause were striking their own blows against the unbelievers, most notably in the sorely tried former French colony of Lebanon. Here, tension between the two main communities, Muslim and Christian, had been exacerbated throughout the 1960s and early 1970s by the presence of large numbers of PLO guerrillas, who had used the country as a base for attacks against Israel. Although most Lebanese sympathized with the Palestinians, Christians resented the PLO setting itself up as a virtual state within a state. In 1975, the tensions had exploded into a full-scale civil war, in which the PLO fighters and their left-wing Muslim allies were pitted against the right-wing Christian militias. Into this vortex of political and sectarian strife were drawn both Syria and Israel—the former to prevent the complete breakup of Lebanon, the latter to eliminate the presence of the PLO.

The Israelis invaded in June 1982 and, having swept aside the opposing Syrian forces, raced on to Beirut, where, after a sixty-seven-day bombardment, they forced the evacuation of some 8,000 PLO personnel. As the Israelis gradually withdrew southward, security inside the shattered city was taken over by a Multi-National Force (MNF) of U.S., French, Italian, and British troops. At the same time, the Americans began rebuilding and reequipping the Lebanese army, which had split along sectarian lines soon after the start of the civil war.

To Lebanon's large Shiite Muslim community, inspired by the Islamic revolution in Iran, the international intervention simply provided further proof of Western perfidy. The militants responded with a campaign of escalating violence against the MNF, culminating, on October 23, 1983, in a spectacular double bombing by suicide drivers. Two vehicles, each loaded with explosives, crashed into their respective targets—the first, the U.S. Marine headquarters in Beirut, the second, the French paratroop base in the city. Two hundred and forty-one American and fifty-eight French servicemen were killed. Within a few months, the MNF had been pulled out, and Beirut had relapsed into murderous anarchy.

But even the carnage in Lebanon faded by comparison with that of the Gulf War. By July 1988, after eight years of fighting, more than 900,000 Iranians and 300,000 Iraqis had lost their lives. On July 18, with still no prospect of an outright victory in sight, the two sides finally agreed to a cease-fire. Making the decision to end the conflict, Khomeini declared, "was more deadly for me than taking poison."

The decision may, indeed, have hastened his death, which occurred less than a year later. His funeral was the occasion for a frenzied outpouring of grief, which ended with 400 people being hospitalized and another 11,000 followers having to be treated for injuries.

Outside Iran it was widely hoped that Khomeini's brand of revolutionary Islam had

Clad in a turban—rumored to hide wounds sustained in U.S. air strikes against Tripoli and Benghazi—the Libyan ruler Colonel Muammar Gaddafi poses in a reflective mood in April 1986. A charismatic mix of Arab nationalist, Islamic fundamentalist, and socialist ideologue, Gaddafi was just twenty-seven years old when he seized power in a 1969 army coup. He subsequently used Libya's oil wealth not only to implement radical policies in his own country but also to fund terrorist activities as distant as the South Pacific and Northern Ireland. The 1986 raids, carried out in retaliation for a series of Libyan-sponsored attacks on Americans, were just one manifestation of the West's hostility to his regime. And even in the Middle East, his methods aroused antagonism—Egypt's Anwar Sadat echoed President Reagan in calling Gaddafi "that madman of the Mediterranean."

A thirteen-year-old boy, hands tied behind his back, sits with other Iranian prisoners captured in the Gulf War between Iraq and Iran. The conflict, launched by Iraq in 1980 amid hopes of a speedy victory, turned into an eight-year juggernaut of death that swallowed an increasing number of troops. On the Iranian side, the personnel shortfall was made up by children. While many volunteered, others were conscripted against their will. According to the boy shown here, he was kidnapped from his school in Azerbaijan, just below the Soviet border, and after perfunctory training, bused to the front line. From kidnap to capture took only three weeks. Others were less fortunate: One Austrian journalist reported seeing waves of children, roped together, being driven forward to clear Iraqi minefields.

been buried with him. However, as the twentieth century entered its final decade, there was scarcely an Arab ruler who was not haunted by the fear of religious upheaval. Even among the one million Palestinians in the occupied territories, engaged since 1987 in an increasingly bloody campaign of civil disobedience against the Israeli authorities, there was growing support for the fundamentalists. It was particularly strong in the Gaza Strip, where many youngsters were attracted by the extremist approach of Hamas—for Islamic Resistance Movement. Unlike the PLO, which in 1988 committed itself to the principle of two states in Palestine, Hamas called for a single Palestinian state and the destruction of Israel. And it showed itself ready to kill Palestinians who spoke out in favor of anything less.

Elsewhere in the Middle East, despite the thawing of relations between Egypt and most of the other Arab states, suspicion and mistrust remained rife. Approximately 20,000 Syrian troops were still embroiled in Lebanon; radicals and conservatives stayed locked in contention; and the radicals continued to vie as bitterly with one another as with their "reactionary" rivals. More than twenty years after his death, Nasser's dream of a single Arab nation was as far from fulfillment as ever.

JAPAN'S EMPIRE OF COMMERCE

On any working day in the last quarter of the twentieth century, in any city of the industrialized world, the signs of Japan's massive economic power were everywhere. Commuters crammed the highways in Japanese-made cars or endured their train and bus journeys with Japanese personal stereos plugged into their ears. Their food was heated in Japanese appliances, their news reports received on Japanese radios. The digital watches that told them they were late for work were, as often as not, produced in Japan. On the walls of the great financial institutions, clocks announced the time in Tokyo, and no dealer on the international stock markets could ignore the movements on the Tokyo exchange. In boardrooms and business schools alike, the case histories of successful Japanese companies were avidly scrutinized, and a stream of books purporting to reveal the mysteries of Japanese management technique issued forth from the commercial press.

Japanese banks dominated the global economy: A country that had once been the United States's biggest debtor was now its largest creditor instead. In Europe's declining industrial regions, local officials eagerly courted Japanese envoys in search of likely sites for branch factories to service their own booming enterprises. Historic landmarks and tourist meccas played host to busloads of well-dressed sightseers from Japan, sushi restaurants proliferated, and the most elegant shopping districts in Europe's capitals housed luxury boutiques and banks that catered particularly to Japanese visitors and businessmen on overseas assignments. In the United States, Japanese investors acquired choice pieces of real estate, including New York's Rockefeller Center, and purchased a famous Hollywood film studio, long a primary exporter of the American dream.

By any standards, the rise of this small, poorly resourced Far Eastern nation to such heights of global power was meteoric. Barely four decades earlier, at the end of World War II, Japan had been a country in ruins—impoverished by an unsuccessful war and humiliated in defeat, with the ports and factories of its major cities bombed to rubble. Its dramatic transformation within the space of two generations would make it one of the world's great economic powers, to be viewed with envy, admiration, and more than a little fear.

It was not Japan's first experience of restructuring and renewal. From the time of the accession of the Meiji emperor in 1867, the state had made strenuous efforts toward modernization. Assiduous study of European political models, as well as European technology, had brought an end to centuries of self-imposed isolation for the island kingdom. The state constitution was updated using Prussian guidelines; British and French models, respectively, were adopted in establishing modern post-office and police services. A corps of young Japanese military officers was sent off for training

In Tokyo's downtown Shinjuku district, center of the city's nightlife, Japan's economic miracle is broadcast in neon lights by company names that have become familiar worldwide. Almost completely leveled by air raids and firestorms in 1945, Tokyo was rebuilt in the image of Western commercial cities, but sheltered beneath the headquarters of mammoth corporations there still were numerous family-run businesses making traditional wares such as kites and dolls.

Stripped of all overseas conquests after World War II, Japan also lost territories that had been part of its sovereign homeland. Okinawa in the Ryukyu Islands was occupied by U.S. forces, for whom it provided a valuable base during the Korean War. The island was returned to Japan in 1972, but in 1990, possession of the northern islands of the Kuril chain was still disputed with the USSR. Japan's postwar economic recovery was mirrored in regions around the Pacific, notably in Hong Kong, Korea, Singapore, and Taiwan, and as the 1990s began, the nations of the Pacific Rim *(inset map)* formed the fastest-developing section of the world's economy.

in the military academies of the West, while their contemporaries of more scholarly bent absorbed the latest technological and scientific advances at Occidental universities. Even the physical appearance of the nation changed: Traditional dress was frowned upon, and flowing robes and kimonos gave way to pinstriped trousers and cutaway coats. The face of the landscape itself went through an equally radical transformation. Railroads and telegraph poles spanned the mountainous interior; shipyards, harbors, and industrial plants were constructed in the low-lying coastal regions. The Japanese then expanded outward, acquiring a colonial empire that included Taiwan, Korea, and the southern half of the island of Sakhalin.

As both a military power and the most powerful economy in eastern Asia, Japan had secured itself a significant position on the world stage by the 1920s. In the next decade, disaffected elements within the military set Japan on a course of aggression that led it first into undeclared war with China, and then into initial triumph and eventual defeat in World War II.

On August 14, 1945, when the emperor's representatives formally surrendered to the Allied forces and clouds of radioactive dust still drifted over the cities of Hiroshima and Nagasaki, Japan began to count the cost of its military misadventures. Its capital city of Tokyo had been laid waste by firebombs; other principal centers of population and industry were now smoking ruins, with homes, factories, roads, and railroad tracks obliterated. The population, demoralized and disoriented, was in a state of shock, and many city dwellers had fled to the countryside as the war ended.

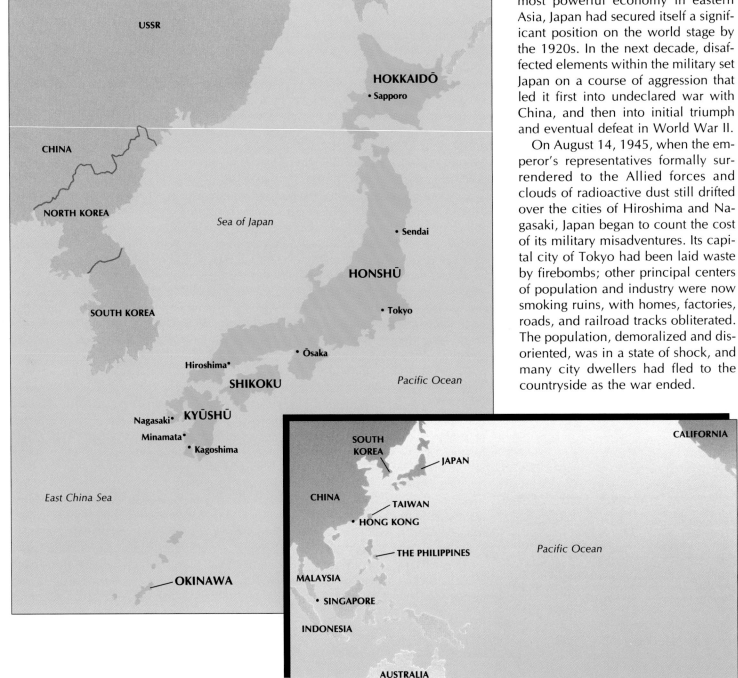

"We lost everything in the firebomb raids," recalled one elderly refugee from Tokyo who had struggled homeward to her native village of Shinohata, 100 miles from the devastated capital. "We were absolutely without food, and the American army was coming, and we thought we would all be killed, so we came back here."

Food, fuel, and the necessary materials for normal life were scarce or unobtainable, and the merchant fleet that had formerly been Japan's economic lifeline was completely wiped out. The years of war had virtually bankrupted the nation; there was little domestic capital left for rebuilding, and Japan's foreign assets and former colonies were stripped away by the terms of the peace treaty.

Stunned by the shock of defeat, Japan lay defenseless before its conquerors. General Douglas MacArthur, supreme commander of the Allied forces, arrived in Tokyo with an army of military and civilian bureaucrats, including specialists in areas from agriculture to women's rights. His mission was not simply to punish the defeated nation but to oversee a program of fundamental reforms designed to ensure that the Japan that would rise from the ashes would never again pose a military threat.

MacArthur's first priority, after the disarming of the military forces, was the distribution of essential aid. The country desperately needed food and basic raw materials to prevent the population from starving and to keep the tottering economy from collapsing. The general's second task was to ensure that Japan could marshal its resources sufficiently to make the necessary reparations to the Asian countries it had occupied. These were paid out either in cash or in kind: 14,000 machine tools, for example, were dispatched abroad to repair war-damaged infrastructure. To pay these debts, it was necessary to get Japanese industry up and running once again. In the view of the American occupiers, these ends could be achieved only by a complete overhaul of the nation's political and economic institutions. Yet, if they were to remake Japan, they would do so in their own image—as a constitutional democracy and a free-enterprise economy.

Political reforms began at the very top. The emperor was retained, as a symbol of the state and of the unity of its people, but it was decreed that he should no longer be treated as a god or as the ultimate source of political power. Instead, sovereignty was vested in the people and decision-making power consigned to a two-chamber parliamentary body, the Diet, composed of democratically elected representatives. As in the United States and other democracies, the judiciary would in the future be separate and independent of the executive branch of government. Local government, too, was strengthened and rendered more democratic, with new administrations controlled by elected mayors and assemblies.

The occupiers also turned their attention to human rights, with a view to breaking down the rigid hierarchical traditions of Japanese society. Women, for the first time, received full political and civil equality, a measure welcomed by survivors of Japan's prewar feminist movement who had been struggling for female suffrage since early in the twentieth century. Trade unions were also brought in from the cold, with new, American-style labor laws giving workers the right to organize and strike, with better working conditions, pensions, and other benefits introduced as a matter of right. By the third year of the occupation, more than 40 percent of the work force was unionized. Educational reforms also reflected an American approach, with nine years of compulsory schooling for both sexes and all social classes, administration by democratically elected local boards, and the establishment of hundreds of new colleges and universities. Not all of these changes ran smoothly: The sudden enlargement of the student population led to a shortage of equipment and buildings that would take several years to rectify. In the meantime, pupils shared textbooks and attended school in shifts.

Radical reforms were also introduced in both the agricultural and nonagricultural sectors of the economy. Land reform, according to the Western specialists attached to the occupying forces, would not only effect a much-needed redistribution of wealth in the countryside, where tenancy had become entrenched, but also would remove some of the internal tensions that had made these rocky, overcrowded islands so aggressive in their dealings with the outside world.

The authorities set about the task with alacrity, ordering the compulsory purchase of all farmland held by absentee landlords, restricting the amount of territory that any resident proprietor could occupy, buying up the excess at an arbitrary fixed price, and selling off the land thus acquired, on easy terms and at low cost, to former tenants. Those farmers who by choice or necessity did not accept these offers were given fairer rents and greater security of tenure than they had ever previously enjoyed. Change came quickly. Prior to 1946, more than 40 percent of farmland had been held under tenancy agreements; by 1950, more than 90 percent was cultivated by its resident owners.

A visit by Emperor Hirohito to a postwar housing project is recorded by journalists and photographers. Formerly regarded as semidivine and rarely seen in public, the emperor—a shy, slight man who wore thick pebble glasses and had a facial tic—undertook such mundane duties as his contribution toward the democratization of his country.

Industry, too, had been dominated traditionally by large power blocs—the family-run capitalist conglomerates known as zaibatsu; these were now officially dismantled and re-formed as smaller, independent concerns. At the same time, as befitted the free-enterprise ideology of the occupying powers, vital sectors of the economy such as steelmaking and electricity generation, which had previously been under state control, were now shifted to the private sector and thrown open to free competition.

These dramatic changes met with a mixed reaction from the nation's former elite. Although most cooperated with the new policies, some right-wing politicians attempted to initiate a "reverse course" movement to undo what they considered unacceptable reforms. But much of the population had seen and suffered the disastrous results of the old system's authoritarian rigidities and imperialist ambitions. They were impatient to rebuild and ready to try democracy.

For the first two years of the occupation, the emphasis—as the supreme command itself described it—was on "punishment and reform": forcing Japan to mend its ways. But by 1947, the relationship between occupier and occupied was changing. The escalating Cold War between the two Great Power blocs—the Communist USSR and its satellites against the capitalist West—gave Japan a new significance in the volatile politics of the nuclear age.

"We are losing Asia fast," warned one American political commentator as China moved decisively into the Communist camp. To prevent this from happening, the pundits warned, Japan would have to be groomed as the capitalist world's Pacific power base. But to play that role, the country would have to regain its economic health; consequently, the rehabilitation of Japan's industrial base now assumed far greater urgency than constitutional or social reforms. At the same time, a systematic purge of left-wing elements, especially within the trade union movement, bolstered the occupiers' sense of security; with Cold War paranoia at its height, the Americans feared the influence of socialists in local or national politics and in the labor force.

Galloping inflation posed problems. Between 1946 and 1948, wholesale prices rose at least ten times, causing ripples throughout the whole precarious economy. But two years later, after strenuous efforts to restrict credit and balance the national budget, prices stopped soaring. Increased economic aid, in the form of imports of crucial raw materials, kept the factory assembly lines rolling and brought manufacturing activity back almost to prewar levels.

But the greatest boost to the Japanese economy came in 1950, when war broke out in nearby Korea. The United States turned to Japan to supply the necessary materials for the war effort. With huge injections of American dollars, as well as American technical expertise, Japanese industry geared up to produce trucks and other vital equipment. The fact that South Korea did not fall to communism was perhaps attributable as much to Japanese factories as to the strategists in the Pentagon. The onetime enemy had become a partner.

In 1951, the wartime Allies (with the exception of the Soviet Union) signed with Japan the treaties that returned full sovereignty to the Japanese government, while giving the United States the right to maintain troops and bases on Japanese soil. By the following year, the occupation had officially ended.

With its military and imperialist ambitions extinguished, Japan redirected its energies and resources into the creation of wealth. The industrial nations of the West looked on in disbelief as Japan's domestic economy expanded at a staggering pace, growing by as much as 10.5 percent annually in the 1950s and 1960s: The average growth rate in the rest of the world during the same period was a mere 4.7 percent. In 1952, at the end of the occupation, Japan's gross national product was just over one-third the size of the GNP of France or the United Kingdom; by the late 1970s, the country could boast the world's third-largest GNP, exceeded only by the United States and the Soviet Union.

This expansion was no lucky accident, but the product of carefully orchestrated economic policies, and the result of a consensus between the state and big business and between the government and the governed. Conscious of the disas-

Scaffold builders using traditional materials—wooden poles secured with ropes—start the monumental task of rebuilding the city of Hiroshima, 90 percent of whose dwellings had been destroyed by the atomic bomb dropped by American air forces in August 1945. Dedicated to world peace, the resurrected city included hospitals that offered free treatment to Japanese victims of the bombing and an institute for research into the medical and biological effects of radiation.

trous end to which their prewar military adventures had brought them, and secure in the knowledge that the United States now took primary responsibility for their defense, Japan's leaders kept military expenditure to a minimum. While other advanced nations poured billions into sophisticated weaponry, the Japanese government directed the lion's share of its resources into capital investment.

In addition, the electorate seemed content to see taxes channeled into the reconstruction of the economy instead of the provision of social services. In the private sector, financial institutions had plenty of money to invest: Faced with the need to provide for themselves in old age or in the event of ill health, Japanese people put a hefty share of their earnings into savings. Nor did the public make any vocal demands for a better range of consumer goods: By common consent, exports, and the earning of desperately needed foreign currency, had to come first.

The guiding hand in these developments was the government itself, through the agency of its Ministry of International Trade and Industry—MITI. Japan, like its patron state across the Pacific, was an aggressively free-market economy, yet no government agency anywhere outside the centrally controlled economies of the postwar Communist bloc wielded so much influence over industry and commerce. Foreign competitors contemplated this formidable engine of enterprise with a mixture of envy and awe, nicknaming it Japan Inc.'s Corporate Headquarters. Its payback was to foster the creation of an industrial structure that could stand as an equal to those of the

MIRACLES IN MINIATURE

From the 1970s onward, elegant and efficient electronic appliances manufactured in Japan flooded the homes of affluent consumers throughout the world, providing conspicuous evidence of Japan's technological expertise. The Japanese capacity to adapt and improve existing ideas had been amply demonstrated during the 1950s and 1960s, when technology imported from the West was refined and mass-produced. After the oil crisis of 1973 increased the costs of heavy industry, the emphasis changed toward the innovation and marketing of Japanese ideas for the overseas market.

Opportunities were seized with aggressive eagerness by the electronics industry, which invested heavily in the production of microchips—the tiny brains inside most electronic equipment, known to the Japanese as "the rice of industry" *(left)*. The manufacturers' products were small and therefore easily exported in bulk, and their work force was highly trained, dexterous, and loyal. By the mid-1980s, each of the leading companies was producing more than 10 million microchips per month, and Japan had 80 percent of the world market.

Designers and marketing managers tried to match their skills to those of the electronics engineers to make the label Made in Japan a sought-after badge of status. Honed by fierce competition among rival Japanese companies, the products here and on the following pages were of a standard that made them hard to combat in the West.

advanced Western nations. Targeted manufacturing sectors—originally the metal, engineering, and chemical industries—were to be reorganized, modernized by the introduction of the latest Western technology, and expanded to manufacture the products the world needed most at the lowest possible cost. Japan, as the men from MITI announced, was to become and remain a "black-ink country."

In its size and complexity, the MITI bureaucracy resembled the vast and intricate hierarchies of an earlier era's imperial court. MITI's official function was to provide guidance for the policymakers; its judgments had no legally binding power. But its civil servants had within their purview export licenses, import subsidies, development grants, and other incentives for outward-looking entrepreneurs. For the edification of the merchants who lined up in its corridors to curry favor with the staff, the ministry posted signs on all office doors declaring Presents Politely Refused.

The efforts of MITI, big business, and the work force soon bore fruit. The tag Made in Japan—which in American consumer parlance had once been an epithet applied to anything gimcrack, cheap, and shoddy—was no longer a badge of inferiority. The Japanese learned fast. Within twenty years, they not only had caught up with Western industry but had surpassed it. Their innovative use of simple but sophisticated components and the application of efficient mass-production techniques allowed them to turn out products that were as good as or better than their Occidental counterparts, and considerably lower in price.

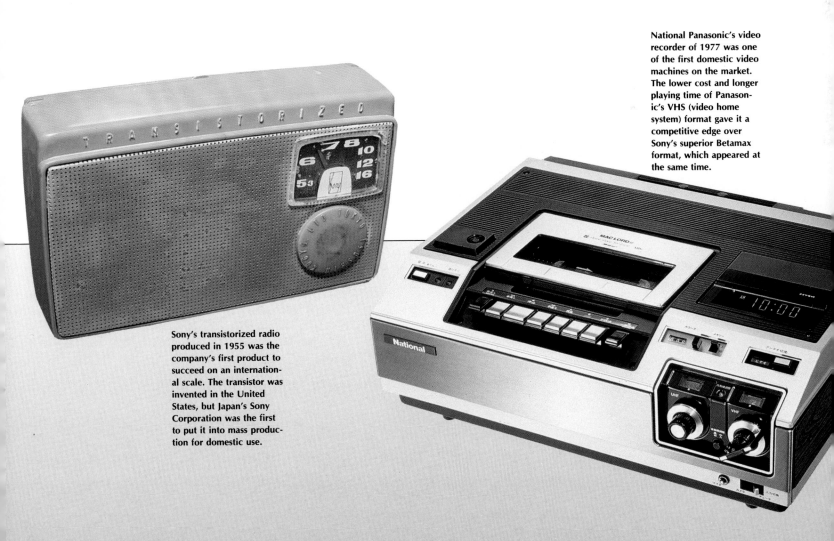

National Panasonic's video recorder of 1977 was one of the first domestic video machines on the market. The lower cost and longer playing time of Panasonic's VHS (video home system) format gave it a competitive edge over Sony's superior Betamax format, which appeared at the same time.

Sony's transistorized radio produced in 1955 was the company's first product to succeed on an international scale. The transistor was invented in the United States, but Japan's Sony Corporation was the first to put it into mass production for domestic use.

Careful planning helped keep production costs down. New factories were built alongside the docks of the upgraded harbors, where imported raw materials could be unloaded from ships at one end, quickly transformed into finished goods, and sent out the other end for immediate export. The economy also benefited from cheap labor. A large pool of workers was readily available, as droves of ambitious migrants moved from the countryside to the metropolitan areas. In 1947, more than one-half of the Japanese labor force had been employed in farming, fishing, and forestry; by 1979, only a little more than one-tenth of the working population was engaged in these activities. The rest had abandoned the shrimp boat for the commuter train, or the rice paddy for the factory floor.

Throughout the 1950s and 1960s, European and American heavy industries waned as their Japanese competitors gathered momentum. The newly built steelworks of Japan rapidly outstripped the output of unmodernized plants in the United States, and the ships that rolled down the ways of the Japanese yards soon accounted for more than half the tonnage—if not half the number—of all new vessels launched. Yet all this growth paled in comparison with that of the automotive industry, which was about to hit the world's highways with all the impact of a twenty-vehicle collision. Between 1960 and the early 1980s, the manufacturers of Japanese cars and trucks would increase their share of the global market from 1 percent to nearly 25 percent, making their country the second-largest automobile maker in the world.

But the boom years of the 1960s, when living standards rose and ordinary citizens began to reap the benefits of their own hard work, could hardly prepare the Japanese

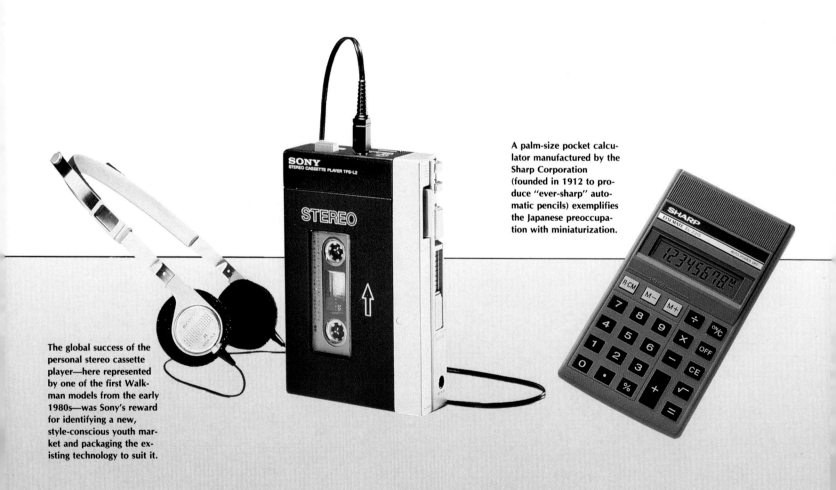

A palm-size pocket calculator manufactured by the Sharp Corporation (founded in 1912 to produce "ever-sharp" automatic pencils) exemplifies the Japanese preoccupation with miniaturization.

The global success of the personal stereo cassette player—here represented by one of the first Walkman models from the early 1980s—was Sony's reward for identifying a new, style-conscious youth market and packaging the existing technology to suit it.

for the upheavals that lay ahead. Throughout much of its history, Japan had succeeded in isolating itself from the turbulent world beyond the seas that formed its boundaries; Kublai Khan's warships, Roman Catholic missionaries, and the merchant-venturers of the Dutch East India Company had intruded only marginally into its private dreams. But membership in the modern world had forced an end to introspection; the country's newfound industrial and commercial success brought its own entanglements. When a cold wind blew through the world economy, it was inevitable that Japan, too, should feel the chill.

The first trauma, which the Japanese named the "Nixon shock," came in 1971. In July of that year, President Nixon announced his intention of visiting the People's Republic of China, which the United States had previously refused to recognize; the following month, the American leader declared a radical change in U.S. economic policy, calling for a general revaluation of world currencies against the dollar, imposing import restrictions, and announcing that the dollar would no longer be freely convertible into gold. Under the new system of floating exchange rates, the yen soared in value on international markets, with disastrous consequences for Japanese exports. In both cases, the Japanese faced a rude awakening; they had neither been informed in advance nor consulted about these moves, and they could no longer expect to receive preferential treatment from their former patrons. Japan plunged into a period of financial confusion and high inflation.

Two years later came the "oil shock," when OPEC, the cartel of international oil producers, initiated a massive escalation in the price of petroleum. No country in the

Like many cameras marketed by Japanese manufacturers in the 1980s, this Minolta model from 1985 incorporates microchip technology for its auto-focus capacity and its liquid crystal display.

A portable radio cassette player with detachable speakers produced in 1990 by Hitachi—Japan's second-largest electronics company—bears the hallmarks of Japanese manufacture: technical sophistication and a design that combines austerity with visual complexity.

Attentive children at a Tokyo cramming school put into practice the slogan on their headbands: Struggle to Pass. So intensive is the competition to pass a series of examinations leading to university entry that Japanese children have little time to spare from study. For those who succeed, high-power career opportunities are the reward: In the 1980s, only 3 percent of Japan's students went to Tokyo University, for example, yet it provided 25 percent of the country's top managers.

world was unaffected, but Japan was particularly vulnerable. It depended on oil, virtually all of it imported, for 75 percent of its energy needs. Japan's saving grace was industrial efficiency. Its modern factories ran on far less energy than their often-antiquated Western counterparts, and its sophisticated manufacturing processes were efficient in their use of fuel. Nevertheless, the implications of Japan's heavy dependence on petroleum became ominously clear, and industry responded with a feverish search for alternative sources of energy, even contemplating the resurrection of the Japanese coal industry, which MITI had deliberately run down twenty years earlier in the palmy days of cheap imported oil.

The writing was on the wall for traditional heavy industries such as steel and shipbuilding, as the cost of their imported raw materials spiraled ever higher. While Western governments sought ways to protect the older parts of their manufacturing sector, the Japanese began to wind theirs down. The so-called smokestack industries, which had restored Japan's economic health in the 1950s and 1960s, were now trimmed in favor of the low-energy, high-technology manufacture of consumer products. Japanese motorcycles, cameras, color televisions, and stereos—better designed, more reliable, and easier to use than their European or American counterparts—soon flooded the markets of the increasingly affluent West.

Brilliant imitation rather than pure invention had long been a hallmark of Japanese culture. When new ideas and skills—the Buddhist faith, for instance, or the art of firing porcelain—drifted across the sea from the Asian mainland, the Japanese had shown a talent for absorbing these novelties and refining them into something uniquely their own. They had done the same with modern technology—studying processes imported from the West, and finding ways to make them simpler, faster, cheaper, and more flexible. But the rising generation of industrialists now saw innovation rather than ingenious adaptation as the best way forward and launched into the exploration of new, high-technology fields such as microelectronics, which could be fueled by homegrown brain power instead of foreign oil.

Academic achievement had become a national obsession. The Japanese understood the pressures that drove the so-called education mama, who vested her own frustrated ambitions in her children. Whether or not they conformed totally to this stereotype, thousands of mothers scrimped to pay for private tutors and harried their offspring—sometimes to the point of suicide—to outshine their classmates in the daunting make-or-break assessments that its adolescent victims called "examination hell." But the rigors of the public school system bore fruit; approximately 94 percent of its pupils went on to upper secondary education beyond the ninth year of schooling, with 35 percent continuing into higher education. No country in the world except for the United States could boast as impressive a record.

By the 1980s, scientists and engineers dominated the boardrooms of the country's leading corporations: About 67 percent of company directors held degrees in the applied sciences or engineering. Under their influence, Japan now spent more money on research and development than Britain, France, and West Germany combined. Instead of paying out substantial sums to Western patent holders for the right to use their inventions, Japanese manufacturers now found themselves earning considerable amounts of foreign currency from royalties and license fees for products they had devised themselves. This was particularly true in electronics and telecommunications, where Japanese microchips and other information-processing technology dom-

Shouting in unison, students from a business training school pause within sight of snowcapped Mount Fuji during a hiking exercise designed to inculcate team spirit. The traditional Japanese respect for authority finds full expression in the commercial world, where company loyalty and corporate effort are stressed to the exclusion of individual ambition. Young managers and salespeople are sponsored by their companies for two-week courses that teach assertiveness, sales techniques, business etiquette, and the English language.

inated the global market. Indeed, as the 1990s began, the nation was poised on the verge of new breakthroughs in the field of artificial intelligence, as private sector scientists—assisted by the government through MITI—pioneered a formidable new generation of supercomputers.

On the international scene, however, Japan seemed to be a victim of its own success. Its European and American trading partners, disgruntled by Japan's simultaneous penetration of their domestic markets and still-substantial defense against foreign exports into its own, enacted a number of protective tariffs and trade restrictions. With now-familiar flexibility, Japanese business leaders countered this move by

Swimmers at a Tokyo amusement park crowd into a pool that reputedly holds 30,000 people at a time. Because of the mountainous terrain, one-third of Japan's population in 1990 occupied only one percent of the land area; in some areas of Tokyo, population density was 22,300 per square mile. Inured to housing that is usually of simple construction but astronomically expensive, most Japanese tolerate their cramped conditions with remarkable resignation and good humor.

entering Western economies as investors. Coffee farms in Brazil, zipper factories in New Zealand, and automobile plants in Wales were all outposts of Japanese industry.

Even the potent combination of private-sector zeal and generous state support could not have transformed Japan so swiftly from war-torn wreck to unstoppable economic juggernaut if the Japanese people themselves had not participated wholeheartedly in the endeavor. Envious Westerners, eager to uncover the secrets of Japan's success, pointed to the differences between Japanese society and their own. A cultural legacy of particular beliefs about group loyalty and collective responsibility, a reverence for education, a rigid etiquette, and a perfectionist aesthetic were all seen to have contributed in their separate ways to Japan's recovery and rise.

The nation that had bred the samurai now supplanted him with the *sarariman,* or "salaryman." This modest folk hero of modern capitalism may have been the victim of stereotyping by foreign observers, but it nonetheless was undeniably true that most Japanese corporate employees took a very different view of work from their Western counterparts. As a loyal team player, the middle-management salaryman often expected to remain with the same organization from apprenticeship to retirement, routinely refused to take up his full entitlement of annual holidays, began the working day with a round of company songs or group calisthenics, and ended it socializing with colleagues or business guests before the long commute home to a cramped home in the suburbs.

Within the company, the salaryman—or, much more rarely, salarywoman, since even highly qualified women usually remained trapped on the lowest rungs of the corporate ladder—inhabited a world of daily briefings and pep talks, made policy decisions by consensus instead of individual executive fiat, and sent suggestions for improvements up the hierarchy as well as down. On the shop floor as well as in the office, workers were given constant updates on new techniques, staff changes, production figures, and sales, and were encouraged to take part in regular brainstorming sessions, known as quality circles, to find more efficient ways of getting things done. Corporations saw their workers as their most valuable resource, offering on-the-job training opportunities and generous performance-linked bonuses, and paying zealous attention to morale. One major electronics firm, for instance, devised such unconventional perquisites as a therapy room containing a life-size effigy of the company president, available for employees to vent their day-to-day frustrations on.

Even the most competitive firms took a highly moral view of their contribution to the common good: "If the company fails to make its profit," said a senior executive in one of the nation's largest corporations, "it has committed a social blunder or sin, according to our philosophy. Profit is the appreciation of society, the reward for what the company has done."

Not everyone shared equally in this industrial paradise, but until the 1970s, there were few outright signs of discontent. Satoshi Kamata, a journalist who spent several months on the assembly line in an automobile plant notorious for its dangerous working conditions, excoriated his fellow workers for their passivity: "Why does everyone work at this goddamned job without complaining?" he asked. "Incredibly, thirty minutes before the second shift, everybody is always ready. They change clothes unhurriedly, begin preparing the parts they'll use in their work, and five minutes before their own shift, they're already working with the guys on the other shift. They're so docile and undoubting that I could almost cry."

Many Japanese workers belonged to trade unions, but these were often little more than staff associations within individual companies, allies rather than adversaries of management. In many firms, election to union office represented a step up the corporate ladder for a shop-floor employee; a term as shop steward could lead to promotion into lower managerial ranks. Labor disputes were not unknown, but they seemed mild-mannered affairs in comparison to European or American conflicts, and they were generally restricted to one brief period in the year. In Japan, the springtime strike-and-negotiation season came to supplant the ritual viewing of cherry blossoms as a fixed point on the national calendar.

Yet no matter how impressive its trade figures or how high its collective standard of living, all was not perfect bliss in the land of the rising GNP. The 1970s and 1980s did not mark the end of conformity or broad consensus, but they did see an upsurge of social unrest. Members of the rising postwar generation, less attached than their elders to old traditions of obedience and patriotic self-denial, demanded a reordering of priorities. Japan's businesses might be booming, but a growing number of its citizens found little to celebrate in the quality of their lives. People choked on the exhaust fumes in their overcrowded cities, sickened from the toxic industrial wastes seeping into their food and water, organized mass protests to block the path of bulldozers destroying farmland to build an un-

The novelist and patriot Yukio Mishima makes an impassioned address to Japan's Self-Defense Forces (the only military force permitted to Japan by its postwar constitution), urging them to reject the debilitating democracy of the constitution and revive the martial purity of Japan's past. The speech was part of a meticulously planned operation in November 1970, in which Mishima and members of his private army took hostage the commander of the forces' base. When the soldiers shouted him down, Mishima committed suicide by ritual disembowelment. This fanatical action struck a chord in those Japanese who were dismayed by the rampant westernization of postwar Japan.

wanted airport, and took their anger into the streets and, increasingly, into the law courts. The bills were coming due for the economic miracle.

In environmental matters, Japan was a victim of its own geography. All the feverish manufacturing activity that had transformed it so swiftly into one of the world's richest nations was confined to a small, overcrowded strip of territory along the Pacific Ocean coast. Only 15 percent of the country's landmass was level enough to support industrial development. In particular, Tokyo's congested sprawl soon merged with the factory zones of neighboring cities to form a giant megalopolis. This territory, stretching 250 miles southwestward to Nagoya, Ōsaka, and beyond, housed approximately 54 percent of the country's total population of about 125 million, and contained nearly three-quarters of its industry.

The manufacturing processes that had fueled the Japanese boom were, inevitably, among the dirtiest: The production of petrochemicals, steel, machinery, and automobiles entailed a massive discharge of dangerous wastes into the air and water. By the beginning of the 1970s, the rivers that flowed through Tokyo, Ōsaka, Fukuoka, and Nagoya were all heavily polluted. Strange new illnesses emerged, caused by contaminated water entering the food chain. In 1972, people living in the neighborhood of Minamata village died of mercury poisoning, caused by eating fish affected by toxic discharges from a nearby chemical plant. In the same year, more than 100 people manifested symptoms of an agonizing disease affecting bones and muscles; the source of the affliction was rice grown in cadmium-polluted paddies.

Environmentalist coalitions sprang up throughout the country, pressuring the government to put more resources into fighting pollution and demanding that big business change its ways. In these organizations, as well as in the new wave of antinuclear groups and the country's increasingly powerful consumer movement, women played a leading role. Despite the civil rights they had received during the occupation, women were still treated in many ways as second-class citizens—''Honor men and despise women'' was the ancient credo. Yet even in the most hidebound households, women had always held the purse strings. The salaryman habitually handed over his paycheck on the grounds that it was a wife's responsibility to balance the domestic budget.

Women had learned how to run their homes as if they were small businesses; the same skills, pooled with friends and neighbors, provided the foundation for hundreds of local consumer cooperatives. These bodies, known as *seikatsu* clubs, were not only bulk-purchasing units giving their members access to cut-rate foodstuffs and clothing, but also pressure groups, demanding that manufacturers improve the quality and safety of their products while taking greater responsibility for the protection of the environment. Political Reform from the Kitchen was the seikatsu slogan.

Women were also becoming more active in the workplace, as the postwar educational reforms

Grouped in calculated postures of listless detachment, punk youngsters hold leaflets advertising a nightclub in Ōsaka, Japan's second-largest city. The generation of children who grew up in the mid-1980s found themselves effortlessly in possession of the affluence that their parents had created during a lifetime of disciplined effort. Some became contemptuous of their elders' ideals of self-denial and group effort and found themselves criticized in turn for their own passive conformity to styles adopted from the West, and for their lack of any philosophy except consumer display.

gradually began to make an impact. Endowed—at least in principle—with the same scholastic opportunities as men, female workers represented a substantial sector of the industrial and commercial labor force. By the 1980s, out of a population of about 49 million adult females, 23 million women held full-time jobs and 15 million more were in part-time employment. Married or single, women's spending power was formidable. A survey done in the late 1980s, for instance, revealed that of eight million Japanese who took foreign vacations, four million were women in their twenties. Nevertheless, their average wages, and their promotion prospects, had a long way to go before they equaled those of men. In many offices and shops, women still fulfilled an essentially ornamental function, as ceremonial greeters and tea makers who were expected to give up their jobs when they married.

The presence of Japanese tourists in the West, photographing the landmarks in European capitals or lining up for the rides at Disneyland, gave positive proof of Japan's increasing affluence. Its citizens came home laden with the cream of Western luxury goods—Italian leather, Scotch whisky, French perfume—while its fine-art collectors outbid the galleries of New York and London for the works of Europe's greatest painters. In the fields of fashion and the graphic arts, Japanese designers no longer copied Western ideas; European trendsetters now looked to Tokyo for inspi-

At the Daewoo shipbuilding company's giant shipyard in South Korea, the vessels taking shape are built by computer-aided methods. The South Korean shipbuilding industry, nonexistent in 1970, had by 1986 become the second largest in the world. Strategic government planning enabled South Korea to become Japan's fiercest competitor in the fields of electronics, shipbuilding, and automobiles; but as wages rose and a middle class with purchasing power developed, Korea itself was threatened by competition from low-wage Asian countries such as Malaysia.

ration. Even Japanese of more modest means enjoyed a standard of living unequaled in the rest of the developed world, with a 62 percent rate of homeownership, and unemployment figures that—though rising—paled in comparison with those of the postindustrial West. In 1987, for instance, 2.8 percent of the labor force was out of work; the equivalent figures in the United States and the United Kingdom were 9.5 and 13 percent, respectively.

Japan's rise had been meteoric, but her neighbors in the Pacific basin were also undergoing rapid change. Housing half of the world's population—some 2.4 billion people, speaking approximately 1,000 different languages—the region known as the Pacific Rim included thirty-four separate countries with enormous political, cultural,

Sleek office buildings in Singapore's financial district and the colonial waterfront buildings huddled beneath them both play a vital role in the republic's economy. In the late 1980s, the latter attracted more tourists per year than the teeming island's 2.5 million population. Banks occupying the former have benefited from government provisions that, from the mid-1960s onward, included tax concessions to nonresident depositors and guaranteed strict secrecy for all transactions.

and economic differences, and it encompassed both eastern Asia and the western coasts of the Americas. Its constituent parts ranged from democracies to dictatorships, from tiny capitalist enclaves, such as Singapore, to the massive, centralized socialist economy of the People's Republic of China. Some of its members were low-income nations such as Indonesia and the Philippines, whose lifeblood was still the export of raw materials; others—such as the English-speaking settlements of Australia and New Zealand—were highly developed industrial and agricultural societies.

The West Coast of the United States had a part to play in the growth of this transoceanic community. California was increasingly drawn into the Pacific sphere as a gateway port for Asian imports and as the U.S. base for many Far Eastern companies and banks. In its relationship to the rest of the United States, California to some extent mirrored Japan's role in East Asia: Both were high-technology dynamos, setting the pace, and stretching the limits of research and development. Indeed, California, with its burgeoning population and energetic sunrise industries, had a state economy larger than that of all but a handful of sovereign nations.

Asia, in its entirety, was the only global region whose overall economic growth actually accelerated, rather than declined, after 1980. The star performers included Hong Kong, Singapore, Taiwan, and South Korea, whose achievements earned them the nicknames the Four Dragons or the New Japans. All four were industrializing at a speed that echoed Japan's performance in the 1950s and 1960s, and they were linked to Japan and to the United States by a web of trading and financial affiliations.

Hong Kong, although moving out of British colonial rule toward political reinte-

With her hand forming the letter *L*—for *laban,* or "struggle"—Corazon Aquino greets her followers during her successful campaign in 1986 for the presidency of the Philippine republic. Her victory toppled Ferdinand Marcos from the position he had held for twenty-one years, during which time his name had become a byword for ostentatious corruption and the kind of pomp displayed in the group portrait of his family shown on the right. On the day that Aquino was inaugurated as president, Marcos fled to Hawaii in a U.S. Air Force plane, bequeathing a troubled legacy. During its first years in office, Aquino's administration was sorely pressed by political division and a series of attempted coups, as well as by the severe economic problems of a country where more than 70 percent of the population lived in extreme poverty.

gration with China in 1997, had risen to unprecedented economic peaks in the previous decade. Thousands of small factories and workshops had made this tiny capitalist enclave the world's largest exporter of clothing, footwear, watches, and various other small consumer goods. By the 1980s, local manufacturers were moving steadily upmarket: Western business executives, for instance, discovered that Hong Kong tailors could produce suits that were nearly of Savile Row quality in a matter of days, and at a fraction of the price. The city had long been Asia's banker, headquarters for numerous financial and commercial services, but was affected by a growing climate of uncertainty as affiliation with China drew closer.

Singapore, meanwhile, stood waiting in the wings, hoping to take over Hong Kong's former preeminence. This small island, with a 2.5 million population, had experienced its own economic boom between the 1960s and the 1980s, first through its shipbuilding and oil-refining activities, later in the lighter, less energy-hungry fields of electronics and computer software. With no natural resources except the intelligence and skill of its predominantly Chinese population, Singapore saw high-technology manufacturing, and services requiring a highly educated work force, as the wave of the future.

Taiwan, too, had developed rapidly in the 1960s and 1970s, offering cheap labor as an incentive. But by the 1980s, its economic position was shaky: Competition from its neighbors, a drop in global demand for its products, and protectionist measures by the United States and other Western nations had dimmed its prospects.

But the strongest contender of all the Four Dragons for the title "Japan Number Two" was South Korea. Like Japan, its own rapid economic development had been given a boost by the Western allies after the Korean War. But the Koreans, with lower labor costs, were able to undercut their more powerful neighbor in steel, shipbuilding, and consumer electronics: Their videos and televisions, for instance, offered customers the twin advantages of lower prices and longer guarantee periods. Like Japan, they enjoyed the advantages of a highly educated work force, poised for developments in such advanced fields as artificial intelligence and biotechnology. But they lacked the social consensus of the Japanese: The country had to contend with a huge income gap between the wealthy elite and the majority of workers, a militant labor force unafraid of prolonged and crippling strikes, and an undercurrent of simmering social discontent. This last problem may be assuaged by the nation's ever-mounting prosperity, as long as the wealth is permitted to spread down through the population by more than a trickle. Even so, the continued political division of the Korean peninsula will remain a source of political unrest.

Like Japan, the Dragons rose by a potent, if paradoxical, blend of free-market economics and energetic state intervention. Their governments provided funding, pulled strings, and intervened to manipulate industry away from old labor-intensive manufacturing into the clean, high-technology disciplines. And, like Japan, they faced a mounting degree of hostility from the West. But for all the pressure exerted on these rising stars by the older-established developed nations, it was clear to most observers that, as the twentieth century drew toward its close, the global center of economic gravity might be facing a radical shift. For 200 years after the Industrial Revolution, Europe and the United States had been the centers of commercial energy and the wielders of economic power. Now it seemed that, barring unforeseen cataclysms, those parts of the world that had first been colonies and later customers for the West were emerging as its most formidable challengers.

"May you live in uninteresting times," said the ancient Chinese, by way of imprecation. Sadly for us, we live in times so interesting many people find them downright alarming. Take a typical week in early 1990. Serious rioting broke out in yet another of the Soviet Union's troubled constituent republics. To the accompaniment of hysterical cheers from a square packed with fundamentalist Muslims, Iran's leader renewed a promise to murder a British novelist who had been accused of slandering the Prophet Muhammad. The dictator of a poverty-stricken African country ordered his high-technology air force to destroy famine-relief shipments en route to rebel districts; it was only one of dozens of murderous little wars that afflicted the five billion humans crowded upon the Earth.

The planet itself was showing dangerous symptoms of ill health: Scientists continued to measure a steadily increasing hole in the atmospheric ozone layer, the Earth's screen against deadly radiation; others plotted the even more ominous rise in global levels of carbon dioxide and warned of the so-called greenhouse effect—catastrophic temperature rises—in the near future. Much of the increase in carbon dioxide was a result of the destruction of the tropical rain forests, where would-be pioneers chain-sawed and burned 54,000 square miles each year, exterminating an estimated 100 species of plant or animal life each day.

The tormented atmosphere of planet Earth was already displaying unusual weather patterns that caused moderate havoc and threatened much worse. Waste and effluent, some highly toxic, some merely unpleasant, fouled lakes, rivers, and even the oceans. Yet despite a widespread awareness of a deepening ecological crisis, the chain saws continued to howl, and pollution still bubbled from factories: Perhaps when the Congress of the United States

agreed to fund an expensive radio telescope designed to search for intelligent life elsewhere in the universe, they were hoping their high-technology receivers might be able to pick up some good advice. For it looked as though the history of the twenty-first century would be very interesting indeed—if any historians were alive at the end of it to record its events.

Just what these future historians will write is, of course, impossible to know, for history by definition involves the study of past events. Nevertheless, even if prediction should be left to clairvoyants and astrologers, a study of the present can give at least a glimmering of the shape of things to come. Even before the Soviet Union's empire in Eastern Europe began collapsing in the late 1980s, the post-World War II bipolar world was being altered beyond recognition. The United States remained the world's most powerful economy; it was at least twice as productive as its old Soviet rival. But as early as 1980, the group of nations that made up the European Economic Community (EEC) was creating more wealth than the United States itself, while the astonishing Japanese economy had overtaken the Soviet Union and was fast approaching American levels.

The Japanese example, and the flood of investment-seeking yen that Japanese industrial exports earned, had inspired similar efforts among Japan's neighbors in the Pacific Rim, leading economists to predict that by the end of the century the whole Pacific area—including a westward-looking United States—would almost certainly account for more than half of the world's production. The implications were dramatic, indicating a tremendous swing away from the transatlantic, Euro-American axis of economic strength that had prevailed for centuries.

Yet there was little sense of impending doom in the Old World. Although the United States could no longer expect to maintain the unchallenged superiority that it had enjoyed in the years following the Second World War, it was still indisputably the world's principal—perhaps its only—superpower. As for Europe, it found itself at the center of a political development of crucial importance to the years ahead: the Soviet experiment with democracy. By 1990, the liberalization introduced by Premier Gorbachev in the years after 1985 had brought political transformation on a scale not seen since 1945. It had also threatened to release some alarming genies from half-forgotten bottles. The specter of nationalism and ethnic hostility was once more looming in Eastern Europe; the plans for a reunited Germany aroused both boundless hopes and deep fears.

But there were powerful forces working against any return to the bad old ways in Europe. First, there was too much to be done: Forty years of economic mismanagement in the East had given urgency to the need for reconstruction. The force of memory was also potent; the devastation caused by nationalism in the years between 1914 and 1945 was not easily forgotten. More positively, the success of the European Economic Community, whose obvious prosperity had helped destabilize the corrupt and incompetent governments of Eastern Europe, clearly depended on the burial of old antagonisms, however bitter and deep-seated they might be.

The United States, the EEC, the Pacific Rim—these were the success stories of the postwar years, an age when living standards in the world's advanced economies had grown faster and more consistently than at any other time in history. There were other countries, though, that had not

of population increase of 2 percent annually, approximately the 1990 level, would require only 1,500 years to convert the entire mass of planet Earth—oceans, crust, core, atmosphere, and all—into solid human flesh. Clearly, the population must stabilize long before that point. It is up to the human race to ensure that its numbers settle at a comfortable level for both people and planet, without the grim intervention of the traditional regulators: war, famine, and pestilence.

There are some apparently ominous signs. Throughout the Third World, cities are expanding at an almost explosive rate. Mexico City, São Paulo, Cairo, and Calcutta are

karta or Nigeria's Lagos have done the same; like their European counterparts a

century ago, they are helping to create new wealth in their new home, while their departure from the countryside eases pressure on rural resources and improves the life of those who remain behind.

Such improvements are modest, and come one small step at a time. But they represent the best hope—perhaps the only hope—of limiting the rise in population. World statistics have long demonstrated that rich people, collectively, have fewer children than poor people.

At first glance, this link between wealth and low fertility might seem a paradox, for human beings, like most large mammals, will usually have as many offspring as they can afford, and that level apparently must depend upon available resources. If there is no food, no one can afford any children, and the population drops dramatically; conversely it would seem only logical that increased resources should mean the population surges.

But human demography is not so simple, mainly because the cost of offspring varies enormously. In an affluent society, child rearing is very expensive, and not only because of the price of feeding, clothing, and educating the young to accepted standards, or even of supplying them with their share of the affluent society's consumer goods. In addition, there are what economists call the "opportunity costs"—in this case, the social opportunities the child rearers, especially the mothers, must forgo while they raise their families. The opportunities lost to an educated, middle-class woman in Western Europe or the United States are obviously vastly greater than the opportunities lost by a farmer's wife in rural Bangladesh. But as Bangladesh slowly grows richer, Bangladeshi children, too, will become more expensive; and in time, Bangladesh will come to have the near-zero rate of population growth that is typical of the Earth's wealthy countries.

The process is a slow one, but it is clearly under way, even in Bangladesh. Demographic predictions are tricky; they depend not only upon the rate of population growth but upon the rate of change of that rate, and the mathematics rapidly become complex. Still, most studies now agree that the latter rate peaked around the early 1970s; although the population continues to grow, the speed at which it is increasing is now diminishing from year to year. Barring accidents or major miscalculations, the growth rate should be negligible and the population should be stable by around 2100. But if the predictions are correct, the human population by then will stand at almost 10 billion, creating a formidable task for even a global economy to manage and probably an impossible one for a world of disparate economies.

While the Soviet Union and its former satellites clamored for admission, there were other nations struggling to avoid the global society's embrace. For Western secular materialism did not appeal to everyone on the planet. The rise of Islamic fundamentalism from the 1970s onward, mainly in Iran and the Arab nations of the Middle East, had largely begun as a reaction against the West by peoples who felt excluded from its benefits at the same time as they were being exploited by its politicians and businessmen. By returning to a fundamentalist religion in which God's holy truth was revealed for all to see in the Koran, they found dignity and self-respect as well as a powerful sense of identity.

But there was a price to be paid for their cultural security: They might despise "Western" science, but without it they could not hope to see their standard of living rise or even remain static. Although Muslim intellectuals talked and wrote lov-

yield all the good things the West enjoyed with none of the drawbacks—for example, female emancipation, promiscuity, and pollution—no one had a clear idea of how to create such a discipline. As a matter of fact, Islamic science made no more sense than had socialist science before it; the methodology that had changed the world sat ill with restrictive adjectives.

The Islamic nations were not the only ones to suffer from contradictions. Elsewhere in Asia, communism retained its grip. In China, in particular, one-quarter of the human race remained firmly under the rule of Mao's largely unrepentant heirs. The massacres following the Tiananmen Square protests in 1989 retarded the political progress of the nation, although they may well have bought its government valuable time. Unlike other Communist economies, China was developing steadily, turning in regular annual growth rates of 8 to 10 percent throughout the 1980s. And although its huge population kept per capita incomes down, China was becoming a substantial industrial power. Future economic expansion would depend on liberal policies that removed much economic decision making from central planners and distributed it instead among the managers of individual enterprises. However, economic liberty and the prosperity it brought were not likely to function well without a level of political liberty that would sweep away the Communist hierarchy at the center of the state—essentially, the inconsistency that had broken the Soviet Union.

Some sort of transition seemed inevitable, for Islam and for Chinese communism alike. It was becoming increasingly difficult for any nation—or any society—to remain beyond reach of the web of electronic communications, not to mention more traditional ties of trade and interdependence.

Global technological society would these people and all the ingenuity could bring with them. For the great political changes that had swept away Cold War tensions had come in the nick of time and human intelligence was now far too important to be locked away behind the walls of absurd and incompetent—or even merely exclusive—regimes. Real dangers had to be faced, and if people could not face them together, then the human race was unlikely to face them at all. For it was no longer only thermonuclear war that threatened humanity daily and directly: There was now also the risk of environmental catastrophe.

In 1989, an American official smugly described the apparent triumph of Western politics and economics over communism as "the end of history." It was an absurd exaggeration. Yet were the worst fears of planetary ecological catastrophe to come true, it would indeed be the end of history, with no exaggeration whatsoever.

The human race has lived without history before. Until the end of the last great Ice Age, approximately 10,000 years ago, people existed in small, scattered family and tribal groups, living by hunting and gathering in much the same way as a number of other large mammals—apes, for example—and occupying a very similar place in the planetary ecology. The big-brained humans—already using tools and capable of some form of organized cooperation—were more efficient than their rivals: Their flint spears and arrowheads had helped push the mastodon, the mammoth, and a host of other prey species toward extinction long before the Ice Age ended. But their role in the landscape—their "ecological niche"—was similar, and a history of our early ancestors would be about meaningful as a history of the polar bears.

the same period: a fascinating study in animal behavior, perhaps, but no more.

Shortly afterward, though, some humans began the systematic cultivation of selected food crops. By inventing agriculture, the human species had, in ecological terms, found a new niche: From being animals that hunted and gathered over a wide area, some had become animals that tilled the soil. For the species, it was a dramatically successful change: Agriculture made it possible for a given area of land to support many more people.

But agriculture meant far more than an increased human population. Itself an entirely new ecological niche, agriculture brought with it the possibility—even the necessity—of more niches still. First, perhaps, was the bandit niche: A strong, aggressive human could make a good living preying upon the labor of the cultivators, at least until enterprising competitors invented the lordship niche and the warrior niche and made their living protecting the tillers of the soil. As social structures began to emerge, newer niches developed with them—by no means all of them violent. There was scope now for merchants, for lawyers, and for scribes—all occupations that would have been quite beyond the comprehension of the hunting bands who had decimated the wildlife of Eurasia a few thousand years before.

Humanity was not only more complex, it was far less uniform. The tension, sometimes creative, sometimes destructive, among different lifestyles, different ways of human development, provided the species with a social dynamic that allowed what we call history to happen.

The rise of civilization found more niches available and made more room for history; the Industrial Revolution more still. Yet despite their new technologies, all these humans owed their livelihoods, and

their very lives, to the same planet that had nurtured their Stone Age ancestors. Thanks to those same technologies, the polluted Earth was teetering on the edge of a climatic shift that could raise global temperatures enough to melt icecaps and swamp the lowlands where billions of humans made their home.

Humans have always had a powerful effect on their environment. Most of the savannas of Africa, for example, were probably created in ancient times by primitive cultivators burning out the original forests to make space for simple agriculture. And atmospheric pollution is nothing new: It made its first obvious appearance in the seventeenth century, when charcoal burning had put enough sulfur into the air to cause silver to tarnish. Early cultivators, however, were not equipped with chain saws and flamethrowers, and charcoal burners did not incinerate millions of tons of fossil fuels every day. The sheer speed of human development has almost overwhelmed the delicate regulatory systems by which planet Earth retains its stability. Now, only humans have it in their power to act quickly enough to restore some of these lost balances—unless, of course, it is already too late.

In the 1930s, when the specter of war was threatening the world, an English poet wrote, "We must love one another or die." Fortunately, nothing quite so difficult was required. But the twenty-first century will make a demand that is almost as hard: We must cooperate, or very many of us will die. Above all, humans will have to think, and think together, for the planet's problems will only be solved by the organ that created them: the large human brain, and the skills it has evolved in the long haul from the cold crucible of the Ice Age to the end of the twentieth century.

1950-1960

1960-1970

Senator Joseph McCarthy heads an inquiry into "un-American activities," i.e., the alleged Communist sympathies of public officials (1950).

The first hydrogen bomb is tested in the Marshall Islands (1952).

Dwight Eisenhower succeeds Harry Truman as president (1953).

A U.S. reconnaissance plane is shot down over Soviet territory (1960). John Kennedy is elected president (1960).

U.S. combat troops are sent to aid South Vietnamese forces against Communist North Vietnamese insurgents (1962).

After Kennedy imposes a blockade of Cuba, Soviet nuclear missiles are withdrawn (1962).

Kennedy is assassinated (1963).

The black civil rights leader Martin Luther King, Jr., is assassinated (1968).

Neil Armstrong and Edwin Aldrin become the first men to set foot on the Moon (1969).

THE UNITED STATES

Soviet dictator Joseph Stalin dies (1953).

West Germany joins NATO; the Warsaw Pact unites the Communist nations of Eastern Europe in a defensive military alliance (1955).

Soviet troops invade Hungary to crush an anti-Russian revolt (1956).

The European Economic Community (EEC) is established by the Treaty of Rome (1957). The initial members are France, West Germany, Italy, Belgium, the Netherlands, and Luxembourg.

Charles de Gaulle is elected first president of the Fifth Republic in France (1958).

Soviet cosmonaut Yuri Gagarin becomes the first man in space (1961).

The Berlin Wall is built to stem the exodus of East Germans to West Germany (1961).

Students and workers in Paris take over universities and factories (1968); the following year, de Gaulle resigns.

Soviet and Warsaw Pact troops invade Czechoslovakia to end the liberal regime of Alexander Dubček (1968).

Britain sends troops to Northern Ireland to police unrest between the Roman Catholic minority and the Protestant majority (1969).

EUROPE

Chinese forces invade South Korea and capture Seoul (1951).

Under collectivization policies, peasants are grouped into agricultural cooperatives; these are later combined into communes.

The Bandung Conference, attended by twenty-nine Asian and African nations, enhances China's international standing (1955).

Following criticism during the Hundred Flowers Campaign (1956), Mao Zedong turns against the intellectuals.

The Great Leap Forward, a program to revolutionize the economy proclaimed in 1958, ends in famine that claims millions of lives.

Soviet advisers and technicians are withdrawn from China (1960).

Links between the Chinese and Soviet Communist parties are formally severed (1963).

Mao launches the Cultural Revolution (1966); charged with enforcing strict ideological conformity, the Red Guards set about destroying all traces of Western or prerevolutionary culture.

Chinese and Soviet troops clash on the northeastern border (1969).

CHINA

The Mau Mau rebellion begins in Kenya (1952).

British and French forces invade Egypt after the nationalization of the Suez Canal but are forced to withdraw (1956).

Ghana under Kwame Nkrumah becomes the first sub-Saharan colony to win independence (1957).

The white South African government designates certain regions as "homelands" for the black community, while continuing to deny political rights to blacks within South Africa (1959).

Seventeen nations win independence from the European colonial powers (1960); eleven more follow in the next five years.

South African troops kill sixty-nine black demonstrators at Sharpeville (1960).

Algeria wins independence from France after eight years of war (1962).

Thirty nations form the Organization of African Unity (1963).

A military coup in Zaire ends five years of civil war in the former Belgian Congo (1965).

The white government of Ian Smith in Rhodesia proclaims unilateral independence (1965).

AFRICA

King Farouk I of Egypt is ousted by a military coup (1952); two years later Gamal Abdel Nasser becomes premier.

Muhammad Mussadeq, nationalist prime minister of Iran, is overthrown with the help of Britain and the United States, who support the pro-Western monarchy of Shah Reza Pahlavi (1953).

Nasser accepts Soviet aid to build the Aswān Dam (1956).

Nasser nationalizes the Suez Canal; Israeli, British, and French forces invade Egypt, but U.S. pressure compels their withdrawal (1956).

King Faisal of Iraq is deposed by a military coup (1958).

The Ayatollah Khomeini, a leader of Muslim opposition to the shah of Iran, is sent into exile (1964).

In the Six Day War, Israeli forces rebuff a planned invasion by Egypt, Syria, and Jordan and occupy the Sinai, Gaza Strip, Golan Heights, and West Bank of the Jordan (1967).

Nasser dies and is succeeded by Anwar Sadat (1970).

THE MIDDLE EAST

A peace treaty signed in San Francisco returns sovereignty to the Japanese government after occupation by Allied forces under General Douglas MacArthur (1951).

JAPAN

TimeFrame AD 1950-1990

1970-1980

U.S. troops invade Cambodia (1970).

President Nixon and Soviet leader Leonid Brezhnev sign a strategic arms limitation treaty (SALT) (1972).

Following a peace settlement signed in Paris, U.S. troops are withdrawn from Vietnam (1973).

The Watergate scandal forces the resignation of President Nixon (1974).

Jimmy Carter is elected president (1976).

Carter and Brezhnev sign a second arms limitation treaty; Congress refuses to ratify the treaty (1979).

Britain, Ireland, and Denmark join the EEC (1973).

Democratic government is reestablished in Portugal following the overthrow of Marcello Caetano (1974).

The Spanish dictator General Franco dies (1975); parliamentary democracy is established under King Juan Carlos.

Margaret Thatcher becomes British prime minister (1979).

Striking workers led by Lech Walesa at Gdańsk in Poland win concessions from the Communist government (1980).

President Nixon's visit to Beijing confirms friendly relations between China and the United States (1972).

Mao Zedong dies (1976). His wife Jiang Qing and other members of the Gang of Four are arrested.

Deng Xiaoping emerges as the new leader of China (1978). Liberal economic reforms encourage foreign investment and permit peasants to sell surplus produce at rural markets.

Biafra surrenders to the federal government of Nigeria, ending three years of civil war (1970).

General Idi Amin seizes power in Uganda (1971) and embarks on an eight-year-long reign of terror.

Angola and Mozambique win independence from Portugal (1975).

The deaths of hundreds of protesters in Soweto and other black townships harden international opposition to the white regime in South Africa (1976).

Marshal Jean-Bédel Bokassa has himself crowned emperor of the Central African Empire (1977); two years later he is toppled by a French-backed coup.

Sadat expels Soviet advisers from Egypt (1972).

Israel repels an invasion by Egypt and Syria (1973).

Arab oil producers halt shipments to pro-Israeli countries; OPEC quadruples the price of crude oil (1973).

In Lebanon, civil war erupts between pro-Palestinian Muslims and Christian forces (1975).
Sadat visits Jerusalem (1977), initiating peace talks with Israel that return the Sinai to Egypt.
The Ayatollah Khomeini returns to Iran after the overthrow of the shah and establishes an Islamic republic (1979).

The novelist and patriot Yukio Mishima, an opponent of the westernization of Japanese culture, commits ritual suicide (1970).

Following a steep increase in oil prices (1973), Japan invests heavily in low-fuel, high-technology industries, such as electronics.

1980-1990

Ronald Reagan is elected president (1980).

Reagan calls for the development of a space-based antimissile program (Star Wars) (1983).

The INF (Intermediate-range Nuclear Forces) Treaty signed by Reagan and Soviet leader Mikhail Gorbachev cuts medium- and short-range nuclear missiles (1987).

George Bush is elected president (1988).

Mikhail Gorbachev becomes leader of the Soviet Union (1985).

The Single European Act (1986) proposes greater political unity in the EEC, to take effect in 1992.

Hungary announces plans for multiparty democracy (1989).

The independent trade union Solidarity wins free elections in Poland (1989).

Communist governments in Eastern Europe are toppled by peaceful revolutions in Bulgaria, East Germany, and Czechoslovakia (1989); after a week of street fighting, the Romanian dictator Nicolae Ceauşescu is also overthrown.

The State Family Planning Commission initiates a campaign to limit families to one child (1981).

Corruption among party officials and rising inflation trigger calls for political reform.

Civil rights demonstrations in Lhasa are crushed by Chinese troops, and the autonomous region of Tibet is placed under martial law (1989).

Students demonstrating for democracy in Tiananmen Square in Beijing are shot down by the army (1989).

Robert Mugabe becomes the first black president of Zimbabwe, formerly Rhodesia (1980).

Famine claims thousands of lives in the sub-Saharan Sahel region; the distribution of relief supplies is obstructed by civil wars in the Sudan and Ethiopia.

After a guerrilla struggle against South African troops, Namibia wins independence (1990).

Nationalist leader Nelson Mandela is released from prison by the South African government (1990).

Saddam Hussein of Iraq launches a war against Iran (1980).

Sadat is assassinated by members of an extreme Muslim organization (1981).

Israel invades Lebanon (1982).

The Libyan ports of Tripoli and Benghazi are bombed by the United States (1986).

Iran and Iraq sign a cease-fire after the Gulf War has claimed more than a million lives (1988).

The Ayatollah Khomeini dies (1989).

Responding to trade restrictions imposed by Western countries on Japanese exports, Japanese companies and entrepreneurs invest in Western economies.

Japan's economic dominance is challenged by the booming economies of the "Four Dragons": South Korea, Singapore, Hong Kong, and Taiwan.

Emperor Hirohito dies (1989).

ACKNOWLEDGMENTS

The following materials have been re-printed with the kind permission of the publishers: Page 128: "With the end of the 1950s . . .," page 131: "The minute Nasser ended his short statement . . ." and "Those who knew Nasser well . . ." quoted in *In Search of Identity* by Anwar Sadat, London: Harper Collins Publishers Ltd., 1978

The editors also thank the following individuals and institutions for their help in the preparation of this volume:

England: Esher, Surrey—Jasmine Birtles. Ewell, Surrey—Kenneth Gatland. London—Peter Bailes, Curator, Department of Computing, Science Museum; David Baker; Mairi Ben-Brahim; Michael Brunton; Professor Lawrence Freedman, Department of War Studies, King's College; Penny Spark, Senior Lecturer, Department of Cultural History, Royal College of Art.
France: Paris—François Avril, Conservateur, Département des Manuscrits, Bibliothèque Nationale.

PICTURE CREDITS

BIBLIOGRAPHY

THE COLD WAR

Ambrose, Stephen E., *The Rise of Globalism*. London: Allen Lane / The Penguin Press, 1971.

Balfour, Michael, *The Adversaries*. London: Routledge and Kegan Paul, 1981.

Chant, Christopher, and Ian Hogg, comps., *The Nuclear War File*. London: Ebury Press, 1983.

Crockatt, Richard, and Steve Smith, eds., *The Cold War, Past and Present*. London: Allen & Unwin, 1987.

Freedman, Lawrence, *Atlas of Global Strategy*. London: Macmillan, 1985.

Gaddis, John Lewis, *The Long Peace*. New York: Oxford University Press, 1987.

Halliday, Fred, *The Making of the Second Cold War*. London: Verso, 1986.

Herken, Gregg, *The Winning Weapon*. Princeton: Princeton University Press, 1981.

Holloway, David, *The Soviet Union and the Arms Race*. New Haven: Yale University Press, 1983.

LaFeber, Walter, *America, Russia and the Cold War 1954-1984*. New York: Alfred A. Knopf, 1985.

Murarka, Dev, *Gorbachov: The Limits of Power*. London: Hutchinson, 1988.

Nogee, Joseph L., and Robert L. Donaldson, *Soviet Foreign Policy since World War II*. Oxford: Pergamon, 1981.

Ulam, Adam B., *Dangerous Relations: The Soviet Union in World Politics 1970-1982*. New York: Oxford University Press, 1983.

Zuckerman, Solly, *Nuclear Illusion and Reality*. London: Collins, 1982.

EUROPE

Ardagh, John:
France Today. London: Penguin Books, 1987.
Germany and the Germans. London: Penguin Books, 1988.

Barzini, Luigi, *The Impossible Europeans*. London: Weidenfeld and Nicolson, 1983.

Berghahn, V., *Modern Germany*. Cambridge: Cambridge University Press, 1982.

Carr, Raymond, *Modern Spain 1875-1980*. Oxford and New York: Oxford University Press, 1980.

Childs, David, *Britain since 1945*. London: Methuen, 1979.

Crouzet, Maurice, *The European Renaissance since 1945*. Transl. by Stanley Baron. New York: Harcourt Brace Jovanovich, 1970.

Fejto, François, *A History of the People's Democracies: Eastern Europe since Stalin*. Transl. by Daniel Weissbort. London: Penguin Books, 1974.

Holland, R. F., *European Decolonization*. London: Macmillan, 1985.

Lane, Peter, *Europe since 1945*. London: Batsford, 1985.

Laqueur, Walter, *Europe since Hitler*. London: Penguin Books, 1987.

Lewis, Flora, *Europe*. New York: Simon and Schuster, 1987.

Milward, Alan S., *The Reconstruction of Western Europe 1945-51*. London: Methuen, 1984.

Sassoon, Donald, *Contemporary Italy*. London: Longman, 1986.

Urwin, Derek W., *Western Europe since 1945*. London: Longman, 1989.

CHINA

Avedon, John F., *In Exile from the Land of the Snows*. London: Wisdom Publications, 1985.

Bailey, P. J., *China in the Twentieth Century*. Oxford: Basil Blackwell, 1988.

Bonavia, David, *Deng*. Hong Kong: Longman, 1989.

Butterfield, Fox, *China: Alive in the Bitter Sea*. London: Hodder and Stoughton, 1982.

Chen, Jack, *Inside the Cultural Revolution*. London: Sheldon Press, 1976.

Fairbank, John King, *The Great Chinese Revolution: 1800-1985*. New York: Harper & Row, 1986.

Fathers, Michael, and Andrew Higgins, *Tiananmen*. London: Transworld Publishers, 1989.

Fitzgerald, Charles P., and Myra Roper, *China*. London: Heinemann, 1973.

Garside, Roger, *Coming Alive*. London: Andre Deutsch, 1981.

Gittings, John, *China Changes Face*. Oxford: Oxford University Press, 1989.

MacFarquar, Roderick, and John K. Fairbank, *1949-1965*. Vol. 14 of *The Cambridge History of China*. Cambridge: Cambridge University Press, 1987.

Rodzinski, Witold, *The People's Republic of China*. London: Fontana Press, 1989.

Wright, Elizabeth, *The Chinese People Stand Up*. London: BBC Books, 1989.

AFRICA

Clapham, C., *Ethiopia after the Revolution*. Cambridge: Cambridge University Press, 1988.

Gilkes, Patrick, *The Dying Lion*. New York: Saint Martin's Press, 1975.

Hargreaves, John, *Decolonization in Africa*. London: Longman, 1988.

Iliffe, John, *A Modern History of Tanganyika*. Cambridge: Cambridge University Press, 1979.

Kahler, Miles, *Decolonization in Britain and France*. Princeton: Princeton University Press, 1984.

Marcum, John A., *The Angolan Revolution*. Cambridge, Massachusetts: MIT Press, 1978.

Munslow, Barry, *Mozambique*. London: Longman, 1983.

THE MIDDLE EAST

Butt, Gerald, *The Arab World: A Personal View*. London: BBC Books, 1987.

Joesten, Joachim, *Nasser: The Rise to Power*. London: Odhams Press, 1969.

Kimche, David, and Dan Bawley, *The Sandstorm*. London: Secker & Warburg, 1968.

Mansfield, Peter, *The Arabs*. London: Penguin Books, 1985.

Meir, Golda, *My Life*. London: Futura Publications, 1976.

Mostyn, Trevor, and Albert Hourani, eds., *The Cambridge Encyclopedia of the Middle East and North Africa*. Cambridge: Cambridge University Press, 1988.

Naipaul, V. S., *Among the Believers*. London: Penguin Books, 1982.

Nasser, Gamal Abdul, *Egypt's Liberation*. Washington, D.C.: Public Affairs Press, 1955.

Pryce-Jones, David, *The Closed Circle*. London: Weidenfeld and Nicolson, 1989.

Sadat, Anwar el-, *In Search of Identity: An Autobiography*. London: William Collins, 1978.

Wright, Mortimer, ed., *Iran: The Khomeini Revolution*. Harlow, England: Longman Group, 1989.

JAPAN

Allen, G. C., *The Japanese Economy*. London: Weidenfeld and Nicolson, 1981.

Buckley, Roger, *Japan Today*. Cambridge: Cambridge University Press, 1985.

Clark, Rodney, *The Japanese Company*. New Haven: Yale University Press, 1979.

Dore, Ronald, *Taking Japan Seriously*. London: Athlone Press, 1987.

Linder, S. B., *The Pacific Century*. Stanford, California: Stanford University Press, 1986.

Nakamura, Takafusa, *The Postwar Japanese Economy*. Transl. by Jacqueline Kaminski. Tokyo: University of Tokyo Press, 1981.

Patrick, Hugh, and Henry Rosevosky, eds., *Asia's New Giant*. Washington, D.C.: Brookings Institution, 1976.

Reischauer, Edwin O., *The Japanese*. London: Harvard University Press, 1988.

Smith, Michael, et al., *Asia's New Industrial World*. London: Methuen, 1985.

Tasker, Peter, *Inside Japan*. London: Sidgwick & Jackson, 1987.

GENERAL

Clark, Philip, *The Soviet Manned Space Programme*. London: Salamander Books, 1988.

Clutterbuck, Richard, *Kidnap, Hijack and Extortion*. London: Macmillan, 1987.

Coker, Chris, *Terrorism and Civil Strife*. London: Aladdin Books, 1987.

The Exploration of Space. London: Science Museum, 1986.

Kennedy, Paul, *The Rise and Fall of the Great Powers*. New York: Random House, 1988.

LIFE in Space. Alexandria, Virginia: Time-Life Books, 1983.

INDEX